*American Film Studios*

# American Film Studios:
# An Historical Encyclopedia

*by*
## Gene Fernett

McFarland & Company, Inc., Publishers
*Jefferson, North Carolina, and London*

*Photo Credits:* Classic Images, Erwin Dumbrille, Burbank Public Library, Marc Wanamaker of Bison Archives, Bruce Torrence, Walt Disney Studios, Film Favorites, H.R. Hertel, Consolidated Film Industries, Cornell University Library, Jacksonville (Florida) Public Library, Florida Photographic Archives of Strozier Library, The Santa Barbara (California) *News-Press,* John LaDue, Filmworks Studios, Anthony Phillips.

**Library of Congress Cataloguing-in-Publication Data**

Fernett, Gene.
  *American film studios.*

  Bibliography: p. 273.
  Includes index.
  1. Motion picture studios—United States—
History—Dictionaries.  I. Title.
PN1993.5.U6F45   1988     384′.8′0973     88-42514

ISBN 0-89950-250-4 (50# acid-free natural paper)

Manufactured in the United States of America.

McFarland   Box 611   Jefferson NC 28640

*This book is dedicated to Samuel K. Rubin
who encouraged this author to seek publication of this work,
and to Erwin Dumbrille
who aided immensely in its research.*

# Acknowledgments

The following people made significant contributions to this book: Erwin Dumbrille, Agoura, Calif.; Nat Levine, Woodland Hills, Calif.; H. Richard Hertel, Orlando, Fla.; Lisa Grigsby, Austin, Tex.; Reginald LaFayette, Mt. Vernon, N.Y.; Marc Wanamaker, Bison Archives, Beverly Hills, Calif.; Carol Nelson, Channel 44, Pittston, Pa.; Ted Erving, Blackhawk films, Davenport, Iowa; Herb Peterson, historian/researcher, Kerrville, Tex.; William Arnold and Paula Wyrick, Department of Commerce Film Office, Raleigh, N.C.; John LaDue, Phoenix, Ariz.; Lynn Foster, Georgia Department of Industry and Trade, Atlanta, Ga.; Ed Spivia, Filmworks Studios, Atlanta, Ga.; and John Massey, Atlanta Production Center, Atlanta, Ga.

These organizations were also extremely helpful: A & M Records, Hollywood, Calif.; Walt Disney Productions, Burbank, Calif.; RKO Studios Archives, Hollywood, Calif.; Film favorites, Canton, Okla.; *The Citizens Voice*, Mt. Vernon, N.Y.; The Division of Commerce and Development (State of Colorado Motion Picture and Television), Denver, Colo.; Arizona Department of Commerce, Phoenix, Ariz.; Texas Film Commission, division of the Economic Development Commission, Austin, Tex.; the reference departments of the libraries at New York City, N.Y.; Burbank, Calif.; Mamaroneck, N.Y.; Kerrville, Texas; Glendale, Calif.; Santa Monica, Calif.; San Francisco, Calif.; Santa Barbara, Calif.; Buffalo, N.Y.; Wilkes-Barre, Pa.; Ithaca, N.Y.; Ft. Lee, N.J.; Cornell University, Ithaca, N.Y.; New Rochelle, N.Y.; Detroit, Mich.; Niles, Calif.; Spokane, Wash.; New Orleans, La.; Jacksonville, Fla.; Fremont, Calif.; Chicago, Ill.; Bronx, N.Y.; Philadelphia, Pa.; Prescott, Ariz.; the historical societies at Ft. Lee, N.J.; St. Augustine, Fla.; Ithaca, N.Y., and San Francisco, Calif.

# Table of Contents

# Foreword

It would have been impossible to include herewith all the American theatrical film studios. If that had been attempted, this volume would have been far too unwieldy.

For this reason you will find no study of the Durango Production Company, organized in 1915 by James Jarvis and W. Goff Black, the outfit which in 1918 filmed a version of General Custer's last stand, employing backgrounds around Dolores, Colorado.

There is no mention, either, of the branch studio operated by Selig Polyscope of Chicago at Cañon City, Colorado, which in 1912 and 1913 operated in the 300 block of Main Street and later at Fourth and Main, with film players Tom Mix, Myrtle Stedman, William Duncan, and Joe Ryan playing in Selig productions made there. When Selig withdrew that company to Prescott, Arizona, in the fall of 1913, the studio at Fourth and Main was taken over by a newly home-grown firm, Colorado Photo-Play Company, which induced former Selig actress Josephine West, as well as producer-director O.B. Thayer and cameraman Owen Carter to remain in Cañon City. Dreadfully underfinanced, Colorado Photo-Play was quickly destroyed in an expensive lawsuit involving the accidental drowning of Grace McCue while she was appearing in a scene along the Arkansas River, just west of Cañon City.

G.M. ("Broncho Billy") Anderson came from Essanay in Chicago to film the first of his westerns near Boulder, Colorado, but after he and his crew had barely begun the series, they pulled out, continuing on to California for completion of their weekly film releases.

Yet the state of Colorado, blessed as it is with awesomely beautiful scenery, has remained a favorite destination for "location shooting" of scenes for such films as *Secret of Convict Lake* (1951), *Viva Zapata* (1952) and the Clark Gable picture *Across the Wide Missouri* (1951).

The neighboring state of Texas has figured more than peripherally in theatrical film production, beginning as long ago as 1913 when the Satex firm was organized, its studio and offices in a decrepit warehouse at 13th and Lavaca streets in Austin. That firm seems to have produced no more than a single picture, a three-reeler titled *Their Lives by a Slender Thread*. It is obvious why such firms as Satex aren't explored at length in this volume!

Of course many on-location sequences for numerous theatrical features have been shot in Texas, perhaps most ambitious and expensive of which was John Wayne's production *The Alamo*, much of which was filmed in and around a full-scale reproduction of the Alamo, Wayne's expensive money-loser having been made near the town of Brackettville, about 120 miles west of San Antonio.

You will find no mention in the text of this volume regarding the Nola Film Company, the 1915 New Orleans studio at which actress Leatrice Joy is said to have made her first screen appearances, nor is there mention of 1914's Esperanto Pictures, which played out its one year of life, during which its titular head, J.A. Servis, grandly held his headquarters at 1613 Dime Bank Building, Detroit.

In Southern California alone there were no fewer than 49 motion picture studios in 1921, according to a count by an enthusiastic Los Angeles Chamber of Commerce.

Exactly why it was that the American film industry chose to gravitate westward to California is not clear even at this date. Arizona, after all, made many attempts at getting itself established as the nations's center for production of theatrical pictures. Selig Polyscope, Eclair (a French firm with main studios in the U.S. at Ft. Lee, N.J.), Lubin (Philadelphia) and others tried their hands at operating branch studios in Arizona, but none chose to make the state its main headquarters.

The delightfully bogus "Colonel" William N. Selig, whose studio headquarters was in Chicago, invested so much in real estate around the city of Prescott, Arizona, that his "Diamond S" ranch evolved from a place where Selig westerns were made, to the status of a movie site within a working cattle ranch, the branding irons of which were a likeness of the Selig motion picture logo.

Tom Mix, as bogus a cowboy as "Colonel" Selig was a military man, not only came to screen fame as a Selig "cowboy," but eventually purchased a ranch near the Diamond S.

Real estate prices were reasonable and land plentiful in Arizona in those days; however that was also true of California, a state with a greater variety of scenery. California won out.

Thus it was that Southern California by 1921 had such film studios as Morosco, Chester Comedies, Pallas, Selig, Bronx Studios, William S. Hart Company, Willis & Inglis, Brentwood Film Corporation, Berwilla, Reelcraft, Francis Ford Studios, Clermont Photoplays, Hollywood Studios, and the busy sprawling lot that in that year was still the Robert Brunton Studios and which now is Paramount.

All those were in operation in those days, though there was some evidence that there were simply too many studios there: one at 651 Fairview in Los Angeles and one situated at Nat Goodwin Pier, Santa Monica, were closed down.

Thoroughly bewildering as this array of studios undoubtedly seems to the reader, it does not touch upon those studios which are given fairly detailed coverage in one of the major entries in this book!

The reader will note that at times this author was forced to use photos and illustrations of substandard quality. While this is regrettable, it is my belief that it is more important to use them to depict the studios, sets and actors, etc., that were a part of motion picture history. However poor some may be, they still aid in the understanding of this book.

# The Studios

## *Actophone*

In 1905 an entrepreneur with the comic-opera name of Mark M. Dintenfass found himself proprietor of a seedy 130-seat Philadelphia nickelodeon named the Fairyland. Believing that his newly acquired enterprise needed some sort of novelty in order to attract larger crowds, Dintenfass purchased from "Cameraphone" a synchronized motion picture projector, phonograph, films and recordings of such tuneful Cameraphone motion pictures as Eva Tanguay's then-current song hit "I Don't Care," Blanche Ring's "The Merry Widow" and others.

The Cameraphone firm was an "independent" studio, operating in defiance of the all-powerful Motion Picture Patents Company (a trust involving such participants as Edison, Kleine, and Lubin). Cameraphone studio equipment embodied a French-made Pathe camera, a poor choice considering that Pathe was at that time a member of the Edison trust rendering Pathe cameras illegal for use by firms outside the Patents Company.

The creator of the Cameraphone, Bert Whitman of New York, had achieved the "talkie" part of his gadget by the use of a recording machine which Whitman had succeeded in getting to record synchronously with the motion pictures being made by the Pathe camera.

Whenever Cameraphone's William Rising, a former Edison employee, went on "location" to film an event, he did so while keeping his Pathe concealed inside a huge corrugated metal box, in case Edison detectives or other members of the "Trust" happened to have spies around the neighborhood.

Al McCoy, an Edison agent, remained doggedly on the trail, and repeatedly tried to capture the culprits in the act; of course, the Actophone firm, which had its studio at 11th Avenue and 53rd Street in New York, was vulnerable at all times, so it was kept locked.

Harassment by the "Patent Trust," together with a lack of exhibitor interest in talking films, eventually led to insolvency, so Dinten-

1

fass bought the Cameraphone assets, including its studio. Renaming
it "Actophone," he set out to try his luck as a motion picture producer.

The inevitable occurred soon after, and a team of Edison's detectives caught an Actophone crew at work, its unlicensed Pathe camera
grinding out hundreds of feet of negative.

On three occasions subsequent to that, Dintenfass was hailed into
court, on two of which he was cited for contempt of court orders to
cease and desist. Thereupon, the filmmaker assured the court he was
abandoning film production, although it appears he was already making
plans to go back into production at his earliest convenience.

It was too risky to set up again at his own studio in New York, so
Dintenfass turned that property into a "rental stage," while he and his
casts and crews made for the famous Palisades area in New Jersey, this
time setting up their home base in a small shack in some woods along
the rim of hills which gave the Palisades its name, though even that
remote spot didn't prove secure from Edison detectives!

Dintenfass might well have stopped entirely except that he
somehow stumbled upon a bold plan: he'd move his operation down to
Philadelphia and there rent studio space from Siegmund Lubin, a
charter member of the Trust Company, but a man who would on occa-
sion lend a helping hand to moviemakers unwilling to play by Edison's
rules. Trust Company detectives were unlikely to snoop around studios
owned by members of the Trust!

While Actophone crews so escaped the Patents Company, it was
to the Actophone studio in New York's "Hell's Kitchen" area that Carl
Laemmle turned when he entered motion picture production; renting
space at Actophone, Laemmle's "IMP" (Independent Motion Pictures)
turned out all the interior scenes for its first one-reeler, *Hiawatha,* a picture featuring Gladys Hulette.

As for Dintenfass, he gradually phased out the Actophone
trademark, supplanting it with his "Champion" label, eventually fusing
it with several others to become the original Universal Pictures. Carl
Laemmle eventually bought out the shares held by Dintenfass, Patrick
Powers and others, continuing Universal under his own leadership, and
retaining Robert Cochrane as his second-in-command.

Admittedly the lifespans of Cameraphone and Actophone were
brief. Both trade names had been abandoned long before Mark Dintenfass began to release his productions under his "Champion" label in the
summer of 1910, but before he abandoned the concept of "talking pictures," the ex-nickelodeon operator had become convinced that the day
of the talkie had not yet arrived. It was a resolve which Dintenfass was
to find that he shared with Patrick Powers, Robert Cochrane, and Carl
Laemmle, who for a time were his partners at Universal.

# *American Film Manufacturing Co.*

Encountering the name "Flying A," you may think of Gene Autry; that's the name he nailed onto his TV film studio. No! The present story goes back to an earlier day, to a pretty, tan, mission-style studio northwest of Los Angeles, to an era just prior to the First World War.

The American Film Manufacturing Company was organized in Chicago and maintained headquarters there throughout much of the history of the firm.

Roy Overbaugh, chief camerman at American Film during its early years, explained during an interview many years ago that the original California studio of American had been at La Mesa, near San Diego, where American produced its films, one-reelers mainly. (Before the San Diego years, American Film had operated a studio in Arizona.)

Remaining there about two years, they exhausted about all the really eyecatching scenic locations near La Mesa, so production facilities were transferred north, to Santa Barbara, the company and personnel arriving there July 6, 1912.

The original stock company included J. Warren Kerrigan, Pauline Bush, Jessalyn Van Trump, Jack Richardson (who played villains almost exclusively), and such character players as George Periolat and Louise Lester (who became quite well-known for her series of *Calamity Anne* short films, made by American). Allan Dwan was the director of that first company of players.

"The producing staff of the American," wrote Terry Ramsaye in his book *A Million and One Nights*, "went into the southwest to make westerns, and started there the 'Flying A' trademark . . . eluding the heated pursuit of the Patents Company."

This rugged, pioneering film unit had begun with S.S. Hutchinson, a Chicago druggist turned-film exhibitor. Soon afterward, he became partner in a Chicago film exchange called Hutchinson and Hite.

Those partners soon decided to undertake a bit of film production, filming their initial one-reeler, *Romantic Redskins,* along the shores of Lake Michigan. It being prudent to hide their filmmaking activities from the Patents Company, Hutchinson and his partner decided to mask such work under the name of "O'Malley and Smith Advertising Company," and as such were licensed by the state of Illinois.

After the release of *Romantic Redskins* they renamed the firm American Film Manufacturing Company, and advertised that fact in film journals of early October 1910.

At its start American Film placed Wallace Kerrigan, brother of J. Warren Kerrigan in position of business manager, and Charles

**The mission-style studio of American Film Manufacturing Co. ("Flying A"), Santa Barbara, California.**

Morrison, brother of cowboy star Pete Morrison, in charge of animals.

When the company took up residence in Santa Barbara it established temporary quarters along the east side of upper State Street, near Pedregosa, on grounds belonging to an ostrich farm.

From that unlikely location, the firm poured forth an average of two one-reel pictures weekly, after while cranking them out so quickly that on occasions two entire two-reelers were shot in a day, allowing personnel to spend the remainder of the week at one of the beaches along the Pacific.

Soon after the Santa Barbara operation got underway, the company headquarters in Chicago decided a Santa Barbara film laboratory would be placed in operation, obviating the necessity for shipping the camera stock back to Chicago for processing. A building on Cota Street near State was leased for this purpose.

Not long after, the Santa Barbara laboratories of American Film got nicely underway; however, the firm decided to consolidate production and laboratory facilities into what the firm was to advertise as the largest film facility in the world.

Plans were drafted for the permanent lots: West Mission Street, the entire block between State and Chapala Streets, where an administration building would be constructed, along with a huge glassed-in studio, numerous dressing rooms, a "green room for the enjoyment of the actors and actresses," a film laboratory, editing rooms, carpenter shops, paint, camera, and machine shops. There would, of course, be cutting, editing, and projection rooms, too, and even a large, lovely rose garden.

The studio's main entrance gate would open onto Mission Street with a gate through which only authorized vehicles would pass, comprising primarily the Simplex and Winton automobiles so highly favored by the firm.

Once all this was begun, it underwent periodic enlargement, as in the spring of 1916 when a $17,000 addition was announced for the Flying A plant, including a 90-foot-tall tower, 30 feet square, with a flagpole atop it to carry the banner of American Film Co. The building itself would have offices, those on the uppermost floor given over to the scenario and editing departments.

So busy and prosperous the studio appeared at the close of 1919, that the Chicago headquarters of American Film announced it had been able to enter into an improved distribution plan by Pathe Exchanges, Inc., whereby the distributor had agreed to assign an additional 150 sales representatives to "help push the rental of American Film Productions."

Players to be seen around the Flying A lot in those goldplated years included Jack Mower, Bull Montana, Harry McCoy, J. Farrell MacDonald, and Eugenie Forde, all of whom joined other famous players such as "Jack" Kerrigan, Eugene Pallette, and Richard Bennett, father of little girls Joan, Constance, and Barbara, whose playhouse still may be seen in Santa Barbara.

Art Acord, too, was working at Flying A, although he proved a trifle troublesome, especially when he'd ride back and forth to Los Angeles, passing the time on the train by smashing windows and glass light globes along the way, though later freely offering to pay for the damage he'd caused.

Acting personnel at American was constantly changing; Mary Miles Minter, Ruth Donnelly, and scores of other players worked at Flying A for a time, only to move on.

Directors, too, left as other opportunities arose. A man who then called himself Reaves Eason, but later was billed as B. Reeves Eason, for a time was a director at American, as were Alfred Santell, Victor Fleming, Harry Pollard, Henry King, and Frank Borzage.

From one-reelers, the American graduated slowly to full-length feature films, pausing in 1915 to turn out a serial, *A Diamond from the Sky*, made from a story by Roy McCardle.

It's often written that the leading role in that serial was first offered to Mary Pickford, at $4,000 per week while the picture was in production. Mary wasn't available, so the story went, at which point Flying A cast Mary's younger sister Lottie in the leading role in the film quaintly described in a press release as "a picturized romantic novel in chapters," 30 episodes, the advance billing promised.

"The mysterious diamond makes its first appearance in the prologue," began the synopsis which accompanied the press release, "when a large meteor falls among . . . Indians about a quarter century before the real story starts. . . ." The release continued with descriptions of how the episode of the serial was "filmed at night at the old Mission Dam in Mission Canyon, with the sky ablaze with lights."

Then, lest readers mistakenly conclude that the blazing arrival of the meteor would be the sole thrill in the serial, studio pundits disclosed many more, including exciting scenes made at the "Old Southern Mansion," which was built especially for the film and constructed at a site near Mission Creek, adjacent to a full-scale gypsy village which would "figure in a sensational incident," the studio promised.

The serial, directed by William Desmond Taylor, who was destined to be murdered mysteriously about half a decade later, involved a good many stunt sequences, one described in the Santa Barbara *News-Press* May 16, 1915: "A sensational fall from horseback took place," reported the paper, which went on to tell how the hero, Irving Cummings, was "doubled" by stuntman Al Thompson who "plunges from the galloping animal, through the window of a rushing train."

Location shooting was usually required for stunt scenes, but also was utilized to provide choice backgrounds for the Flying A productions. Large estates around Santa Barbara often served, at no charge to the studio, for "society" sequences. For westerns nearby Hope Ranch was the usual spot. Whenever an exotic "South Sea island" was needed, one of the Santa Barbara channel islands did the cinematic trick.

And as with most film producers in the era of silent movies, Flying A filmed hair-raising sequences of runaway autos, traffic accidents, and street brawls in sections of Santa Barbara which had been roped off so that onlookers could watch, but at a prudent distance.

Along a street adjacent to the studio, an impressive shell of a "mansion" was constructed by carpenters from the studio to serve in a scene for the feature *The House of a Thousand Scandals.* Crowds estimated at nearly 2,000 watched as the camera captured the mansion being blown to pieces with dynamite and black powder, intermixed with quantities of loose dirt.

While location shooting was frequent, American Film's studio was a commodious one, allowing more than two or three productions to be made there simultaneously. The gigantic greenhouse-type stage endured long after filmmakers had given up permanent quarters at Santa Barbara. At one time or another, that stage was later used as a roller rink, an auditorium, and even as the local National Guard Armory.

Before those things occurred, however, an attempt was made to revitalize the place as a motion picture studio. Years after American Film had churned out its final productions in 1920 and moved to Hollywood to expire, Frank W. Cole had taken a short-term lease on the Flying A studio in the spring of 1927, on March 19, local newspapers announcing excitedly that no fewer than three motion picture producers "from Hollywood" were planning to move to Santa Barbara.

Fred Church, the paper stated, was already in town, filming a "society-western" to be titled *Wiles of the West*, in which a local high school girl, 17-year-old Martha Jane Steele, was featured.

The flimsy plot involved a down-on-its-luck dude ranch inherited by the hero who tries to get the place back on a paying basis.

In mid–April 1927, Fred Church and producer Frank Cole, having completed their picture, rented Santa Barbara's Granada Theatre and there premiered their film. If Church's picture were typical of other productions made at the Flying A lot during its "revitalization," it probably would have been far better to let the old studio stand empty.

"Mountain, valley, and garden scenes are shown in profusion," wrote a local journalist about the Fred Church "society-western," observing "the cast appeared a trifle amateurish . . . none of its members except Fred Church, W.J. Tedmarsh, and Emanuel 'Nig' Sampson having appeared in films before."

Even before *Wiles of the West* had its premiere showing, an outfit which called itself Atma Productions came to the Flying A studio to continue filming scenes for a feature titled *Eyes of Envy*, the first scenes for which had already been shot aboard a battleship in San Pedro Harbor.

And about the same time there was still another feature, *The All-American*, in production at the former studio of Flying A. Location scenes for that production were considerable and involved a local high school assembly program and a Boy Scouts gathering in Santa Barbara.

Such efforts proved far too feeble for the Flying A facilities ever to see permanent renewal as a film production center.

In June 1948, most of the remains of the studio were brought down, levelling most of one side of the 2000 block State Street. Ironically, demolition was by local contractor Charles Richardson, who had poured much of the concrete for the studio structures just 35 years earlier.

As for Hutchinson and Freuler, they lost fortunes in Mutual Film, the firm in which they'd been partners with Harry Aitken. Both Flying A and Mutual disappeared long before the sound picture craze seized America.

Part of the studio of American Flying A may still be viewed, though it's a private residence now. Part of one other structure remains, incorporated into a section of Bible Presbyterian Church.

Report has it that what remains of the rose garden of the studio also is in evidence, its blossoms waxing seasonally into rich beauty only to fade and wither as did the firm which brought the garden into being.

# The American Mutoscope and Biograph Co.

The history of Biograph started much earlier than the time of its acquisition of its first indoor studio at 11 East 14th St., New York City. Before the firm added the word "Biograph" to its corporate title, its headquarters had been at 841 Broadway. There, in 1896, it had established both a rooftop "studio" and below that, its own film laboratory facilities and offices.

The firm had started operations as American Mutoscope shortly after its founding on December 27, 1895, a partnership involving W.K.L. Dickson, a former associate of Thomas Edison. Besides Dickson, there were Herman Casler, Harry N. Marvin and Eliza Koopman. The declared purpose of the new firm: to utilize certain cameras which the partners patented under the name of one of their group, Herman Casler. Such cameras were to be used in making sequential moving pictures for a peep show device known as a Mutoscope.

Edison should perhaps have paid more heed to the rise of this new competitor, for it was to grow swiftly. "The most alert competitors of (Edison's) Kinetoscope," wrote Benjamin Hampton, film historian, "were the men who devised the Mutoscope ... and the Biograph...."

In order to avoid possible infringement upon Edison's patents, the earliest moving pictures made by Biograph utilized a camera driven by an electric motor, exposing a negative in which each frame of film was about 2¼" by 2¾", the film exposed at 30 and 40 frames per second. (The film stock measured 62mm in width.) The camera was cumbersome and heavy; the resulting negative size was incompatible with the 35mm width film which had already come to be a "standard."

After American Mutoscope and Biograph outgrew its rooftop, outdoor studio in New York, it acquired this brownstone at 11 East 14th Street. Once a palatial residence, the place had a large dance hall inside that served as the stage for countless films.

In 1897 the firm began using its new "Mutograph," a camera which bore an exterior likeness to Pathe cameras of that period, but which circumvented Edison patents by using a raw film stock which was placed in the camera unperforated. As the camera was cranked to expose the film, the machine punched its own rows of perforations along the edges of the 35mm ribbon. This unorthodox camera also produced photographic images which bore inconsistent widths for each frame— another precaution against lawsuit.

At its rooftop studio, Biograph set up its camera under an open-front shack mounted on a set of metal tracks, an arrangement permitting the heavy "Mutograph" to be moved when necessary. The stage area was similarly mounted.

Biograph prospered, its Mutoscope peepshow devices rather quickly outstripping the sales of Edison's Kinetoscope.

So successful was the Biograph operation that in 1906 it was able to lease a venerable town house situated at 11 East 14th St., not far from Union Park. Lillian Gish, who as a child appeared in films made by Biograph, described the 14th Street studio as "a Victorian brownstone solidly built and well laid out, originally the townhouse of a rich, self-indulgent bachelor. The ballroom—now the studio (of Biograph)—had been the scene of lively balls and glamorous parties. . . ."

At the time that the ballroom was being converted for studio use, powerful new Cooper-Hewitt mercury vapor lamps became the artificial light sources, casting sharply white, glaring illumination at once so cold-looking as to render the setting in stark bas-relief; the camera, with its equally unsubtle old orthochromatic film stock, producing sharp contrasts between black and white images.

By 1907, Biograph was employing two cameramen, Arthur Marvin and G.W. "Billy" Bitzer, neither of whom wanted to direct the productions they filmed. Henry Marvin, president of the firm, thereby proceeded to offer a position as screen director to David Wark Griffith, a second-string stage actor who came into the organization as a player and occasionally a writer of screen stories.

During two days in June 1908, Griffith directed his first film, *The Adventures of Dollie,* a one-reel melodrama released the following month. The budget for the picture was $65.

A year later, with Griffith firmly established as its chief director, Biograph had begun to build a stock company of players for its little films. Mary Pickford, Mack Sennett, Owen Moore, Marion Leonard, Florence Lawrence, Linda Arvidson, James Kirkwood, Billy Quirk, Lionel Barrymore, Henry B. Walthall, Arthur Johnson and others were employed regularly at the studio.

As her work continued at Biograph, Mary Pickford succeeded in finding employment there for sister Lottie and brother Jack—though their employment at the studio at first seems to have been confined to appearing in Mutoscope subjects, which were made on postcard-sized photographic "flip cards" shown in the coin-in-the-slot machines made and sold by the company. The teenaged Miss Pickford also introduced her boss, Griffith, to a couple of children named Lillian and Dorothy Gish—who immediately became members of the Biograph "stock company."

A particularly cold and bitter New York winter in 1910 prompted Biograph to dispatch Griffith, together with a small company of his players, to California in order to continue outdoor photography of their pictures. Theirs was by no means the first motion picture company to search out the climate of Southern California. Selig, New York Moving Picture Company, Kalem, IMP, and Essanay all were shooting pictures there before Griffith journeyed to the West Coast.

The first Biograph "studio" in California proved to be nothing more than a vacant lot at the corner of Grand Avenue and Washington Street in Los Angeles, a lot which was circumscribed by a high board fence and equipped with a revolving "shed" which could be rotated to follow the sun. It was to be Griffith's "stage" for use in making whatever interior scenes were needed to accompany the outdoor sequences for his productions that winter.

In April 1910, Griffith and other personnel left California, returning to New York City with an impressively large array of completed films including *Ramona, The Thread of Destiny, A Romance of the Western Hills, Love Among the Roses, The Unchanging Sea* and *The Two Brothers,* all of them 15-minute pictures.

By this time both Griffith and Biograph were riding high in popularity and rich financial success. It was, unfortunately for the company, a largesse which was to endure but one decade. Griffith was to leave Biograph in the early autumn of 1913, not many months after Mary Pickford had left for a time to take employment with IMP (only to return to Biograph at the beginning of 1912). Once Griffith had severed his ties with the firm he did not go back. Pickford finally left Biograph for good after completing the one-reeler *The New York Hat* in 1913. Before she did so, Mary had gone to California as part of Griffith's entourage. Temporary "studios" for Biograph had been established at 312 California St. in Santa Monica and, later, at 906 Girard St., Los Angeles.

While Griffith was in California accomplishing exterior shooting for the four-reel Biograph production *Judith of Bethulia* (released subsequently in four separate one-reel "episodes"), Biograph moved from 14th Street to more spacious quarters on 175th Street in the Bronx. There Griffith completed interior shooting for *Bethulia* (1913), a production costing $36,000.

The release of *Judith of Bethulia* as four separate films instead of as a four-reel feature drove the final wedge into a widening rift between the studio and Griffith.

The stubborn refusal of the firm to produce pictures in excess of one or two reels in length was to be the death knell of the studio.

Even while Griffith was still in Biograph's employ, the firm attempted to branch into feature picture production by a rather unique procedure: it arranged to photograph Klaw and Erlanger stage plays (which quite naturally employed famous Broadway actors). Griffith neither was consulted on the plan, nor was he employed as producer or director of such motion picture versions.

Klaw and Erlanger produced many successful plays, and profitably translated a few to motion pictures; however, Biograph's simplistic scheme was not to prove financially successful. If it had, the idea might well have saved Biograph from extinction. Alas, movie audiences did not enjoy seeing stage plays transferred onto film.

Biograph marketed its final releases in 1916, the lifespan of that firm measuring 21 years.

# Astoria Studio

Once a business largely restricted to the East Coast of the United States, motion picture production had begun migrating westward early in the 1900s. When the migration was complete, only a few studios remained in the East, one of which eventually was the Paramount studio at Astoria, Long Island, one of the busiest New York studios especially after the talking picture first became *de rigueur.*

Indeed, much of Paramount's early output of sound film came from here, including its newsreels and considerable "insert footage" for its feature films. The Marx Brothers appeared in their initial two feature films, *The Cocoanuts* and *Animal Crackers,* at the Astoria lot. The now nearly forgotten comic Jimmy Savo made at Astoria the feature *Once in a Blue Moon* (1936) for the partnership of Ben Hecht and Charles MacArthur.

If there were any single fault with films made at Astoria, it was that nearly all had an intangible something which separated them from their Hollywood counterparts: sets seemed smaller, more fraught with the "cardboard" look than Hollywood productions. Then, too, there was a sharp lack of exterior filming which, in the end, made the Astoria product almost claustrophobic to watch.

A phrase from the lyrics of the song "Paper Moon" seems strangely to apply to the pictures which issued from Astoria: "It's a Barnum and Bailey World, just as phoney as it can be. . ." for there was unquestionably an artificiality about Astoria productions which placed most of them in a category of cheap, loosely hung canvas.

Yet, several motion picture stars who found Hollywood restrictive, among them Rudolph Valentino and Gloria Swanson, at one time or another fled to Astoria, Valentino making his film *Monsieur Beaucaire* (1924) in Astoria, while Gloria Swanson did likewise in the case of her feature *Manhandled.*

Officially opened in September 1920 as the Famous Players–Lasky Studios, the place became Paramount's Eastern Studio late in the same decade, eventually becoming one of several studios which Paramount

**Lee Strasberg, George Burns, and Art Carney hold up a bank guard in the 1979 Martin Best production *Going in Style*. George Burns surely felt nostalgic as he came back to the Astoria Studios where he and his wife Gracie had appeared in comedy shorts in the early 1930s.**

operated besides its Hollywood one. There were Paramount studios, for example, near London and at Bombay, India.

When the studio at Astoria began production, the first film to be made on its main stage was George Fitzmaurice's production, *Paying the Piper*, released in 1921.

Eventually Paramount began to lease space to other firms for one or more productions, although in 1927 Paramount had shut down this operation at Astoria, reopening it as a facility for the production of the new talking pictures, the earliest of these the Jeanne Eagels 1929 feature *The Letter* co-directed by Jean de Limur and Monta Bell.

A great advantage which Astoria had was its proximity to Broadway, which gave easy access to talent which otherwise might not have been easily available for pictures, especially the many Broadway luminaries who were employed in some of the Paramount short subjects made at Astoria, among them Bob Hope, Fred Allen, Jack Haley, Willie and Eugene Howard, Jack Benny, Danny Kaye and others.

Joseph Ficarrotta, an instructor of motion picture photography at Fort Monmouth, N.J., from 1952 to 1954, recalls that one course he taught included a field trip to the Astoria Studio, which he recently described as "a real event for my class, which often was able to observe actual production taking place on the huge sound stages." The Army continued to use the facility as late as 1972, by which time the army had been there for thirty years.

The five-and-one-half acre facility then fell into the hands of the city of New York, which tried assigning the place to La Guardia

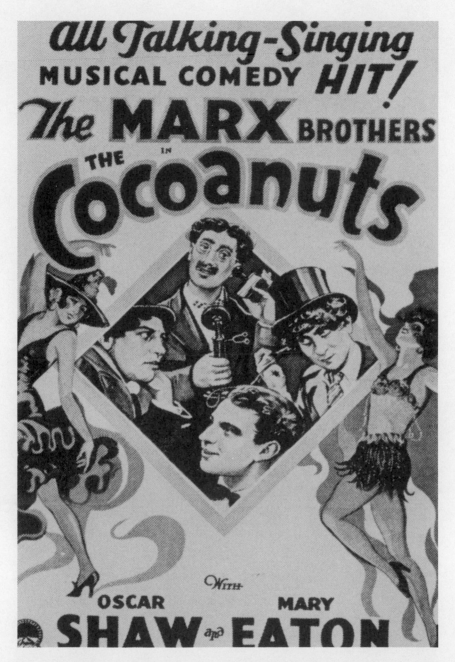

*Opposite:* A part of the back lot at the Astoria Studios as it appeared in 1929; the set is for Robert Florey's *The Battle of Paris. Above:* One of the two Marx Brothers feature pictures made at Astoria Studios, this 1929 film spoofed the Florida land boom; the state in 1925 had also been hit by a hurricane.

Community College, which never used it. By 1975 the city was preparing to tear down the studio and outbuildings, at which point a cooperative group comprising city planners, TV unions and others came forward and formed the nonprofit organization which saved the studios.

Since then, several films such as *Fort Apache, the Bronx* with Paul Newman; Bob Fosse's *All That Jazz* and several other pictures have been made at the facility, using one or more of its seven sound stages. The present group in charge of the facility pays the city of New York $350,000 a year in rent, with a promise of 35 percent of profits over $2 million per year.

Presently the studio, now designated Kaufman-Astoria, is competing rigorously with Silvercup Studios, the latter operation preferred by producers of commercials for television.

For more than half a century, Astoria Studio has survived, brave but poor cousin of its Hollywood counterparts, stubbornly unwilling to give up the dream of becoming a major U.S. film center.

## Astra Films

Both Kalem and Diando Motion Picture studios had proven but brief residents of the Los Angeles suburb of Glendale. Still another outfit, Astra Films, was next to attempt to establish itself in that community, occupying the former lot of its two predecessors.

Buying buildings and equipment but not the property, Astra moved to Glendale early in 1919—almost on the heels of the Diando firm's departure. Partly financed by Pathe, Astra was headed by Louis Gasnier, who pointed out that Astra's parent company was "one of the big concerns with studios in New Jersey." Astra leased additional land in Glendale, giving the firm about 22 acres for stages, offices, laboratories and back lot.

The studio quickly undertook a serial starring Ruth Roland and George Larkin, a Glendale man who'd already appeared in many films, including several Vitagraph productions. *The Tiger Face,* directed by Paul Hurst, also a Glendale native, was finally released under the title *The Tiger's Trail.*

"A small city will arise as if by magic," stated the *Glendale Evening News* in referring to Astra's arrival in California. "Hundreds of extras will be used in many of the scenes; it is confidently expected that this great studio will rival any of those in Hollywood or other parts of Los Angeles."

As if to underscore those enthusiastic predictions, actor Lewis

Cody, together with his director, W. Christy Cabanne, speedily began production of pictures at the Astra lot, prompting rumors that it was Cody who actually owned the lot.

Astra's activities at Glendale occasionally wrought rather zany happenings in the town. There was, for example, an unusual "butterfly day" when both Glendale kids and grownups were requested by Astra to corral hundreds and hundreds of butterflies for use in the feature picture *The Butterfly Man,* which required about a thousand of the winged insects. Someone named Opal Peck turned up at the studio with 21 butterflies, Jack Wright with 18, and an Edward Stockbridge with 16 (eight of which were Monarchs). That the butterfly hunt was successful is evidenced by a story two months later: "*The Butterfly Man* with Lew Cody is in the Astra cutting rooms, as script readers are at work trying to select the script for Cody's next film."

Elsewhere on the Astra lot, scenes were being shot under the guidance of James Horne for the serial *The Third Eye,* while Mae Marsh, it was announced, would begin work at the Astra Studio in February 1920.

Oddly, though, 1920 began for Astra with a decided lull in production, the firm announcing to the industry and the public that while it was in some sort of "quiet routine," it envisioned big things for the future.

*The Third Eye* was almost finished by mid–January, while another serial, *The Broadway Bat,* was announced for Ruth Roland, in spite of the fact it was becoming gradually clear that Astra had hit upon difficult times. At the beginning of 1920, Lew Cody and Astra chief Gasnier returned to Glendale following a flight to New York City, a trip necessitated by financial problems.

As 1920 wore wearily on, there was little production activity at the Astra lot, although a Glendale newsman reported, a trifle too glowingly it now appears, that some of the members of the Ruth Roland Company were doing location scenes for the fourth episode of *The Broadway Bat.* At the same time light comedian Lloyd Hamilton was busily completing a block of comedies at Astra, creating the appearance of considerable activity there.

Possibilities for continued production were gloomy, though in April 1921 Astra enthusiastically announced plans for enlargement of the facilities: "Demands are great at present," studio heads optimistically reported, "for one- and two-reel, high-class pictures." James Adams, James Horne and Lloyd Hamilton all were reportedly working on comedies at Astra, and producer Jack White (brother of the better known Jules White) had just completed a series of *Mermaid* comedies at the Astra lot.

Just what transpired after mid–1921 can only be guessed at, but by

1922 Astra had degenerated into a rental facility for makers of one- and two-reel comedies. Even serial production had ceased, while feature production had become almost nonexistent.

Then the bombshell burst. "Old Kalem Plant Here Being Razed," headlined an article in a Glendale paper of August 1922. "Soon the old Kalem plant on Verdugo Road will be no more," the paper solemnly reported. "One of the original cradles of the motion picture industry, situated on the Woodbury Ranch, in the eastern section of the city, is giving way to progress, while the barnlike buildings of the best western street' are being wrecked by the White-Mead Company."

"For the last several years the plant has been known as Astra Studios, where many photoplayers of note have worked," the story continued, "Carlyle Blackwell, George Melford, Marin Sais, Helen Holmes, and heaven knows what a host of others flitted across the stages . . . or through the company street."

The reporter closed his report, "In the closing of the studios recently, almost a score of permanent residents have had to shift to other employment or else go to Hollywood."

# Balboa Studios

The year: 1916. The place: Long Beach, California. Near the corner of Alamitos and Sixth Street there is a fancy sign atop a gateway: "Balboa Films." Balboa Amusement Producing Company had started out in Hollywood back in 1913, a really down-at-the-heels outfit put together by a former stage producer named H. M. Horkheimer, who possessed, it is said, a total capital of but $7,000 when he started film production. By knocking out a fast, cheap group of one- and two-reel films, and a serial titled *When Fate Was Kind* that Pathe released, Horkheimer and his brother, Elwood, scraped together enough cash and landed enough credit to hie themselves with their Balboa outfit out to Long Beach in 1914.

Once there, the Horkheimers proceeded to acquire an old Thomas A. Edison outdoor stage and tiny office building, several acres of space for their "lot," and as time scurried onward, a nearby 11 acres at Signal Hill, the latter for use in shooting sequences in outdoor films.

Both the Horkheimers were originally from Wheeling, West Virginia. As young men they'd worked with circuses and theatrical groups, sometimes in jobs as modest as those of ticket takers, and like so many others, became enamored of show business — and eventually a new and novel branch of the business, motion pictures.

Balboa Amusement Company, as the front of its studio at Long Beach, California, appeared in late 1919. Note the large, glass-enclosed stage at right rear of the photo, said to be the largest glassed-in stage west of New York.

Apparently it was H.M. Horkheimer who first ventured into film production: he set himself up in 1913 as president of Balboa, and was joined soon after by his brother Elwood, who became treasurer of the firm. Together, the two began to quickly build Balboa into a busy, expanding and viable operation, though in their haste to expand the firm they were almost always without cash.

Balboa came to comprise by 1917 an operation which occupied about 15 buildings situated around all four corners of Alamitos and Sixth. Balboa's true heydey began at a time when the firm's brand new glassed-in stage was leased to comedian Roscoe "Fatty" Arbuckle, who was then residing in Long Beach, at 1830 E. Ocean Blvd., close to actress Theda Bara.

Big and busy as it became, it was never to be more than a shoestring operation, with increasing cash flow all the time, but little went beyond meeting the burgeoning payroll and the costs of expanding and enlarging the studio and facilities.

As early as 1915, Balboa had an output of around 15,000 feet of finished negative film each week, making it one of the largest independent film producers in the U.S.

Balboa had many actors and creative personnel directly under contract, including Henry B. Walthall, Ruth Roland, Neva Gerber, Lew Cody and others. Directors Henry King and William Desmond Taylor (the latter destined to be victim of a murder which shook the film world) were Balboa employees, too.

In personnel and physical assets, Balboa Amusement Enterprises, in 1917, showed every sign of becoming a permanent and profitable company.

So successful was Balboa for a time, that founder and president H. M. Horkheimer was able to tell a reporter for the *Long Beach Daily Telegram* in 1917, "While I do not pose as a prophet . . . I have every reason for believing that the biggest improvements in pictures [are] ahead. We of Balboa would not be spreading out if we did not have faith in the industry."

Horkheimer and his brother proved that his words were not simply an idle boast, by plowing into the studio and its facilities $300,000 within only a few years after they had established the studio, a figure which was upwards of $2,000,000 by the time the Horkheimers were financially insolvent, a few years afterward.

Throughout the years 1914 through 1917, however, Balboa rode high, turning out serials and short films before longer feature pictures came into vogue during World War I, at which time the Horkheimers switched to making full-length films.

In 1915 Balboa turned out *Who Pays?*, a 12-part film released serially by Pathe, and followed by *Neal of the Navy*, a 14-chapter Pathe serial which proved timely in that it came almost on the eve of America's participating in World War I, and at a time when patriotic fervor ran high.

*Red Circle*, another 14-chapter serial, proved particularly memorable in that it offered the public the serial queen Ruth Roland in a not-entirely-sympathetic role in which a birthmark on her hand leads the character portrayed by Miss Roland away from the path of righteousness.

Balboa's next chapter play again comprised 14 episodes. Issued in 1916, *Grip of Evil* starred the then-popular actress Jackie Saunders (who married Elwood Horkheimer, treasurer of Balboa). Miss Saunders was not only assured of work at Balboa by her marriage to one of the Horkheimers, but was a more agreeable person than was the temperamental Miss Roland.

Despite Roland's somewhat less-than-pleasant personality, she was the featured player in the Balboa serial *Neglected Wife* which, it turned out, was the final chapter play in Balboa's brief history.

There were countless one-, two- and three-reel films made by Balboa all during its years of operation, two of them in full color *(Shrine of Happiness* and *Rose Among the Briers)*.

The bewilderingly large output of films from the Balboa lot speaks eloquently of the feverish tempo of production there, especially in the busiest years of the studio (1914–1916). It was the sort of production pace which made adequate work schedules for such players as Baby

Marie Osborne, Anita King, Gloria Joy (whom Balboa advertised as "the child wonder"), Cullen Landis, Kathleen Clifford and many others.

Somehow Balboa seemed almost to become a runaway machine, pumping out its products at such a dizzying pace that by 1916, Pathe officials were warily advising the Horkheimers to slow their pace of production. Once in high gear and at full throttle, however, Balboa seemed unable to slacken its pace. Before long, the market was so badly glutted with Balboa products, that the Horkheimers and Pathe separated. That separation of producer and distributor was to prove the Horkheimers' downfall, though it didn't immediately become apparent.

By the time America recovered from the effects of World War I, a nationwide recession swept in; the Horkheimers were forgotten. They had last been active in motion pictures when in 1917 they had supervised a group of feature films, each four reels in length. There were about a dozen such pictures, all of which were distributed by General Film as parts of a group of releases that General called "Falcon Features" (and some of which were also made for General Film by Vitagraph).

The titles of the 1917 features which the Horkheimers supervised bore, for the most part, uninspired titles such as *Best Man, Clean Gun, The Phantom Shotgun* and *Zollenstein.* A few were directed by Henry King, others by William Bertram, Harry Harvey, Otto Hoffman, Bert Brackin and Edgar Jones. They were the final pages of the brief, busy history of Balboa films.

The Horkheimers' studio existed but a dozen years; its spot in film history minuscule. Demolition of the buildings which once housed Balboa occurred around the middle of 1923. Before that a few others tried to make a success of the studio but, like the Horkheimers, they failed.

And while the Horkheimer brothers had financed the way of Balboa largely with the firm's profits, they were forced to turn frequently to local bankers for added financing, so that when Balboa ultimately lapsed into insolvency, three Long Beach banks emerged as Balboa's largest creditors. One of the institutions, Security Bank, was the chief holder of liens against the studio.

There were various salvageable assets left, chief among them the property on which the studio stood. The stage properties contained in the "prop department" of Balboa remained, too. About 100,000 pieces of furniture, pictures and other items were sold at auction in 1922.

Just how hastily the Horkheimers had left the Long Beach area may be gleaned by the fact that they are said to have left behind in Balboa's film vaults some 17 feature pictures, all new and unreleased! Some 14 of these pictures later fell into the hands of Charles W. Harlow, a wealthy oil man who found the films after he'd purchased the corner of the old Balboa lot on which the film vault stood. Representatives of Mr. Harlow took the films to New York where they succeeded in selling them, it was later reported. Presumably, the films were eventually released, though not to the Horkheimers' financial betterment, it would seem.

The Balboa lot had functioned for a time after the Horkheimers disappeared from the scene, but primarily as a "rental stage facility" on which various independent motion picture and educational film productions were churned out on budgets even smaller than those the Horkheimers accorded their productions.

When a Mr. D.A. Graybill appeared in Long Beach, he was able to buy what was left of the Balboa lot for $200,000. Graybill subsequently authorized demolition of the stages and other buildings, subdivided the property into smaller parcels and sold them, relegating Balboa Amusement Company to American cinema history.

# Balshofer's Studios

Entry into the world of photography occurred for Fred J. Balshofer when he was only a boy, apprenticed to a small New York firm which made and sold glass lantern slides, hand tinted, most of them lettered with the words to up-to-the-minute song hits for showing in nickelodeons, taverns and such.

His occasional contacts with movie houses convinced Balshofer that motion pictures were soon to outstrip glass lantern slides; consequently, when he was in Philadelphia in 1905, the youth made his way to the crowded and shabby optical shop of Siegmund Lubin, a sign in the window proclaiming that Lubin made and sold motion pictures.

Once inside, the youthful Balshofer gave Lubin an account of how he photographed and prepared lantern slides and performed laboratory work. Lubin, without hesitation, gave the boy a job as a laboratory technician operating the Lubin lab, and soon afterward, photographing titles, as well as scenes about the city, with the primitive and bulky Lubin motion picture camera.

Much of Lubin's activity lay in "pirating" negatives and prints of motion pictures made abroad, many produced by the famed and imaginative magician and moviemaker George Melies of Paris. Illegal though such Lubin activities were, Balshofer remained with the pioneer filmmaker for three years during which the young man learned the rudiments of the motion picture.

In the spring of 1908 Balshofer returned to New York City, where he formed a partnership with Herman Kolle, a youth whose father owned Prospect Hall at 272 Prospect Avenue, South Brooklyn, a rental auditorium of a type which flourished in those days. The hall consisted for the most part of a large auditorium with balconies around three walls, a stage, and a generously proportioned dance floor. Adjacent to the hall itself was a large summer garden which Balshofer and his partner certainly could use, Kolle's father said, on whatever sunny days the boys chose to make moving pictures with their field model Pathe camera.

A motion picture lab was set up beneath the stage of the hall with tanks, film racks, and a motion picture printer for copying prints from negatives. Kolle and Balshofer hastily came up with a trademark for their film productions: a crescent moon against a dark firmament, with the accompanying words "Crescent Film Company." The modest firm began turning out split-reel subjects with titles such as *A Desperate Character*, *What Poverty Leads To*, and *Young Heroes of the West* (the latter a western starring neighborhood youths in a not-too-convincing scenario of derring-do).

Surprisingly, all the Crescent subjects found a ready market; one New York film exchange even bought multiple prints of some Crescent subjects, that particular firm being invariably provided with prompt, efficient service, and with personal delivery by Balshofer. In this way Balshofer came to know well the owners of that exchange, one a former horserace bookie, the other an ex-trolley car conductor: Adam Kessel and Charles Bauman.

The partnership which had resulted in Crescent Film abruptly broke up a few months after it was formed. Although it had been successful, Kolle became terribly frightened once he discovered that detectives hired by Thomas A. Edison and the Motion Picture Trust Company were strongarming independent filmmakers like Crescent, dragging them into court and otherwise harassing them. So fearful did Herman Kolle become that he encouraged his partner to close their operation.

So while Balshofer suspended work as a partner of Kolle's, he bought the motion picture camera which Crescent owned, and set out to join Kessel and Bauman in the formation of the grandiosely named New York Motion Picture Company, another outlaw firm. (The term "outlaw" implies a filmmaker who was not allied with Edison's Motion Picture Patents Company.)

The new organization grew swiftly, establishing numerous production groups which turned out a variety of one- and two-reel pictures under such trademarks as Bison 101, Keystone Comedies, Kaybee, and Domino. Thomas Ince, a former stage player, along with Mack Sennett, a former actor and assistant director at Biograph, joined N.Y.M.P.C. in positions as heads of film units.

Soon, both Ince and Sennett were overseeing production at two California locations, Ince at a canyon location between Santa Monica and Los Angeles, Sennett at a studio in Edendale, a suburb of L.A.

N.Y.M.P.C. profits were immense, helped no doubt by the stock companies of players employed by Kessel and Bauman. Faces soon to be familiar around the world—Charlie Chaplin, Ben Turpin, William S. Hart, Mabel Normand, Charles Ray, and scores of others—worked for N.Y.M.P.C. producers.

As profitable as his partnership with Kessel and Bauman had proven, Balshofer saw a very large, dark cloud on the horizon, a cloud which he decided would soon bring a storm, perhaps a destructive one: a former film exchange owner named Harry Aitken, having bowed out of Mutual, was organizing a new firm soon to be christened Triangle, the three points of that geometric figure representing D.W. Griffith and two N.Y.M.P.C. outfits—Keystone and Ince. Before that merger took place, Balshofer sold his holdings in N.Y.M.P.C. and was on his own.

New, hastily made plans caused Balshofer to visit Carl Laemmle of Universal, Balshofer proposing a contract under which he would form a studio devoted to making short comedy films for release by Universal. Moreover, having just been part of the firm which employed both Ford Sterling and Mabel Normand, Balshofer told Laemmle he was aware that neither had a contract with producer Mack Sennett; they were, in effect, free agents, and Balshofer claimed he could easily sign either one to a contract. Laemmle was impressed; accordingly, he granted Balshofer terms under which Universal would agree to handle Balshofer comedies.

Unfortunately, Balshofer soon discovered that he was too late to sign Mabel Normand; she'd already put her name on a contract with Sam Goldwyn. So, gritting his teeth, Balshofer set out to find Ford Sterling and offer the comic $250 per week. That contract signed, Balshofer hastened to issue still another contract: comedy director Henry "Pathe" Lehrman at $200 per week to direct the Sterling comedies.

Balshofer contracts were issued for other Mack Sennett discoveries including Louise Fazenda, Peggy Pearce, Bob Thornby, George Jeske, Chester Franklin, Beverly Griffith, and a child actress named Olive Johnson.

In February 1914, incorporation papers were signed, establishing the Sterling Film Company. The personnel and the paperwork set, Balshofer went to find a studio for the firm, his search the former Nestor Studio at the corner of Sunset Boulevard and Gower Street. Price of that entire property, buildings included, was $11,000, on terms of $500 down, the balance payable at $125 monthly.

The property measured 180 feet along the dusty thoroughfare one day to be known as Sunset Boulevard, and 280 feet along its sides, one of which was on Gower. Included within these boundaries were a stable, a carriage house and, by the time Balshofer acquired the place, an outdoor stage built by the former occupants.

Balshofer wasn't long in getting into production. Within months after starting operations, the Sterling Film Company was profiting so on its comedies that Balshofer sought to spread good cheer by giving his comic, along with director Lehrman, a good-sized bonus.

Taking the $1200 he acquired, Sterling made off at once for New York City, not returning for three weeks, at which time he was, as Balshofer described him, "flat broke." What "Pathe" Lehrman did with his largesse isn't generally known, but presumably it was expended in no wiser a fashion.

The prodigals, back at work, quickly began nearly constant feuding. If Lehrman was ready to start filming by 8 a.m., Sterling wasn't anywhere about until after 10 a.m. Soon Lehrman was not able to turn out even a split-reel comedy (half a 1000-foot reel) in an entire two weeks, although in that time director Bob Thornby had completed two "kid" comedies with little Olive Johnson.

Matters reached such an impasse that Balshofer fired Lehrman, retaining Sterling, while Balshofer directed several more comedies.

George Jeske, another comic on Balshofer's payroll, often had drawn laughs around the studio by doing imitations of Sterling in costume. In fact, Balshofer decided, it might be difficult for movie audiences to discern a Jeske imitation from a Ford Sterling original, providing those shots which employed Jeske included no closeups.

So, dismissing the troublesome Sterling, Balshofer began screening all the outtakes of earlier Sterling comedies, and around that discarded footage, concocted new comedies in which Jeske, mimicking Sterling, appeared in sufficient additional material to permit the studio to continue production until early in 1915, at which time all the outtakes had been exhausted.

In April 1915, Quality Pictures Corporation took over the studio of Balshofer. That unit, a partnership involving Balshofer, Richard Rowland (at that time president of Metro Pictures) and Joseph Engel, with capitalization at a modest $25,000, had as its avowed purpose the production of dramatic feature films.

Balshofer knew of a popular actor who, at the moment, was not under contract: Francis X. Bushman. Quickly Balshofer went to Chicago where he succeeded in obtaining Bushman for two years at $750 per week and a percentage of the profits from each picture which Bushman was to make.

So the lettering on the studio at Sunset and Gower was changed, this time proclaiming a new studio. At the same time, a railroad train speeding westward carried cloth banners on its baggage car announcing that on that train was Francis X. Bushman, star of Quality Pictures.

By spring of 1915, Bushman was appearing before the camera for scenes of a drama, *The Second in Command,* the negatives and prints for which were processed at Balshofer's studio, for distribution by Metro.

Bushman's second picture for Quality was shot largely on location in California's Big Bear Lake region. Before the camera rolled, however, Bushman began agitating for Beverly Bayne as his co-star (Miss Bayne was not yet married to Bushman). Somewhat perturbed to find that his new star was already appearing as if he might be as troublesome as Ford Sterling, Balshofer shrugged his shoulders and added Miss Bayne to his list of contract players. Big Jim Jeffries, the prizefighter, also appeared prominently in the next film, *Pennington's Choice,* a five-reel feature completed and released within the allowable time limit.

But Balshofer's troubles were not ended. Bushman proved to be increasingly bothersome, having conveniently forgotten his new employer advanced him considerable cash with which to pay a mountain of bills in Chicago before Bushman came west. So serious did problems between the pair become that Balshofer seemed unable (or at least unwilling) to undertake the production of *Rosemary,* the picture which was intended as Bushman's third one at the Quality lot. Balshofer eventually sent Bushman packing to Balshofer's partners, thus looking to other hands to deal with the temperamental player. Thereafter, *Rosemary* went into production with Lester Cuneo cast in the role which had been intended for Bushman, and with a supporting cast comprising Marguerite Snow, William Clifford and Frank Bacon.

With the addition of Lloyd Bacon to play the leading role, Balshofer's studio next made *A Corner in Cotton,* released March 9, 1916. For that film, Balshofer and eight of the cast in the picture journeyed to Jacksonville, Florida, for the purpose of shooting parts of the film; Howard Truedell was assistant director, Balshofer the director. The players involved in the location scenes included Marguerite Snow, Zella Call, John Goldsworth, Ed Rausch, and Ray McDermott. Trade journals of that time indicated that once the location work was completed, cast and crew returned to the Quality Pictures Studio in Hollywood for the purpose of filming the remainder of the picture.

During this time, Francis X. Bushman was yet under contract to Quality Pictures, but was filming at studios other than Balshofer's, making pictures such as *In the Diplomatic Service,* which was released October 1916. Concurrently, Balshofer's studio made *The Wall Between, A Million a Minute,* and *The Masked Rider* before abandoning the studio, which Al Christie eventually bought, paying Balshofer $22,000, double what he had paid for it.

Years afterward, Balshofer produced the 1922 feature *The Isle of Love,* which he wrote, produced, and directed. By that time he had acquired another studio, this one situated at 1329 Gordon Street, Hollywood, where the film pioneer rented out space to such other producers as Reggie Morris, Billy West, and Chester Conklin.

In the mid–1950s, long after his retirement from the film industry, Balshofer co-authored a book, *One Reel a Week,* in which he gave his version of how he was mistreated by Francis X. Bushman, Ford Sterling, and Henry Lehrman, his rationalizations possibly having a strong basis in fact.

# The California Motion Picture Corp.

Its first feature, *Salomy Jane,* went into release November 1914; its final production, *The Kingdom of Human Hearts,* began its discouraging rounds in April 1921.

Between those films there were 16 other feature-length productions, variously distributed by Al Lichtman's Alco Film Corp., by World Film, Ultra Pictures, and others.

As the story of the California Motion Picture Corporation began, the *San Francisco Chronicle* announced on January 6, 1914, the formation of two new studios, something which had "developed in a few months." Capitalized at $1,000,000, CMPC initially was headed by 27-year-old Herbert Payne, heir to a mining fortune; finances thus were obviously not ever to be a problem, or so it appeared.

Marin County, California, was selected as the site for the studios of the new corporation. An impressively large property near the town of San Rafael was purchased, and construction started on a sprawling layout, eventually to consist of numerous frame buildings, most of them painted virginal white, the largest of which was a glass-enclosed stage 30 feet high, with 6,000 feet of floor space.

Along with its main studio, CMPC created a ranch in California's Big Tree country, close to Boulder Creek in Santa Cruz County, where westerns and other outdoor pictures could be made amid authentic surroundings.

It had been the original intent of the firm to attempt to make pictures which dealt only with some phase of California history, a laudable but very limiting aim. *The Pageant of San Francisco,* made by CMPC in 1914, was an example of such, and was scheduled to premiere in San Francisco at about the time that city was to hold its Pan-Pacific International Exposition in 1915. The picture was liberally sprinkled with caballeros, scenes of the Gold Rush of 1849, of Indians, monasteries and monks.

Most surprising about the story choices for many of the company's subsequent pictures was that a large number were simply love stories set against the picturesque sweep of California backgrounds. (Beatrize Michelena, a Latin-American who entered films following an earlier career as a stage actress, was the most frequently seen leading lady in such CMPC feature films.)

It is likely that studio chieftains at CMPC carefully studied just which film stars were reigning favorites elsewhere in filmdom. Of course, Mary Pickford, Mary Miles Minter, Clara Kimball Young and other players must have surely come to mind, spurring CMPC officials to attempt to transform their own Beatriz Michelena into another such box-office favorite.

In addition to its less-than-famous feminine "star," the new California firm hired such players as Jack Holt, House Peters, and William Nigh (Nigh also functioned as one of a trio of CMPC directors).

Stories by local author Bret Harte yielded such CMPC films as *Salomy Jane* (1914), *The Lily of Poverty Flat* (1915), *The Rose of the Misty Pool* (1915), *Minty's Triumph* (1915), *The Heart of Juanita* (1919), *Just Squaw* (1919), and *The Flame of Hellgate* (1920).

Other famous authors' works were frequently filmed, too; in 1914 there was a version of *Mrs. Wiggs of the Cabbage Patch* (from the novel by Alice Hegan Rice), and in 1915 the feature *Mignon* was filmed, adapted from Goethe's poem "Wilhelm Meister."

While location shooting near the studio provided breathtaking backgrounds, casts and crews many times journeyed to other parts of the state, including Monte Rio in Sonoma County or to San Francisco.

Essaying the history of CMPC would be incomplete without noting the attempts at color films which were made there, the earliest of which was an advertising film, *Winning a Peach*, a hand-colored picture made as a promotional film for California Packing Corporation.

In the fall of 1918, the studio encouraged inventor/producer Leon Douglas and his Natural Color Motion Picture Co. in the creation of the color feature *Cupid Angling*, with Ruth Roland and Albert Morrison. Mary Pickford and Douglas Fairbanks made guest appearances.

The picture was made at CMPC studios and distributed by W.W. Hodkinson but proved to be unprofitable, owing to the fact that the special projection equipment needed for showing that film was something theatre owners just didn't want to invest in.

The triumvirate then heading the studio, President Herbert Payne, Business Manager Alex Beyfuss and Executive Producer George E. Middleton, was erroneously led to believe that Lewis J. Selznick, general manager of World Film Corporation of New York, could obtain bookings for CMPC releases, putting such pictures into the best movie houses throughout the world. Alas, early in 1916 World Film was reorganized and Selznick forced out; in the takeover, William A. Brady, longtime theatre magnate, took control of World, cancelling the contract with CMPC.

Deprived of having World Film distribute its new pictures, the northern California firm hastily turned to a smaller distributor, Ultra Pictures Corporation of New York City, for distribution.

Exhibitors Mutual contracted for the distribution of *Just Squaw* (1919), while the few later pictures from the CMPC were distributed simply on a "states rights" basis.

As early as 1914 CMPC studios had been used as "rental stages" by various other producers, including some with such unlikely titles as Bear State Co., J. Frank Hatch Enterprises, and Christian Philosophical Institute. Such outlandish outfits could never hope to garner any big-name screen players, and so contented themselves with such thespians as Velma Whitman, Mae Gaton, Frances Burnham, Hugh Metcalfe, Lona Good, and Seldy Roach (although occasionally employing "name" players such as Crane Wilbur and Ruth Roland).

The rumored wealth of President Payne did not extend to refinancing California Motion Picture Corporation: by the time the firm turned out the picture *The Woman Who Dared*, Payne's firm had extended its bank balance to the point where the company's checks were being returned stamped with the heart-stopping words "insufficient funds."

Treasurer Beyfuss kept the firm temporarily afloat by promises of funds to come, but soon found his efforts to no avail.

Beatriz Michelena states she had the perfect scheme for keeping CMPC alive: she and Middleton would simply accept, in lieu of back salaries due them, the studio facilities, meaning land, buildings, contents and all equipment.

Absurdly brazen though the proposal now sounds, the other figures in the CMPC organization accepted the proposal, leaving the studio to Miss Michelena and her partner. These interlopers turned out *The Heart of Juanita* (1916), *Just Squaw* (1917) and *The Flame of Hellgate* (1917), a trio of ill-starred feature films which sealed the fate of the Marin County Film Studio.

Subsequently, a disastrous fire broke out in the film vault, destroying originals, masters, and release prints of all the productions which had been made at the California studio. A few feet of such productions as *The Flame of Hellgate* have since come to light, but this footage is insufficient to reveal whether the overall output of CMPC was truly as good as many lovers of the film would like to believe.

Like many other early-day motion picture studios, California

Motion Picture Corporation is today only a small, nearly forgotten corner of American motion picture history, its nitrate ribbons lost forever in piles of dust and ashes.

# Cayuga Pictures

"New Movie Company Is Capitalized at $525,000" was the heading above an item on page five of the *Ithaca* (N.Y.) *Journal* of June 3, 1920. Cayuga Pictures, the news story explained, was chartered by the state of New York. Having leased a studio in Ithaca's Renwick Park (one previously occupied by the Whartons, then by Grossman Pictures), Cayuga Pictures was to be managed by James Naulty of New York City. Naulty, the newspaper stated, had been with Famous Players–Lasky Co.

"The firm will start its operations around June 15," a spokesman of Cayuga announced. "All exteriors for our films are to be filmed around Ithaca, the interior scenes probably in a studio in New York City."

The declared aims of the new company were lofty indeed; it would produce "only the highest grade feature pictures such as are now being released through Paramount and Artcraft, First National, etc."

In setting forth his qualifications for the position as president of Cayuga, Naulty cited part of his background in films: 1898–1906, he claimed, were years when he'd been in charge of production and sales for Thomas A. Edison, a position he left to establish "the rental end of the business with 'store theatres'." He cited a total of more than 20 years in film.

In 1912, Naulty said, he'd left General Film (a distributing combine of which Edison and others were members), to become vice president and general manager of Mutual Film. He resigned that position to help organize Triangle Film Corporation.

Naulty, together with longtime writer and editor Gardner Hunting, would produce pictures exclusively for Cayuga Pictures for five years. In their first year alone, the pair anticipated producing six full-length feature films.

At Renwick Park, Naulty announced, Cayuga would have a "fully equipped studio" (no studio ever has been known to be less than "fully equipped"!). It would have 45 acres of forest and river land, with 1200 feet of frontage on Lake Cayuga, for which the corporation was named. Ithaca suddenly was to become the "finest picture producing center in the East" according to one newspaper story.

"The directors feel . . . that this is the first high grade company ever brought to Itahca for motion picture production," an unnamed source told reporters. In an additional bit of fluff, Cayuga Pictures was to possess "two leading motion picture producers . . . at its helm."

Cayuga's initial production was to be directed by a Mr. Griffith, not the famed "D.W." but instead by one E.H. Griffith of New York City, who was to have as his assistant one A.F. Bernadec. Neither was famous in film production circles, nor was the head cameraman, William McCoy of New York City. McCoy's assistant, Ray June, was destined to become one of Hollywood's most famous cameramen.

The firm's initial production was an Americanization of a famous French novel. The film's title was not at first disclosed, although eventually *These Women Loved Him* was the working title of the picture.

Cayuga Pictures publicity indicated that the production would contain "a number of scenes of college atmosphere, with appeal from a plot involving strong love and familial ties."

Cornell University campus at Ithaca was to play a large part in the diverse backgrounds. "In this connection, we hope to photograph Ithaca's beautiful scenery as it never has been photographed before," one studio official told the press.

Early in July 1920, press releases by Cayuga Pictures claimed that the area of Ithaca was well suited to the needs of a motion picture company; film director E.H. Griffith was being enthusiastic over the natural scenery which abounded in and around Ithaca.

The first Cayuga Pictures production moved into its initial 10 days of shooting July 7, 1920, with seven principals of the cast appearing in scenes shot at Cornell's swimming pool, in Fall Creek Gorge, at Enfield Falls, and in the community of Cortland.

A week of unfavorable weather then moved into the Storm Country. With insufficient sunlight, it did not allow acceptable exterior scenes, so while personnel awaited the arrival of Frederic Burton and Charles Lane, an indoor set was hastily prepared in the Renwick Park studios. Still another exterior set was being readied for use in what studio publicists called a "truly spectacular fire scene."

While *These Women Loved Him* hardly sounds exciting, the Ithaca newspaper on August 3 announced that the Cayuga Pictures production would be highlighted by the filming of a "specially constructed [fraternity] house . . . the burning [of which] is in connection with the picture." Sections of a duplicate of an actual fraternity house at Cornell University had been constructed on the back lot at Renwick Park studios.

In describing the replica which was to be sent up in flames, the *Journal* explained, "The porch contains two electric lamps of the Old English type and a street has been provided in front of the building where a boulevard light . . . has been placed. The building is elaborately painted with special decorative effects and includes real glass windows and window curtains."

Because a fire unfailingly draws a crowd of onlookers, special trolley cars had been scheduled by the Ithaca lines to accommodate the expected hordes of viewers.

"J.N. Naulty [president of Cayuga Pictures] announced that the public will be welcome." Shooting was expected to commence around 7:30 p.m. or as soon as it was dusk.

The studio reported that many gallons of gasoline and oil would be added and numerous smoke bombs set off. As a precaution against having insufficient water for use by Ithaca's fire department, a deep ditch had been dug from nearby Lake Cayuga.

To provide proper illumination for the scene, high platforms had been erected on which powerful arc lamps were placed, providing a total of 7,000,000 candlepower. (One of the arc lamps had supposedly been tested by shining its beam along the water. Its light beam extended 16 miles, and within five miles of it one could easily read by that light.)

"The fire scene concludes local work of Cayuga Pictures Inc. for its first production," stated the local newspaper, which went on to say that the remainder of the picture would be filmed in a studio in New York City.

The fire scene was not filmed as per schedule, this footage finally being made on the evening of August 13. Some 3,000 visitors who'd been on hand in the region of Cayuga's "lot" on August 6 again showed up for the event, which had by then been delayed nearly two weeks.

With assurances to the citizenzry of Ithaca, N.Y., that he and Cayuga Pictures would be in the community for years to come, Naulty, like every other motion picture producer who moved into the pretty Finger Lakes region, quietly disappeared.

By early 1921, the mayor of Ithaca, convinced that his city would never be a filmmaking capital, advised his fellow townspeople to buy for the city of Ithaca the area then known as Renwick Park. As for the "old motion picture studio," as the *Ithaca Journal* quaintly termed that structure on April 21, 1921, the building "may be fitted up as an athletic hall for indoor contests and an adjacent building as a bath house."

The city eventually acquired Renwick Park. The total cost of the purchase? A mere $10,000.

That would seem to have closed the book on Cayuga Pictures, were it not for a story which appeared in an Ithaca newspaper on Wednesday, April 6, 1921, headed "Ithaca-made Picture to Be Released April 21." It stated that the unreleased film, retitled *If Women Only Knew*, was scheduled for release through Robertson-Cole, which the *Journal* described as "big distributors."

"The picture features such well known players as Robert Gordon, Madeleine Clara, Virginia Lee, Fred Burton, and others," concluded the news story.

In mid–September the management of Ithaca's Lyceum Theatre released a terse announcement that in early October that theatre would show *If Women Only Knew,* based upon Balzac's story "Meditations on Marriage." The management of the Lyceum reminded readers that the feature was the "last picture filmed in this city . . . with hundreds of local residents and [college] undergraduates . . . in the picture."

When the film played the Lyceum in Ithaca, a highly favorable review appeared in the local paper, which reported "The picture pleased large audiences at its matinee and evening presentations," adding that the feature contained "plenty of local color."

Ithaca's former "film studios" were gone by 1921, but memories of those intense activities still live on.

# Champion and Others Along the Palisades

The frame hotel was hardly impressive, nor was the potholed, dusty street which flanked its front. Looking more like a hostelry in the Old West than one just across the river from New York City, Rambo's served admirably as an exterior for early westerns, just as the nearby New Jersey Palisades had served Edwin S. Porter in filming *Rescued from an Eagle's Nest,* when D.W. Griffith was acting in such films.

If Rambo's was an early symbol of the part New Jersey played in the history of the American film, then the later glass studios in and near Ft. Lee were an elaboration of that.

The earliest of the "greenhouse" type studios in the Ft. Lee area generally is conceded to have been the Champion, built in 1909 for film producer Mark W. Dintenfass.

From the Champion studios poured an almost incredible number of Eastern-made westerns, including *At Double Trouble Ranch* (1911), *Caught by Cowboys* (1910), *The Cowboy and the Easterner* (1910), and a rare appearance by "Broncho Billy" Anderson in other than an Essanay western, *The Cowboy and the Squaw* (1910).

Many of Champion's non-westerns featured a youthful Irving Cummings, later an important Hollywood director. When Champion made its few movies which didn't feature cowboys, the results were often such action offerings as *An Aviator's Success* (1912), *Saved from the Titanic* (1912), or such melodramas as *An Italian Romance* (1912), and *A Daughter of Dixie* (1911).

**Rambo's Hotel at Coytesville, N.J., often doubled as a western hotel and bar. This is how it appeared in 1910 when it was serving as a setting for an Eastern-made western.**

So successful were Champion films that Dintenfass became one of the original founders of Universal and an important stockholder, until Carl Laemmle bought him out.

Two women figured in the establishment of a pair of Ft. Lee studios. Florence Lawrence, originally known to the filmgoing public as the "Biograph Girl," who with her husband, Harry Salter, founded the Victor studios in 1912. French actress-director Alice Guy Blache, in company with her husband, Herbert, established and operated the Solax studio, first at Flushing, New York, in 1910 and, in 1912, at its new studio in Ft. Lee.

The Solax operation in Ft. Lee entailed construction of a $100,000 glass studio, where the firm accomplished indoor filming for comedies, adventure films, and an occasional "big" production such as the 1912 picture *Fra Diavolo (The Devil's Brother)*.

In 1914 the Blaches organized United States Amusement Company for the purpose of making only feature-length films, releasing that output through Pathe and Metro. Such film players as Mary Miles Minter, Olga Petrova, Bessie Love, and Ethel Barrymore were starred in Solax productions.

Metro occupied facilities at the Solax studio from 1918 through 1920, turning out such pictures as *Eye for an Eye* (1918), *The Brat* (1919),

These interior views of two of the Ft. Lee studios reveal how much glass was needed in the construction of the "greenhouse" type stages for motion pictures.

**Blanche Bates emotes in a scene for *The Seats of the Mighty* filmed at Ft. Lee, N.J., in 1914.**

and *Out of the Fog* (1919), in which the heroine was Nazimova. At the same time, Solax made for Metro release the 1919 feature *Stronger Than Death,* a feature film which was co-directed by Herbert Blache and Charles Bryant.

The first few Keystone comedies were filmed in New Jersey. Mabel Normand was at Ft. Lee to make such shorts as *Cohen Collects a Debt* (1912), *The New Neighbor* (1912), *Riley and Shultz* (1912), and *Fatty and Mabel Adrift* (1916), which was directed by Arbuckle. Even after Mabel Normand left the Keystone firm to join Sam Goldwyn, she made a number of her pictures at Ft. Lee, as witness *The Venus Model* (1918) and *Sis Hopkins* (1919).

Not all New Jersey studios were at Ft. Lee and adjoining Coytesville. Herbert Brenon, the Irish-born director, had his Ideal Studios at Hudson Heights, where in 1916, he directed the six-reel feature *War Brides.*

Kalem had one of its several studios, at Cliffside, 1912 through 1915. E.K. Lincoln (not to be confused with Elmo Lincoln, the screen's first "Tarzan"), a well-to-do stage actor, built a motion picture studio between Ft. Lee and Cliffside, where he produced eight of his own films from 1916 to 1922, releasing them through such firms as Goldwyn, Affiliated Pictures, Mutual, Pathe, Associated, and U.S. Motion Picture Corporation. The Lincoln studio, later renamed the Royal Studio, was subsequently used for production of many Hope Hampton features.

The French firm of Pathe Freres set up its American branch under manager J.A. Berst, taking over a former cash register factory at Bound Brook, New Jersey, in 1910. For years afterward this modest plant housed the newsreel plant of Pathe; in 1912 part of Pathe's operation moved to a new glass-walled studio at 1 Congress Street, Jersey City.

The Pathe Freres firm was not destined to operate in America for long, however: In 1914 its U.S. operation was sold to Merrill Lynch and Company, which altered the name slightly, calling the firm "Pathe Exchange" and in 1919 establishing its headquarters in New York City.

During the winter of 1914–1915 Arthur Spiegel of the Chicago mail-order house put together a motion picture firm called Equitable. With the financial assistance of a conservative banking house, Spiegel next organized World Films Corporation, naming himself as its president, and Lewis J. Selznick its vice president and general manager. World Studios' general offices were established at Ft. Lee; William Brady, the Broadway producer, was named director of production. Spiegel's other motion picture firm, Equitable, channeled its output through World, as did Peerless Pictures, which was controlled by Jules Brulatour. Brulatour had amassed a personal fortune first as a distributor for Pathe film stock, later that made by Kodak.

During its first year of operation, World showed itself to be suffering from problems incurred through Selznick's immense ego; "money men" behind World Film acted quickly to force Selznick out. (Soon after the firm was further shaken by the death of Arthur Spiegel.)

In the meantime, Selznick went about organizing his own picture firm, and not any too soon; World Pictures collapsed soon after.

Selznick then acquired the film exchanges of the World Corporation, renaming the system "Republic Pictures," through which Selznick began release of medium- and low-priced features; his class "A" productions through Selznick-Select exchanges. (The Selznick operation had no connection with the much later Republic Pictures, which had studios in North Hollywood.)

Eclair, a French firm, established an American studio at Ft. Lee, and was active in the years 1914 and 1915 when it occasionally distributed its American product through Universal. Its Ft. Lee studio was considered one of the most modern and complete ones ever constructed although in all probability the Pathe studio at Jersey City was far better equipped once the Pathe operation was completed.

William Fox operated a studio in West Ft. Lee, along Main Street, a layout comprising a pair of glass "barns" (so called because both had quaint gambrel roofs styled after common barn designs). These studios were in use by Fox until sometime in 1919, having been leased to that firm by the owner-designer C.A. Willat.

The studios of New Jersey are only memories now, the parade of directors, movie stars, film laboratory technicians and other film workers having long gone, along with names such as Centaur, Triangle, Emile Chautard Productions, and the many others.

# The Chaplin Studios

What has often been described as the most aesthetically pleasing of all Hollywood film factories is that which once housed the Charles Chaplin firm. Built at the end of World War I, a time when Chaplin was at his height of popularity with audiences, its construction also coincided with the establishment of the United Artists Corporation, a firm in which Chaplin was one of the principals.

Unfortunately for the comic, his studio came into being at almost the time when he was becoming widely known as something of a leech upon American ways—a man who didn't mind gathering tubsful of U.S. dollars, but who insisted upon remaining a British subject.

Still, the momentum of his fame as a screen star well served both the artist and his purse, even during the years of the Great Depression when unemployment, hunger, and deprivation were rampant.

Chaplin was, in those years, rolling in money.

But more than a decade prior to Wall Street's collapse, when Chaplin had been deciding upon a place on which to build his studio, it wasn't clear what the comic had in mind for that gigantic place whenever he wasn't using it himself. For even in 1918, when the studio was opened, Chaplin's output of films was a trifle sporadic and besides was comprised of only "short subjects."

It is possible that his ego led him to consider that the studio would somehow serve as a sort of shrine to himself and his art, a place where he could have his name in large letters announcing him not as "Charlie" but as "Charles Chaplin."

At 1416 La Brea, a blocklong facade for the Chaplin studio quickly took shape. The studio's site had formerly been the estate of R.S. McClennan. Chaplin acquired the 5-acre tract for somewhere between $30,000 and $35,000. Instead of a protective wall along the front, Chaplin chose to have built an unbroken row of unimaginative imitations of Tudor-styled houses, one of which sported a window poking through the face of an exposed fireplace chimney. To Chaplin, however, the design was innovative and attractive. He afterward wrote of the place: "At the end of the Mutual contract (1917) I was anxious to get started with First National, but we had no studio."

He goes on to describe the property he selected: "The site was at the corner of Sunset and La Brea and had a very fine ten-room house and five acres of lemon, orange, and peach trees. We built a perfect unit complete with . . . cutting rooms and offices." The layout also included a film processing plant, a generous "back lot" on which to film exterior scenes, and the usual indoor stages and allied facilities.

Produced at the Chaplin studio, 1920's *The Kid* was distributed by First National.

The three-reeler titled *Sunnyside*, the picture *A Day's Pleasure* (both 1919), and Chaplin's milestone, the six-reel feature *The Kid*, were early products of the new studio, as were *The Idle Class* (1920) and the two remaining films which the Cockney clown turned out in order to fill his contract with First National.

In 1923, Chaplin turned to releasing his pictures through United Artists, the firm in which, for so long, he had been an equal partner with Mary Pickford, Douglas Fairbanks, and D.W. Griffith. Because Chaplin's output was slow and sporadic, there was scarcely a cornucopia of product from the Chaplin lot. *A Woman of Paris* (1923), *The Gold Rush* (1925), *The Circus* (1928), *City Lights* (1931), *Modern Times* (1936), and *The Great Dictator* (1940) were made at the Charles Chaplin Studio. Chaplin made but three films after that time, and these were made elsewhere.

The intervals between productions were far too great to justify the existence of a separate studio for such a small output, with so many employees being idled between their periods of activity. Still, it probably would not have been feasible to offer "rental space" to other producers; there were, after all, better equipped rental stages already going begging around the Los Angeles area. Surely Chaplin realized all this when he launched the elephantine project, though he may cannily have reasoned that such an operation would provide a good many tax loopholes, places where costs of depreciation and other factors could be turned into profitable items on tax ledgers. At the end of World War II Chaplin at last began offering studio space for rent; customers eventually included

**Although not a high-quality photograph, the imitation Tudor-style architecture is evident in the facade of the Charles Chaplin Studio.**

Cathedral Films, Walter Wanger Productions, and the soapmaker Procter and Gamble.

But even with these factors at work on his behalf, Chaplin was proud to point out later how he would, at a whim, shut down his studio completely whenever he chose to do so. Such was the case just after he completed *The Idle Class*, a time when, as Chaplin put it, "I could concentrate no further. I did not realize how tired I was . . . I told Tom [Chaplin's aide-de-camp] to pack my things and Alfred Reeves [who was in charge of the studio] to close the studio and give the company a holiday. I intended going to England."

Such decisions must have proven expensive, for the Chaplin studio regularly employed quite a number of personnel. Even Chaplin's cameramen, Roland H. Totheroh and Karl Struss, remained on call and on the studio payroll even when the studio was totally idle.

But as Chaplin's films became fewer in number, more dated in their techniques, the "Little Fellow" as Chaplin used to call his screen character, began to lose luster at the box office, furthered by Chaplin's appearance in the headlines as everything from an income tax evader, a leftist, and a defiler of young women. Whether all such charges were true is unimportant here; the results were, however.

Chaplin found himself becoming exceedingly unpopular, and moved to Vevey, Switzerland, into a self-imposed exile.

In 1966, after months of operation of the Charles Chaplin lot as "Kling Studios" (a rental stage), the La Brea studio was transferred to Herb Alpert and Jerry Moss for operation as A & M Records. (Chaplin is said to have sold the studio in March 1955 for $700,000, the sale taking place just the same month the comedian sold his remaining interest in United Artists Corporation.) By that time, the place had been designated by the city of Los Angeles as "Historical Cultural Monument No. 58," proclaimed by a bronze plaque near a gate to the studio. By that time, Chaplin's former house had been destroyed already and that part of the lot turned into a supermarket.

# Columbia Pictures

Denigrators of the late Harry Cohn say he was uncouth, suspicious-natured, thoughtless and vicious. Perhaps he was. Yet he overcame his many shortcomings while he turned Columbia Pictures from a very smalltime independent studio along "Poverty Row" into one of the majors, making and remaking stars in the process, even as he produced more than a few memorable films.

There were two Cohn brothers involved in the formation of Columbia, Jack (a less stormy personality than his brother) and Harry, both of whom were born in New York City in the late 1890s. Although the two never had gotten along well, they formed in 1920 a partnership with their cousin Joseph Brandt, first calling their outfit C.B.C.

Jack Cohn had entered film production through an early association with Carl Laemmle's "Imp" studios, where Cohn became a co-producer of the early "exploitation" feature *Traffic in Souls,* released in 1913. Remaining with Laemmle until well after Imp had become part of Universal, Cohn left the latter firm only when he started his own company.

Harry Cohn, formerly a "song plugger" for a New York music publishing firm and a cousin of Joseph Brandt, a former business executive, joined the other Cohn in building their C.B.C. firm mainly around a series of shabbily made "Hall Room Boys" two-reel comedies and cheaply made "Stars on Parade" short subjects, which for the most part were simply edited together out of newsreels and other readily obtainable material. By 1922 the C.B.C. Film Sales Corporation had branched into release of a few feature pictures, of which *More to Be Pitied* and *Only a Shop Girl* were early examples.

In 1924 the C.B.C. nomenclature was dropped (it is frequently said the name was abandoned because wags dubbed the company "Corned

**Even major firms often distributed pictures not made directly by their own studios. The Columbia release *Wide Open Faces* (1938) was made by David L. Loew. Shown in the foreground are Sidney Toler, Joe E. Brown and Jane Wyman.**

Beef 'n' Cabbage"), and the name "Columbia Pictures" substituted. The name was chosen in spite of the fact that there had already been a "Columbia Pictures," although that firm had expired less than a decade earlier.

While Jack Cohn operated the New York office of the firm, Harry took charge of studio operations. By 1927, Joseph Brandt had withdrawn from Columbia, although by that time the firm had become well enough established to acquire its own studio and offices at 1438 North Gower Street, between Sunset and Santa Monica boulevards, Los Angeles.

The Cohns were fortunate to acquire some highly creative personnel, craftsmen such as director Frank Capra (formerly a gagwriter at the Mack Sennett lot), who, though totally inexperienced in film, had bluffed his way into the industry as a director on a short film made in 1921 by San Francisco's Fireside Productions, filmed at a crude "studio" which had formerly been known as Jewish Gymnasium.

When Capra went to work as a director for Columbia he discovered that the lot was made up of a vast disarray of structures,

MIGHTIEST OF ALL MOTION PICTURES!

FRANK CAPRA'S
GREATEST PRODUCTION
RONALD COLMAN
in
LOST HORIZON

with
JANE WYATT · JOHN HOWARD
MARGO · THOMAS MITCHELL
Edward Everett HORTON · ISABEL JEWELL
H B WARNER · SAM JAFFE
From the novel by JAMES HILTON
Screen Play by ROBERT RISKIN
A COLUMBIA RELEASE

*Lost Horizon* (1937) was one of several top-drawer feature films which succeeded in raising Columbia from its status as a poverty row producer to the
lofty heights of a major Hollywood studio.

which he described as "additions to additions . . . two sides were now
three stories high; the third, two stories; the fourth, one and a half."

Capra describes the interior of the office building as possessing
"narrow halls rising and falling with the uneven levels, tunneled
through the maze." Capra's own office at Columbia consisted of a six-by-
eight-foot cubicle on the ground floor. The wonder of it all is, perhaps,
that amid such tawdry surroundings persons of Capra's imaginativeness
could place before the lens of the cameras spun dreams of nearly pure
gold, as magic and as captivating to film audiences as were films made
at far more attractive, better equipped studios where budgets were far
greater.

Operating in the early pre–Capra years, Columbia at first had no
studio facilities. Instead, the firm operated out of modest, inexpensive
offices, renting studio space only when filming a picture.

After acquiring the studio on North Gower, Columbia began making remarkable strides toward entry into the select circle of major
studios. Eventually there came the day, thanks to directors such as
Capra, when the studio attracted top-flight casts of players, although
Columbia always was a curious admixture of bad releases and good, of

"Now they all know what I am..."

COLUMBIA PICTURES presents
RITA HAYWORTH
*as*
*Gilda*
*with*
GLENN FORD
GEORGE MACREADY · JOSEPH CALLEIA
Screenplay by Marion Parsonnet
*Produced by* *Directed by*
VIRGINIA VAN UPP · CHARLES VIDOR

**Glamorous and sultry Rita Hayworth (who had earlier played in Republic "quickies" under her real name Rita Causino), was a favorite pinup queen of American soldiers during World War II, and a hugely profitable property of Columbia.**

independently made features and short subjects, and throughout most of the "sound era" offered very nearly the worst chapter plays ever foisted on a gullible public.

Harry Cohn had long been aware that film titles go a long way toward selling even a bad picture, although occasionally he found, too, that quite ordinary, almost trite titles also did well at the box office, as witness *Mr. Smith Goes to Washington, It Happened One Night, Golden Boy,* and others.

When the studio had edged its way into what was just barely the stature of a small major outfit, Harry Cohn discovered that he could often wheedle a major player or two from one of the big studios, especially when that player was becoming somewhat of a problem to the larger organization. In order to chasten such film stars, the big studios simply loaned their troublesome players—for a hefty fee of course—to Cohn's frayed-cuff outfit for a film or two.

By such means, Columbia landed Clark Gable for his role in *It Happened One Night,* an amusing, light comedy from director Frank Capra, and a picture which turned out to be an Academy Award winner.

By about a decade after Columbia was founded, the studio had a respectable number of players under contract, persons on whom the firm might call frequently if it chose, or might "loan out" to other studios for more money than the salaries it paid the actors under the terms of their contracts.

There were no fewer than 43 players under contract to Harry Cohn's little studio during 1936 and 1937, names which ran the gamut from the Three Stooges to such dramatic talents as Lew Ayres, Ralph Bellamy, Melvyn Douglas, Lloyd Nolan, Jean Arthur, Grace Moore, Fay Wray, and Thomas Mitchell. Even such western "stars" as Ken Maynard, Charles Starrett, and Leo Garillo had inked Columbia contracts by then, though Maynard's westerns were turned out by Larry Darmour Productions. (I never was on a Columbia stage," Maynard once said.)

Budgets on Columbia Pictures have ranged from those which were so minuscule as to make a Monogram producer appear a spendthrift, to those which aped M-G-M's class "A" productions. Still, even by the mid–1930s, Columbia offered few blockbusters of the caliber of Ronald Coleman in *Lost Horizon.* Instead, most were likely to be "B" features like *Death Flies East,* which offered moviegoers a cast headed by Florence Rice and Conrad Nagel, or of the "Blondie" category, which became a staple of the Columbia studio in 1938.

A widely diverse list of releases permitted Columbia to provide a respectable group of "A" budget pictures for playing time in large first-run theatres, and many "B" films to be seen in small-town and side-street theatres, often double-featured, of course, in this case with the latter group.

Along with a constant flood of feature films of both the "A" and "B" types, Columbia remained loyal to its commitment of supplying a regular output of serials and short subjects, the latter primarily the work of Jules White's comedy unit. Chief among White's comedy capers of course was his Three Stooges series, begun in 1934. Along with these many two-reelers, Columbia offered short comedies with Andy Clyde, El Brendel, Hugh Herbert and others. There also were "Screen Snapshots," and a diversity of other one- and two-reelers.

Producer Jules White, who operated his comedy unit almost as a completely separate arm of Columbia production, had grown up in California. Even as a child, White had been associated with motion picture production (he'd appeared in a good many silent films as a "bit" player). Jules and his brothers Jack and Sam all became associated with screen comedy. As long as Jules White's productions proved profitable and were turned out with unbroken regularity, Harry Cohn seemed satisfied not to interfere with the operation.

The studio's 57 sound serials, nearly all of which were 15-episode ones, did not begin appearing until 1937 (Frank Buck in *Jungle Menace* was Columbia's initial offering in this category). Some of them weren't produced by Columbia, as was the case with the Weiss Brothers' chapter play *The Mysterious Pilot* (1937) directed by veteran Spencer Gordon Bennet and made largely on location around a large lake to the north of Hollywood, where there was a strong resemblance to the wilds of Canada.

By seizing upon such locations near Hollywood, Columbia's serial producers, like those at competitive Republic and Universal lots, were able to produce some exceedingly diverse backgrounds, particularly for action sequences in their chapter plays. Columbia's serials, unfortunately, lacked story values and production qualities of even passable merit, placing them far down the ladder from Republic's serials, and a cut below those of Universal.

All Hollywood enjoyed boom years around World War II, in spite of the closing of many overseas distribution markets. Probably Columbia enjoyed the greatest studio growth of any of Hollywood's "big five" during these several critical years.

It was during these five years that Columbia really reached its peak as a true "major" studio. Its narrow alleys between sound stages were crammed always with players and other personnel, with props, scenery, cameras, autos and a staggering array of equipment and entities. All the sound stages were scheduled for day and night shooting. Scoring and editing departments worked feverishly as Columbia poured forth from its cornucopia such wartime films as *Adam Had Four Sons* (1941) with Ingrid Bergman and Warner Baxter, *Cover Girl* (1944) with Rita Hayworth and Gene Kelly, *Flight Lieutenant* (1942) with Pat O'Brien and Glenn Ford, *Here Comes Mr. Jordan* (1941) with Robert Montgomery, *The More the Merrier* (1943) with Jean Arthur and Joel McCrea, and *My Sister Eileen* (1942) with Rosalind Russell and Brian Aherne.

By the time the war ended, while Columbia still occupied its crowded lot along Gower Street, the firm had acquired recognized status as a major, with financial reserves and backing sufficient to gamble on such postwar technicolor features as *The Jolson Story*, in which Larry Parks played the part of the famous entertainer, *Bridge on the River Kwai* (1957) with William Holden and Alec Guinness, and *Guns of Navarone* with Gregory Peck and David Niven.

In 1968 Columbia was completely reorganized as Columbia Pictures Industries, Inc., with Columbia Pictures and Screen Gems (now called Columbia Pictures Television) as its major divisions. Harry Cohn, fiery head of the firm, was deceased by then, and the presidency was in the hands of David Begelman who, while he was to see the firm through some difficult years and with some outstandingly profitable feature releases, saw his career with Columbia crash but a few years later in financial disgrace on embezzlement charges by the corporation.

By that time, the original Columbia studio on Gower had long since been abandoned, the firm occupying space at the Warner studios. Today, as the firm jockeys for a solid, profitable share of the motion picture and television industries, countless motion picture enthusiasts and film historians recall with genuine fondness the days when an artist's concept of the "Lady Liberty," torch asparkle, stood draped in the Stars and Stripes, her stalwart likeness the proud evidence of what wonders a couple of boys named Cohn had fiercely wrought.

# The Cosmopolitan Studio

He loved the words "cosmopolitan" and "international." Both stood for hugeness, all-embracing power. So it's little wonder William Randolph Hearst founded a magazine called *Cosmopolitan* while naming his film studio that too. And his gigantic news bureau? That was "International News Service," of course.

For some reason, virtually all other film historians have ignored Hearst's role in film production, such scribes choosing also to overlook Hearst's nearly continual presence in newsreels beginning as early as 1913 when he teamed with "Colonel" William N. Selig in the regular release of Hearst-Selig newsreels.

Naturally, with such omissions the usual thing where Hearst is concerned, it is not surprising that film histories often overlook mentioning Hearst's film production unit at MGM which made such Metro features as *Ceiling Zero* (1936), *Young Mr. Lincoln* (1939), *Men in White* (1934), and *Manhattan Melodrama* (1934), the latter two pictures featuring Clark Gable.

Hearst comedies and animated cartoons based upon characters in Hearst newspaper comics were released to theatres as early as 1916, which such early chapter plays as the Edison Company's *Active Life of Dolly of the Dailies* (1914), *What Happened to Mary* (1912), and *Who Will Marry Mary?* (1913), as well as Pathe Wharton's serial, *Perils of Pauline* (1914), *Patria* (1917), *Beatrice Fairfax* (1916), and *Mysteries of Myra* (1916), all were productions with which Hearst was connected, at least peripherally.

More germane is that Hearst for a time had his own studio. To trace its beginning one has to go back to a period preceding World War I, though Hearst didn't announce formation of his Cosmopolitan

**An abandoned dance hall called Sultzer's was turned into the first studio of William Randolph Hearst's Cosmopolitan Pictures. Shown in production there is Marion Davies' *When Knighthood Was in Flower* (1922), directed by Robert G. Vignola.**

Productions until 1919. He had been dealing in motion pictures for years by that time, his International Picture Service distributing one-reelers such as the Katzenjammers, Judge Rummy and numerous other subjects. By the time playboy Hearst became acquainted with the petite showgirl Marion Davies he had purchased a gigantic barnlike building in Upper Manhattan which was previously a German–American club and dance hall named Sultzer's. The building was ideal for conversion into a movie studio, in as much as a large portion comprised a massive dance hall, unencumbered by pillars or similar impediments which might have created problems in obtaining long shots of large sets or interfered with the free movements of cameras and floor-level lighting units.

As Hearst's extramarital love affair with Marion Davies continued, he watched lovingly as the youthful charmer came to the screen in a film titled *Runaway Romany* (1918). He featured her in *Dark Star,* a seven-reel romance directed by Allan Dwan and distributed by Paramount under its Artcraft label, filmed at the newly occupied Cosmopolitan Studios.

Numerous other Cosmopolitan feature films followed, including

*The Miracle of Love* (1919) and such 1920 pictures as *The Restless Sex, Humoresque, The World and His Wife,* and *Heliotrope.*

As the flow of such films continued, Hearst spared no expense. *When Knighthood Was in Flower* (1922) was unusually lavish; the sets were as expensively designed and decorated as possible. Robert G. Vignola directed Hearst's ladylove painstakingly through 12 reels, 180 minutes of ersatz history of the never-never variety in which Hearst loved to star the girl for whom he'd gladly made himself the subject of endless gossip. All the Marion Davies pictures became insanely lavish. By 1924 Hearst cheerfully laid out a vast sum for literary rights to the second-rate novel *Janice Meredith* and commissioned Lynn Reynolds (whom he later replaced) to direct the film in which Marion Davies starred, supported by a cast which included W.C. Fields and Ken Maynard.

Maynard recalled his work in *Janice Meredith,* telling this writer, "Lynn Reynolds got me the part of Paul Revere in that picture. I went from California to New York City where the picture was to be made. The trouble was that while I went 'on salary' from the moment I reported at Cosmopolitan, my role in the picture didn't occur for a long time after the shooting of the film got underway.

"At the director's suggestion, I spent days and days at the New York Library researching Paul Revere—while old man Hearst was bankrolling my studies! When I finally got called for my role, I knew more about Revere, I'm sure, than he knew about himself."

Maynard's comments illustrate one reason why Hearst's pictures were so costly; no cost controls seemed ever to have been exerted.

Even Hearst himself did not seem to apply restraint where budgets for Marion Davies' films were concerned. Once, when Hearst viewed a set involving a replica of a ship, his countenance clouded when he observed that the set designer had attempted to scale down the cost by causing the ships to be painted in monochromatic paints, as were used on virtually all sets made for films which were in black-and-white.

"Didn't ships have bright colors?" asked the newspaper magnate. The set designer nodded. "Well, then," Hearst went on, "let's get this set completely repainted. Bright reds. Greens. Whatever else will make the players feel they're on real ships." The set was repainted at Hearst's expense, of course.

While the Cosmopolitan Studio operated, it turned out a flow of features distributed by various firms including Paramount/Artcraft, Sam Goldwyn, and MGM.

Long before sound films became *de rigueur,* Hearst observed sharp changes in the neighborhood in which his New York studio was situated, and noted, too, that the capital of the film world was no longer in New York; it had shifted to California. He also noted how many of the film directors he was employing in his productions, Frank Borzage for instance, were obliged to travel from the West Coast each time Hearst chose to make a picture.

Deliberating carefully, Hearst chose to close the New York studio, transferring personnel and equipment to a part of the large MGM lot in Culver City, with that decision leaving his studio to become merely a huge warehouse wherein Hearst stored part of the art objects he often purchased (he purchased so many art objects that not even his massive "castle" San Simeon in California could contain them all).

The Hearst-Davies love affair was to continue right up to the time of Hearst's death, his production of Miss Davies' elaborate films enduring almost as long, love being a powerful, pervasive force, even in the cold-blooded industry of the motion picture.

# Crystal Studio

Crystal Studio at Wendover and Park Avenue in the Bronx was one of many early film studios which once existed in New York City. Crystal functioned both as a production entity and rental facility in 1909, when movies were not longer than one or two reels.

In 1911, the studio briefly had the services of a young, former stock company player named Pearl White, one of her early pictures at Crystal being *The Lost Necklace*, released November 23, 1911. By that time, Miss White had already been employed at another New York studio, Powers Picture Plays, where she reputedly made but $30 weekly.

In 1911, she'd been employed at the Lubin Studio in Philadelphia, a job from which some historians say she was discharged, reasons unknown. In 1912 she worked briefly for Pathe, but in October of that year again signed on at Crystal Studio, where she appeared in such pictures as *The Girl Next Door* (1912) and split-reel comedies including *Pearl's Adventure*, *Pearl's Dilemma*, and *Pearl and the Tramp*.

Always careful with a dollar, Miss White managed to accumulate savings of around $6,000, truly a small fortune in 1913; it was then that she announced that she was leaving to tour Europe. Indeed it was not until about seven months afterward that she returned to Crystal Studio and the leading role in the 1914 picture *The Lady Doctor*. At about that time, she happened to encounter an old acquaintance, film producer Theodore Wharton, who introduced her to Louis Gasnier of Pathe. That introduction led her to a contract at $250 weekly to star in the serial *Perils of Pauline*.

Officials at Crystal apparently felt no animosity toward Pathe for hiring Miss White; Joseph Golden, head of Crystal Studio, continued to release many pictures through the Pathe exchange, among them the 1914 chapter play *The Great Gamble.*

By 1918 there was also production of feature-length films at Joseph Golden's studio, Golden himself directing *The Libertine, The Prima Donna's Husband,* and *Redemption,* all of them early examples of American-made feature pictures.

Actor/director Charles Hutchison, before achieving fame as the hero of numerous silent chapter plays, worked both as a leading man and a director at Crystal, where he met actress Edith Thornton, whom Hutchison directed, along with actor Chester Barnett, in countless light comedies. Hutchison married Miss Thornton some time prior to 1918, the year when Joseph Golden contracted to produce for Pathe the Charles Hutchison serial *Wolves of Kultur.* Another Hutchison serial, *The Whirlwind* (1920), was also made by Golden, who released it on the Allgood Pictures label. It was distributed on a states rights basis by the original Republic, owned by Lewis J. Selznick.

During its existence, Crystal Studio often rented space to outside firms, among them an outfit whose chief organizers were Edwin S. Porter, Adolph Zukor, and Daniel Frohman, who called their firm Famous Players, which later became part of Paramount Pictures.

If the end of Crystal Studio may be attributed to one cause, it is that the operation was allowed to dwindle into that of a mere "rental stage," thereby losing its place as a prime producer of films. Rental stages, alas, are seldom long-term successes.

# The Larry Darmour Studio

A shabby, deserted old studio in Los Angeles now is something of a legend, having been touted by TV and radio stations of the region as being haunted. The notion of the cavernous stages of a studio being sorely in need of an exorcist is more than fascinating.

In all probability, however, the spirits which supposedly haunt the premises designated as 5823 Santa Monica Boulevard may be little other than those of photographic chemical solutions mixed there in the days around World War I, when the place was headquarters and plant of Pacific Film Laboratories.

Nowadays Santa Monica Boulevard is too busy a thoroughfare for motorists to do more than glance at the cheerless, faded green facade of the Larry Darmour Studio, perforated with outdated window designs which in spots have been truncated to permit installation of small air conditioner units.

**Built in 1916 this Los Angeles structure at first housed Pacific Film Laboratories. It was later occupied successively, by National, Bull's Eye, Berwilla, and Larry Darmour Productions. After World War II it briefly was the home of Family Films and Key West. Today it is vacant.**

In the back of this low, lanky office building of the studio tower the massive stages which can be glimpsed from the street, at least their roofs, retarred sloppily through the years.

Unimpressive though the place is today, it once was headquarters of Ben Wilson's production enterprise, which spun out numerous chapter plays and more than a few feature films, in the days before movies had hurriedly adopted a voice. Back then Bull's Eye Comedy also occupied quarters there, in 1919 employing as a director the inventive Charley Chase, whose films were released by Bull's Eye through a new firm calling itself Universal.

It remained for producer Larry Darmour, who acquired the studio early in the 1920s, to undertake the expensive task of fitting the stages of the studio for sound recording. (Darmour's ownership of the studio commenced at the close of the silent film era and continued into the sound film era.)

Darmour produced several series of comedies, one with Karl Dave, another, longer-lived one featuring a young boy whose real name was Joe Yule, Jr., who while under contract to Darmour was renamed Mickey Rooney, a surname derived from the comic strip character "Mickey McGuire."

The "Mickey McGuire" pictures began in 1927 and first were released by Darmour through R-C Pictures. When R-C metamorphosed into F.B.O. the series went along. In 1932, however, Standard

Cinema's label was on the series, at the time RKO began the distribution.

In 1933 Columbia Pictures assumed distribution, although only for about 18 months; in mid–1934 Mickey Rooney had outgrown the part and continued his screen career elsewhere.

Besides, by about the mid-thirties, it had become clear to Larry Darmour that the market for short subjects was shrinking rapidly, at which juncture Darmour Studio geared up for production of full-length feature films. A fast-growing Columbia Pictures agreed to the distribution of such "B" budget features.

By 1934, Darmour produced one of those *almost* "A" budget pictures, *The Scarlet Letter*, releasing it under the Majestic logo. The film featured Colleen Moore and Henry B. Walthall.

In 1936 Darmour's feature film schedule had been diversified to include westerns for Columbia distribution and such melodramas for release through Empire as *Shadows of the Orient* with Regis Toomey, *The Fire Trap* with Norman Foster, and *Mutiny Ahead* featuring Neil Hamilton. Spencer Gordon Bennet was signed in 1935–36 to direct a group of cheap westerns which starred aging cowboy Ken Maynard.

At the beginning of World War II all of Hollywood learned quickly that the wartime audience for films of any type whatever was an immense one. Darmour found wide distribution through Columbia for his many "Ellery Queen" detective films, a series in which William Gargan and Charles Grapewin were featured.

Columbia itself was operating at peak capacity in those years, forcing it to occupy adjacent lots, including at times the Darmour studio.

What scribes often nicknamed "the Moneymoon" ended soon after World War II ended. It was difficult to market "B" features only a couple years afterward, a condition which was aggravated by the coming of television in the fifties with its plethora of programs, almost all of which were neither better nor worse than Hollywood "B" budget films.

It was then that the Larry Darmour stages went dark for the final time as a theatrical film production center.

A religious film unit, Family Films, occupied the Darmour lot for a time, followed by an even shorter-lived firm, Key West Studios.

Today the studios at 5823 Santa Monica Boulevard remain vacant, echoing only to the footfalls of the watchmen, at least one of whom stoutly maintains that he is never alone in his nightly rounds, accompanied as he is by the ghost which by now has made such publicity that the late Larry Darmour would surely have laughed heartily at the publicity.

# *J. Charles Davis Studios*

The aging stucco structure at 9147 Venice Boulevard in Culver City nowadays houses a pasta factory; once, however, it was the J. Charles Davis Studios, a 1920s lot devoted primarily to making westerns and other action films. Its president and director-general boasted that his operation covered three acres, which by 1929 offered two stages fully equipped with "Sound Art" equipment for recording "talkies" onto discs or film. Davis claimed at that time to have under contract such players as Marilyn Mills, Yakima Canutt, and Art Mix, and five years before that, he'd employed a new cowboy actor, Ken Maynard, for a series of westerns. Several of these Davis subsequently re-edited into a 10-chapter serial titled *The Range Fighter.*

J. Charles Davis II, like every other producer in show business, had grandiose plans for his enterprises. He envisioned Davis Distributing Division as developing into a large distribution outlet for his firm. Alas, that idea died almost as quickly as it was announced; by 1928 Davis had to content himself with distributing his productions through such firms as Bell Pictures. Although Davis attempted the changes required by the coming of sound to films, his studio, like so many others, ceased to exist by the time of the collapse of world stock markets.

When the former Davis Studio was resuscitated it was as the Bryan Foy Studio. Foy, one of many sons of vaudevillian Eddie Foy, had already made something of a name for himself in Hollywood during the years when he'd been in charge of "B" productions at Warners. Leaving them, Foy opened his own studio, producing inexpensive but mildly profitable exploitation films which lured moviegoers to theatres by seeming to promise shocking, titillating fame (as suggested by the title of Foy's 1936 production *Highschool Girl,* in which Cecilia Parker portrayed the seduced and abandoned ingenue). Perhaps something more of an actual shocker to movie audiences of the 1930s was his film *Elysia,* filmed entirely in Elysian Park, a California nudist camp.

William Austin, now retired after a long career as a film editor, worked at the Bryan Foy Studio, "a short-lived . . . operation," Austin says, adding, "the market for exploitation films has always been a limited one."

Foy attempted to enlarge that market by producing a pseudo-educational picture about the controversial and Utopian scheme known as technocracy, which promoters claimed would put an end to economic depressions and unemployment. Foy's one-reel film on the subject was distributed to theatres under a plan whereby an onstage lecturer explained technocracy and extolled its promised virtues, while

**J. Charles Davis II, president and director-general of the studio that bore his name.**

playing down the fact that technocracy was supposedly based upon rule by scientists and engineers, types to whom exploitation subjects were an anathema, to put it mildly. Nevertheless Foy's film was financially successful for its producer.

The Foy studio was under the management of Lewis Golder, Foy's business partner. Sam Katzman, who had been a production supervisor for A.W. Hackel's Supreme Pictures, came to Foy as an assistant director. When the Foy studio ceased operation, Katzman hastily put together a small corporation, Victory Pictures, and possessed sufficient backing to take over the vacant Foy lot.

Contracting with screen cowboy Tim McCoy, film bogeyman Bela Lugosi and a few other such players, Victory Pictures began producing skimpily budgeted westerns and a series of action melodramas, the latter of which headlined one-time Olympic athlete Herman Brix, who later changed his name to Bruce Bennett.

In 1936 Victory turned out the 15-chapter serial *Shadow of Chinatown* with Bela Lugosi, and followed it in 1937 with the Ralph Byrd 15-episode picture *Blake of Scotland Yard*.

The Victory label existed from mid–1935 through the spring of 1939, although in 1938 a large fire swept parts of the Culver City lot, leaving no stages and forcing Katzman to move his operations to 1509 Vine Street, Hollywood. Katzman went on to produce pictures for Monogram and later for Columbia release.

# Diando

When Kalem ceased business in 1917, its Glendale, California, studios were taken over by Diando Film Corp., an outfit which was to build its corporate fortune largely around child actress Baby Marie Osborne who had been a "star" at Balboa. It wasn't likely that Baby Marie would ever quit Diando or demand excessive pay; her father was one of the owners of Diando (a name compounded from the letters "D" and "O," which stood for Douglas and Osborne).

In 1918, the Glendale newspaper proudly pointed out that "Glendale is on the motion picture map and is going to get much favorable publicity . . . through Baby Marie Osborne . . . youngest star now in the film world."

Baby Marie completed in mid–January 1918 a 5-reel feature, *A Little Patriot,* and was scheduled for a series of other "feature plays," as the local paper described them.

In addition to its juvenile star, Diando boasted the black child Ernest ("Sunshine Sammy") Morrison, and such technical and creative personnel as director William Bertram and technical director Richard Johnson.

While *A Little Patriot* was in production, the Diando firm also had in the works a western titled *A Daughter of the West,* which the Pathe firm was interested in purchasing, as it did all the Baby Marie films.

There was other evidence of a bright future ahead for Diando: the famous Bryant Washburn, who'd risen to such fame and adulation in Skinner Steps Out and many other Selig and Essanay pictures, now was independently producing films. He, too, moved onto the Diando lot.

Meanwhile, studio manager Norman Manning viewed with both pride and alarm the fact that the production of *Daughter of the West* was costing Diando for 300 "extras" and immense amounts of blank cartridges (then costing $40 per thousand rounds). To add to Manning's handwringing budget problems, much of *Daughter of the West* had been shot on location, utilizing backgrounds at Long Beach, Pasadena, Eagle Rock, and other areas adjacent to Glendale.

But sudden profits were pouring in, so Diando president W.A.S. Douglas announced the employment of a landscape gardener for the "studio," a group of frame structures situated on the outskirts of Glendale. (However, shortly after that, the less imaginative studio manager at Diando chilled Douglas by announcing there'd be no landscape gardener at Diando, at least on a fulltime basis. In fact, Manning claimed, he'd perform the role of gardener himself in order to hold down the costs of operation of the then-busy studio!)

Diando, its studios on Verdugo Road, next announced the acquisition, late in 1918, of a tract consisting of 50 acres about a mile south of
the Diando studios. The property comprised a rugged area within a
dead canyon running east and west and flanked on three sides by
precipitous mountains. The valley to the west was backed by blue hills
reaching distantly skyward.

On that property Diando workmen began construction of a large,
two-story log house, several stables, corrals and other buildings. These
were parts of an outdoor "set" at which was to be made a new chapter
play the company was making for Pathe release. The working title of the
new serial: *The Wolf-faced Man,* a fifteen-chapter western fashioned
from a story by W.A. Douglas and Lucian Hubbard.

Because there was a one-mile gap separating the Diando studio
from its new "back lot," a private phone line was constructed between
the two, and heavy capacity power service was provided for the canyon
operation.

As the site was being readied, the cast for the serial was announced:
George B. Larkin (known as "Daredevil Larkin" for the great chances
he supposedly took doing his own stunts for films), Betty Compson, Ora
Carew, William Quinn, and Fred Malatesta ("the well-known Italian actor," the studio publicity department called him). The director was
Stuart Paton, of whom Diando was unusually proud owing to his former
directorial credits with Universal, where he had filmed *Twenty Thousand Leagues Under the Sea, The Grey Ghost, Voice on the Wire* and
other pictures.

Late in 1917, Baby Marie, supposedly then earning a cushy $1,000
weekly salary from her dad's firm, passed her fifth birthday. "The
wonderful acting of the baby grand star," proclaimed the Glendale
evening newspaper, "the heart grip she gets on her audience, tends to
[bring] merits to a picture." Naturally the child was regarded by most
Glendale citizens as "one of their own," and thus worthy of considerable
local newspaper publicity, even when her current antics consisted of
nothing more adventuresome than an outing at nearby Camp Baldy,
where, according to a lengthy story in a March 1918 paper, she went and
"had some sport in the snow."

Baby Marie, the story noted, was currently at work on the feature
*The Soul of a Child.* She'd also recently donated to a local charity a
photograph and a pair of her silk stockings that promptly fetched a
whopping $25 at a Red Cross auction benefit (this was during World
War I, when such benefits were common).

In April 1918, America was heavily involved in the First World
War. The Diando studios were losing personnel to the draft. One such
draftee, Harry F. MacPherson, left his post at the studio, bearing a $75
gift and a wristwatch from the staff.

In preparing to depart, MacPherson clasped Baby Marie in his arms à la Victorian behavior brought on by Baby Marie's little speech to him to the effect that all the Diando people hoped the watch, as it ticked, would evidence that "hearts were beating in unison for his safe return at the end of the war." Who said moviedom never possessed one iota of heart?

In the middle of June 1918, Roscoe "Fatty" Arbuckle and his whitefaced brindle bulldog visited the Diando lot. His ostensible reason for calling there was to see the child star Baby Marie Osborne, but it is more than probable he was looking over facilities there with an eye to moving production of his Comique Films (which released through Paramount) to Diando. Arbuckle had doubtless become aware of the deep financial problems of the Balboa Amusement Co., at Long Beach, where he was renting space for his company.

Alas for Glendale, and Diando, too, Arbuckle's beloved dog disappeared while the comic was touring the Diando facilities, causing him to regret having ever seen Glendale. In leaving the town, he posted a reward for his lost pet which, happily for everyone concerned, was returned safely to Arbuckle "through publicity given to this loss by the *Glendale Evening News,*" the paper announced proudly in its June 18, 1918, issue.

Early that same month two important officials of Pathe, Ferdinand Zecca and L.E. Franconi, visited the Diando facilities in Glendale. While there, Zecca purchased for Pathe an unreleased 6-reel western, *Texas Rose,* which Stuart Paton directed, and in which George Larkin, Betty Compson, Frank Deshon and Claire DuBrey were featured.

Both officials remained in Glendale for about two weeks, although part of that time they went to visit other Los Angeles area studios where other Pathe films were in production.

When the pair returned to New York City, Diando announced a change of policy, as did other Pathe producers in the Los Angeles region. Just what the changes were isn't known today, though it is known that Pathe was engaged in adjusting the output of its producers, causing such outfits as Balboa to retrench so much that their output of pictures thereafter was unable to support the cost of operating the studio.

It is possible that, indirectly at least, Pathe's action with regard to Balboa caused Arbuckle's Comique Films to leave that Long Beach facility and, in the late summer of 1918, to announce that he henceforth would be producing his pictures at the Diando studios. Arbuckle's decision brought the number of companies producing at the Diando plant to five.

Even as W.A.S. Douglas, president of Diando, joined the Marine

Corps, his partner Leon T. Osborne indicated that he would continue operation of the studio.

Stuart Paton was at work at this time (June 20, 1918) directing his second western for the studio: *The Death Trail*, with a cast headed by George Larkin and Betty Compson.

At the same time, the studio launched a new series of 2-reel comedies featuring "Sunny Sammy," who up until then had been appearing as the comic relief in Baby Marie Osborne's feature films.

The month of July 1918 proved newsworthy for Diando in other ways: it was the month in which Roscoe Arbuckle, having completed his final picture at Balboa Studios, moved his company to the Diando lot, although only a tentative agreement had been made between W.A.S. Douglas, Diando president, and Lou Anger, business manager for Arbuckle.

It was the month, also, when Gale Henry, an actress who'd rolled up a five-year association with Universal, brought her production company to Diando and set up shop, her first comedy at Diando beginning production in mid–July 1918.

In the meantime the Arbuckle unit got ready to produce his next Paramount feature at the Glendale facility. Though a one-picture deal with Diando, there were strong possibilities that the obese comic would make the Diando lot permanent headquarters for his Comique Film Corporation.

As Diando continued to lure independent film units such as that headed by Arbuckle, the studio was turning out its own productions, including the western *The Coming of the Law* (another entry in its series with George Larkin and Betty Compson), and Baby Marie's newest, a William Bertram picture titled *The Old Maid's Baby*.

The Diando lot was opened to the public for the filming of Baby Marie's mid–1918 feature film about life with a circus. Ed Unger, billed as a "famous balloonist and parachute jumper" was to be on hand for his role in the new film, as was the youthful comic "Sunshine Sammy." About 500 Glendalians were later said to have been guests of Diando to witness the making of key scenes for *The Old Maid's Baby*.

Amid such activity at the lot, financial problems suddenly appeared, some so seemingly trivial that they now appear almost laughable. Nevertheless, by January 30, 1919, Diando pulled out of its studios in Glendale, dispatching its "star," Baby Marie Osborne, on tour, while the ailing firm set up offices in the H.W. Hellman Building in Los Angeles.

John English, publicity chief for Diando, was promptly questioned by newsmen as to whether the studios at Glendale might ever be reopened, to which he replied, "That will depend. We would like to reestablish ourselves in Glendale, but are waiting to find out what the final action of the Pacific Telephone Company will be in regard to toll rates between Glendale and Los Angeles. At $.02 a call, our tolls averaged $24 a month. Under the schedule now proposed they would exceed $200 a month which is more than we feel like contributing to that corporation."

Whether Pacific Telephone really was the proverbial straw which broke the camel's spinal column can only be guessed. What is apparent, however, is that Diando's days as a film producing firm ended at that time. Diando thereby gave up its studios, relinquishing the nearby "canyon location" where it had been shooting most of its westerns, withdrew for a time to offices in Los Angeles, and soon afterward became swallowed up by the mists of motion picture history.

# *The Walt Disney Studio*

On October 16, 1923, young Chicago-born cartoonist Walt Disney secured a contract with film distributor Margaret J. Winkler of Kansas City. Under the terms of the agreement, Disney was to turn out a series of one-reel "Alice" subjects in which a real youngster would cavort among and beside cartoon figures on the motion picture screen.

Walt set out to make those films in a small backroom, rented at $10 per month from the Holly-Vermont Realty firm at 4651 Kingswell, Hollywood. But, by February 1924 the Disney brothers, Walt and Roy, had found their first studio far too small for their needs. So they mved next door into larger quarters, above the door of which they posted a sign, "Disney Bros. Studio." The rent: $35 per month.

The "Alice" films proved popular with audiences, profitable enough so that in July 1925 the Disneys made the purchase of property and soon afterward started construction of a Mediterranean style building at 2719 Hyperion, which was ready for occupancy in February 1926.

In 1937, Walt Disney released his pioneering animated Technicolor feature *Snow White and the Seven Dwarfs,* the box-office bonanza which made it possible in 1938 for the Disneys to make a modest cash deposit on 51 choice acres in nearby Burbank, and to undertake drafting plans for the studio complex which today includes 77 buildings ranging over 44 acres along two sides of Riverside Drive, not far from the Warner Bros. studio.

The Disney studio in Burbank began operation in May 1940, a corporately owned community with its own pipelines for natural gas, a vast storm drain system, a telephone network, and its own fire and

**When Walt Disney established its first studio operation of any size, it was this one at 2719 Hyperion Avenue, Los Angeles. Shown here in 1935, it was the studio headquarters until 1940 when the firm moved to Burbank.**

police departments. Within the area there is even a 597-seat movie theatre which, while used mostly for special screenings such as those for journalists, serves as an occasional re-recording facility as well.

There is a spacious commissary on the lot, providing seating for 200 in the cafeteria portion with two banquet facilities, the Coral Room (built in 1959), and the smaller Gold Room also in the same building.

The studio was built at a time when animated cartoons were the firm's chief source of income; today there is comparatively little such activity. One entire building, which once was devoted to preparation and filming of the Disney cartoon short subjects, is now used as a wardrobe area and for the makeup and music departments.

The sweeping changeover from animation to live-action subjects began when, in 1940, Stage One was constructed, serving initially for production of live-action sequences for the Disney feature *Fantasia*. Today, having been added onto, this stage measures 71' x 157' — a 60' x 40' x 8' subterranean "tank," appended in 1976.

Just three years after adding onto Stage One, the Disneys set about the construction of a second huge stage, this one in part designed to meet the requirements of rental customer Jack Webb, who for several seasons used that facility for filming his *Dragnet* TV shows. (The

The Burbank, California, studios of Walt Disney. Most of the firm's feature films have been shot here including *Mary Poppins*, and similarly, many of its latter-day animated subjects.

same stage was used in filming the 1950 and 1951 Walt Disney Christmas shows for television.)

A third massive sound stage at Disney was constructed specifically for filming a quite specialized feature which was in production during parts of 1953 and 1954. *20,000 Leagues Under the Sea* paired James Mason and Kirk Douglas under directors Richard Fleischer and Earl Feldman for a film based on a popular novel by the Frenchman Jules Verne. For the underwater scenes and special effects, a huge tank had to be constructed on Stage Three, a 60' x 60' x 8' unit, alongside which was a camera pit with viewing ports. The combined unit consumed most of the space on the 102' x 195' stage.

The water tank was fitted with heaters; pumps filtered and chlorinated the water while maintaining a flow rate of 4,000 gallons of water per minute.

In the more than three decades which have passed since that stage was built, a single additional sound stage has been added to the Disney lot, a stage which measures 133' x 243', as does Stage Two. (These two stages are among the largest at any studio in California.)

Because the Disney lot is in the vicinity of Burbank-Glendale-

Pasadena Airport, it was particularly important that the sound stages be of the "building within a building" type, employing double walls, floors, and roof so as to separate the twin "shells" of the structures completely, thus isolating the inner shell from outside noises.

But these sound stages are not of such great interest to visitors as are the areas of the "back lot" where outdoor, permanent sets are to be found. Here may be seen the sprawling set used originally in filming the 1960 theatrical feature *The Sign of Zorro*, the set comprising the Pueblo de los Angeles, replete with church, fort, town squares, jail, and inn. The layout was also used in filming the television series *Zorro*, and, with modifications, to represent the city of Monterey in another of Disney's pictures. (One of the town squares, further modified by artisans, was used as a French village.)

Just around a corner from this, there is a Western street, beyond which is an outdoor set representing a Midwestern town, circa 1920.

If one continues along that street, the way leads to what proves to be an exceedingly flexible representation of a town square, its fake business facades readily convertible to match almost any period in history, any business establishment.

Not often seen by visitors to the Disney studios are the paint shops, the lumber department, woodworking plant, and the department where statuettes, vases, picture frames, facades of structures, pillars, staircases and the like are cast out of plaster, fiberglass, and similar materials. These shops are close to the property department and to the special effects shop where may be seen under construction such devices as the Model T in which Fred MacMurray zoomed skyborne above the college where the "absent-minded professor" taught.

Much of this massive dream factory was planned and developed soon after World War II, and much of it in the late 1940s and early 1950s.

During the years of the global conflict, two of the Disney features, aimed specifically at Latin American markets, proved almost unbelievably popular: *Saludos Amigos* (1943) and *The Three Caballeros* (1944). Both happened to combine live action with animated footage. This experience proved invaluable to the Disney organization in postwar years and prompted Disney to offer more and more feature pictures with either part live action or, in more and more cases, with live action exclusively.

The 1947 Disney offering *Song of the South* marked the clear subjugation of animation to live footage, animation serving but as a child's daydream within a feature picture built primarily around live actors, including James Baskett and Hattie McDaniel, together with two talented children, Bobby Driscoll and Luana Patton (both later being signed to longterm contracts with Disney).

After the release of *Song of the South* things were never quite the same at the Disney studios. While the firm continued to make occasional animated features, most of the output of the Disney lot eventually consisted of feature films of a live-action type.

In 1950 the studio produced at D & P Studios, England, *Treasure Island*, a deep-toned Technicolor offering made from the classic Robert Louis Stevenson novel. The film starred Bobby Driscoll together with a very hammy Robert Newton, who appeared to be burlesquing the late Wallace Beery (who had essayed the same role in the 1934 MGM picturization of the novel).

Probably not of the same great interest to youthful Disney audiences were *The Story of Robin Hood* (1952), *The Sword and the Rose* (1953), and *Rob Roy, The Highland Rogue* (1954), a trio of swashbucklers which starred British actor Richard Todd. These pictures, along with the earlier *Treasure Island*, were utilized by the Disneys as the means of getting "frozen funds" out of Britain. (That country did not like to return cash for the many U.S. films it exhibited.)

One of these British imports, *Rob Roy*, was to prove the final Disney picture distributed through RKO, the firm which had handled Disney products for many years. With the release of *20,000 Leagues Under the Sea* in 1954, another Disney operation, Buena Vista Film Distribution, began flexing its corporate muscles preparatory to becoming a major distributor, with exchanges in more than two dozen cities.

Other Disney ventures soon followed. On October 4, 1955, the televison show *The Mickey Mouse Club* bowed in via the ABC network, following by less than a month *Disneyland*, an evening TV program which was to prove a potpourri of made-for-television subjects and footage taken from the backlog of old Disney films. The afternoon *Mickey Mouse Club*, hosted by personable Jimmy Dodd, proved something of a cornucopia for new acting talent for Disney's later films, kids who lived in the Los Angeles area. One of these was a child with the unattractive last name "Funicello" (wiseacres in the TV audience quickly took to referring to the child as "Funny Jello"). No matter, little Annette, an attractive girl except for her prominent nose, was accorded surgery for her proboscis, and the equally truncated name "Annette." (Audiences persisted in employing both her surname and last name, however.)

Tommy Kirk and Kevin Corcoran, also members of the club entourage, made their ways into theatrical films at the Disney studios, which suddenly was a money mill!

In early summer 1955 Buena Vista began distribution of a Disney feature which was to make licensing and merchandising history for the incredibly profitable fees which Disney began raking in soon after that picture was in circulation.

The feature, *Davy Crockett, King of the Wild Frontier,* was strictly a "B" budget affair, happily not half so lengthy a film as its title. (It was edited from three TV segments of Disney's TV series.)

Exactly how it was that U.S. patent and copyright laws permitted Disney exclusive rights and profits from a name and person from the pages of history isn't exactly clear, although it may have been because Disney's screen personage bore absolutely no likeness to the true Davy Crockett, who was a coarse, unschooled backwoods braggart and wife deserter; the complete antithesis of Disney's representation as personified by actor Fess Parker.

Other screen newcomers besides Parker were to achieve fame at the Disneys' factory. David Hartman, Dick Van Dyke, Brian Keith, Dean Jones, Suzanne Pleshette and the late Bob Crane were others who found that Walt Disney's kingdom profited more than its monarch.

Possibly even the Disney brothers were surprised at how quickly little-known players could achieve stardom through "family pictures" made at the Disney lot. London-born Hayley Mills had been but a minor screen figure when Disney hired her; Disney magic worked similarly for the adopted son of Helen Hayes. James MacArthur quickly became a favorite with Disney audiences. Jody Foster seemed to be on a similar course when her career was cut short by events over which Miss Foster had no control.

The Disney studio reached its busiest years in theatrical film production at the start of 1958, although it proved to be a period in which Disney released no new animated features. The sentimental paean to the canine, *Old Yeller,* opened that year, followed by the Alan Ladd picture *The Proud Rebel;* a documentary, *White Wilderness,* and a couple of live-action features, *The Light in the Forest* and *Tonka.*

For more than a decade thereafter the studio continued operating at nearly peak capacity. Animated features, live-action ones, and made-for-television shows were in production. Feature pictures enjoyed top budgets; no matter how inane the plots and titles they made money and they delighted audiences.

*The Absent-Minded Professor, Son of Flubber, The Monkey's Uncle,* and a feature with the cumbersome and lengthy name *The One and Only, Genuine Original Family Band* brought the Disneys respectable profits, some of which were plowed into such projects as the Disneyland theme park near Anaheim and later, Disney World near Orlando, Florida.

Not all of the feature films from Buena Vista have been financially successful, of course; like every other studio, Walt Disney invested in a great many pictures which the firm would probably prefer to forget. *Scandalous John* (1971), *Charley and the Angel* (1972), *One Little Indian* (1973), *Superdad,* and such earlier turkeys as *Smith!* (1969), *The*

*Barefoot Executive* (1971), and *The Boatniks* (1970) are not likely to be spoken of inside the boundaries of the wonderful world of Disney, even today.

Oddly, these box-office forget-me-nows often possessed quite good casts, at least as Disney films go. Yet, the foregoing pictures were such losers that such players as Fred MacMurray, James Garner, Bob Crane, Jody Foster, and Brian Keith were unable to defuse these bombs.

Yet, coursing through those Disney wastelands there seemed always to be a refreshing stream of excellent color offerings, most of them based upon novels which were classics in children's or young adults' literature.

Disney films which were fashioned from such literature include *Kidnapped* (1960), *Swiss Family Robinson* (1960), *Third Man on the Mountain* (1959), *Greyfriar's Bobby* (1961), *Babes in Toyland* (1961), and one of Disney's most acclaimed and largest grossing pictures, *Mary Poppins* (1965), colorfully and tunefully marking the Disneys' apogee in feature film production.

*In Search of the Castaways* (1962), *The Moonspinners* (1964), and *Emil and the Detectives* are other examples of successful combinations of literature and Disney imaginativeness, flare, and production values, though not such topbudget productions as *Mary Poppins*.

It is beyond the scope of the present series to discuss Disney's many animated feature pictures; suffice it to say, all during the years of Disney live-action offerings the studio has also contributed to motion picture history cartoon features including *Peter Pan* (1953), *Sleeping Beauty* (1959), *101 Dalmatians* (1961) and *The Jungle Book* (1967).

The four massive Disney sound stages are silent many days per year now; the theatrical market for "family type" movies has long since dried up.

Rumors long have been rife within the film industry that the Disney empire wishes to divest itself of its film studio — another case of the once sinewy arm of a friendly giant having metamorphosed into a withered, shrunken limb.

Then again, there's a flurry of excitement about how the Disney empire may build new studios near Orlando, Florida, and will proceed to revive its film studio enterprises. As rental stages perhaps? Certainly not to make another generation of "family type" feature films!

Are Davy Crockett, Long John Silver, and the absent-minded professor about to be revived? Or are the Disney studios at Burbank to remain sepulchers for generations of films for the young and their parents?

# The Thomas Dixon Studio

At Western Avenue and Sunset Boulevard, Los Angeles, the Reverend Thomas Dixon operated for a short time the motion picture studio bearing his name. A Baptist preacher and also a lawyer and writer, Dixon was a popular lecturer on the Lyceum circuit from 1899 through 1903 (this organization presented popular entertainment intermingled with public lectures, concerts, and the like, similar to that provided by the Chautauqua presentations of that time). His many books included *The Leopard's Spots* (1902), *The One Woman* (1903) and *The Clansman* (1905), the latter yielding the story which producer-director D.W. Griffith made into his 1915 film masterpiece, *Birth of a Nation*.

In 1916 Dixon penned *Fall of a Nation*, a story and screenplay which he turned into a feature picture with Arthur Shirley and Lorraine Huling. Obviously, Dixon was attempting to cash in on the immense popularity of the Griffith film, or at least to suggest that the picture was a sequel to that picture; however, *Fall of a Nation* was an account of the bleak future America would face if it ever lost a war.

Dixon's success with his novel *Birth of a Nation* caused him to become involved in other film activities besides the establishment of his own studio in Los Angeles; he entered into a short-lived partnership to build a large studio near San Francisco (see Pacific Studios entry on page 155), a plan that Dixon and his partners withdrew from even before that studio was completed.

The Thomas Dixon Studio in Los Angeles occupied a highly desirable Hollywood site. Thus, after using the studio for only a handful of productions, Dixon found the property easy to dispose of. William Fox purchased it and abandoned his previous quarters on Allesandro in Los Angeles. For years, the Dixon lot functioned as the William Fox Studio, even after the firm moved to what was at the time known as "Movietone City," where a new, larger studio designed for the new "talking pictures" had been built.

During World War II, the former Dixon Studio was leased by 20th Century–Fox to the Army Signal Corps for use by its 834th Photo Unit, the commander of which was Hollywood director Frank Capra; he shared these facilities with the now-legendary Armed Forces Radio.

So ensconced, Capra produced and edited the noted series of Army films *Why We Fight*.

As for the Reverend Mr. Dixon, who had almost disappeared from the film industry before the end of the First World War, he returned to his home state, North Carolina, where he continued work as a writer, turning out such minor novels as *A Man of the People* (1920), *The Man in Gray* (1921) and *Companions* (1931). In 1932 he co-authored, with Harry M. Daugherty, *The Inside Story of the Harding Tragedy.*

Besides the films already referred to, Dixon wrote the story for the film *Bolshevism on Trial* (1919) and *Foolish Virgin* (filmed in 1917 by the Clara Kimball Young Film Corporation, and in 1924 by Columbia Pictures).

Dixon died at his home in Raleigh, North Carolina, April 3, 1946.

# The Edison Studio

When Thomas Alva Edison chose to get out of the film production business, he was withdrawing from an industry which was destined one day not many years afterward to be the fifth largest in the U.S.

One of Edison's co-workers, W.K.L. Dickson, had in the 1880s spearheaded development of the motion picture as a peepshow device; when Edison later bought rights from an inventor named Thomas Armat for a projection device which showed films onto large screens, Edison succeeded in getting his name affixed to the moving picture so securely that even to this day the wily tinkerer is widely accepted as "father of the moving picture."

The original Edison "Kinetoscope" was nothing more than a coin-in-the-slot viewer, by means of which one customer at a time could view a short belt of celluloid film (in another version of the machine—again a development of Dickson—the Kinetoscope was "lashed" onto one of the crude cylinder-type Edison phonographs so as to allow the film viewer, who'd donned earphones, to have a bit of musical accompaniment with the show being watched).

Not long before Edison's factory at West Orange, New Jersey, began turning out production models of Armat's 35mm projector, it became clear that the facilities for film production would need considerable enhancement. Numerous films and longer productions were needed, not the short belts of film the Kinetoscopes required.

Originally, indoor production of Edison films had been accomplished in what employees termed the "Photographic Building," but later was transferred to a hump-backed, tarpaper-covered structure about 48 feet in length, mounted on a revolving base so the building could be rotated as necessary to allow the slant-roof with its large glass window to be oriented to the sun during most of the daylight hours. The bulky, heavy motion picture camera inside the "Black Maria," as the

**The first American film studio, the "Black Maria" of the Thomas Edison Company, West Orange, N.J. Built atop a turntable base, this entire building could be rotated in whatever direction favored the sun. The camera was positioned in the low-roofed part of the structure (at right).**

building was nicknamed, was mounted on a pedestal which, in turn, was mounted on tracks to facilitate its movement in relation to the stage.

Black Maria, built at a cost of $637.67, was the world's first building designed exclusively for motion picture production. Built under the supervision of Edison's hardworking associate, William Kennedy Laurie Dickson, Black Maria served admirably in the production of the short films made for Kinetoscopes, but it never adapted well to the making of longer productions.

In Edison's employ, besides Dickson, was Edwin S. Porter, who developed into quite a cameraman and an imaginative director. Sheer luck was smiling on Edison, for Porter turned out to be something of a creative visionary where the moving picture was concerned. If Edison himself bore the responsibility for exploiting the machinery of the

**After the Edison studio moved to the Chelsea district of New York City, the firm began to produce a diverse group of films, including this farcical comedy of about 1901.**

moving picture, it was Porter who led the movies toward a form of enduring popularity with the public—something Edison would not and could not have done by himself.

It was relatively simple and inexpensive to set up branch studios in the days of silent pictures, particularly where those pictures were made outdoors on simple muslin-topped stages. Little wonder that before Edison phased out his moving picture enterprises in 1918, he had possessed branch studios, at one time or another, in New Jersey, New York, Jacksonville, Florida, Long Beach, California, and other places. Such studios might have operated for a season or two, then their personnel, "properties," and equipment suddenly moved elsewhere.

Were it not for the early film production activities of Porter, it remains somewhat questionable that the Edison firm would have developed nearly so well as a motion picture producer. It was Porter who conceived the idea of editing together various existing short Kinetoscope films dealing with fire stations and their activities; by inserting new sequences specially made for the film *The Life of an American Fireman,* a one-reel picture came into being and proved conclusively that nickelodeon audiences would prefer "story films" to mere movement on the motion picture screen.

In 1903, Porter turned out another monumental one-reeler, *The Great Train Robbery,* a crudely made western which was in part shot "on location" in what was then a relatively undeveloped area of New Jersey. Even today *The Great Train Robbery* seems remarkable, not only for its pioneer storytelling and editing techniques, but for its early

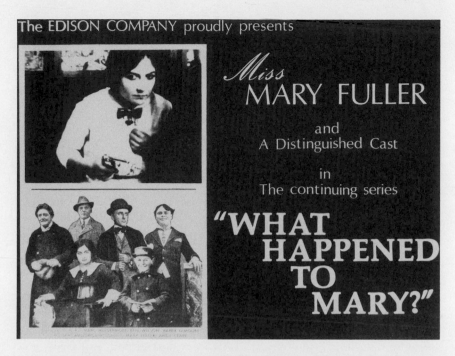

*Top:* In 1912, the Edison Company issued the world's first "continuing series," a filmic idea which later evolved as the movie serial, replete with "cliffhanger endings" for all but the final episode. *Bottom:* The Edison Studio in the Bronx section of New York City, 1912.

use of "matte" — devices which overprinted certain scenes onto others to produce a seemingly single image.

Just two years after the release of *The Great Train Robbery* (a picture which was widely imitated by such competing firms as Lubin), Edison erected a "greenhouse-type" motion picture studio, a vast, sprawling place situated in New York City's Bronx suburb.

Motion picture production was proving one of the most lucrative of Edison's many businesses. Between 1912 and 1918, for example, Thomas A. Edison, Inc., submitted for copyright close to a thousand film subjects, a figure which doesn't include all of the firm's many earlier subjects, primarily those of Kinetoscope length.

In addition to those releases made by Edison film crews, the firm began offering pictures made by outside firms such as film animator Paul Terry's company whose 1917 one-reel cartoon, *Farmer Al Falfa's Wayward Pup*, launched a series of Terry films which was to last for decades thereafter.

Comedies, cartoons, travel subjects, history, westerns, adventure, melodrama, literature, drama, chapter plays — all were among the numerous Edison releases, just as they were in the cases of virtually all large-scale film producers and distributors of that time. Edison even offered a few films in color — hand-painted, and terribly expensive.

By 1913, feature films had begun to appear in America, most of the early ones imported from Italy or elsewhere. At about the same time larger, more comfortable movie theatres began appearing, at first in larger metropolitan areas, then in ever smaller, more remote towns and cities. By 1915–16, it was clear that old-type "storefront" movie houses, nickelodeons and other such operations were soon to be things of the past.

Historians often maintain that the Moving Picture Patents Company, of which Edison was one of the organizers, fought the introduction of the so-called "full-length feature picture," preferring to continue with release only of short productions. Investigation proves this false; the Edison Company released many feature films, among them such titles as *The Unbelievers* (1918), a seven-reel feature produced with the cooperation of the United States Marine Corps, and based upon the novel *The Three Things* by Mary Raymond Shipman Andrews. Earlier, in the fall of 1917, Edison released *The Awakening of Ruth* directed by Edward H. Griffith, and *The Apple Tree Girl*, a five-reeler directed by Alan Crosland.

The experiment with long pictures came too late for the firm to hope for survival. Edison himself had been satisfied as long as his "step-child" was able to turn a fat profit on a skinny investment, but the old man now proved unwilling to risk large sums of money in order to allow his studio to work up a steady output of expensive feature pictures.

Besides, there were few "stars" on Edison's roster of players. Mary Fuller, who'd played the lead role in Edison chapter plays and in many one-and two-reel subjects, was the sole player with any sort of star value.

Edison, lacking any interest in the storytelling type of motion picture, lost interest in pictures, especially since his share in the Motion Picture Patents Company had soured ever since the federal government began looking into some of its highly irregular tactics.

Before the Edison film interests could be cast aside, many of its personnel had gone on to greater fame, and in a few cases to fortune, as had Gilbert Aaronson [Anderson], known as "Broncho Billy," and W.K.L. Dickson, who'd helped found Biograph. Edwin S. Porter had quickly made his name important among screen directors, as had Alan Crosland.

World War I had changed moviegoing habits of America, and indeed the world; "storefront" movie shows, needing one-and two-reel films changed daily were a thing of the past.

By the time the 1920s had become a sharp, jazz-ridden reality, the "Wizard of Menlo," as Edison frequently was called, no longer operated film studios.

# Essanay

When he was 19, George K. Spoor began working for the North Western Railway at the Wells Street depot in Chicago. A train "caller," he announced arrivals and departures of nearly 250 trains daily. Evenings, he managed the Phoenix Opera House in nearby Waukegan. Those opera house activities led Spoor to the movies.

"In Waukegan, I got to know a man named Amet," later explained Spoor. "He was a mechanic and worked during the day for the Chicago Scale Works. But in the evening . . . he was working on a projection machine. I lent him $100 to complete his machine . . . that was in February, 1895."

At first, Amet and Spoor demonstrated the projector by simply utilizing 50-foot films which had been made by the Thomas Edison labs for use in the coin-operated peepshow machines which Edison called Kinetoscopes. But from 1897 through 1902, Spoor said, he and Amet worked out problems relating to their projection machine, and undertook production of their own line of motion picture films, as well.

"I remember one of the first films we made," Spoor often recounted. "I got my boss at the railroad office to get permission to use

*The Bearded Bandit*, Essanay, 1912. G.M. "Broncho Billy" Anderson made a long series of these, filming them in Colorado, Hollywood, and Niles, California.

a new, deluxe, million dollar train. Down a long hill on the outskirts of Waukegan came the train, with Amet set up on some pilings." Such a mundane scene, enlivened by the inclusion of a track repair crew at work as the train passed, was sufficiently interesting for.early-day film audiences.

The making of such short, crudely photographed scenes eventually gave way to that of filming "incidents," even newsreel scenes, although the clumsy motion picture cameras of the era usually were too cumbersome, too heavy to allow them to be on hand whenever and wherever unstaged events happened to take place. "When the Spanish-American War came along," Spoor reported, "we got an idea. Amet built a large [water] tank, 35 feet square, and placed scenery around it. From newspaper pictures we built various models of the warships in action at that time . . . May, 1898. This represents, I think, the first work in miniatures." One of those model vessels used by Amet and Spoor survived at least until 1944, when the six-foot-long copy of Dewey's flagship was still preserved in the home of Spoor's brother-in-law, Enoch J. Brand, of Winnetka, Illinois.

Work with miniatures at Spoor's studio wasn't confined to the re-creation of the battle at Manila. In 1902 when Mount Pelee at St. Pierre, Martinique, erupted Spoor used newspaper photos to make a large scale model of the volcano and with the use of compressed air, soap-suds, gravel, ashes and small rocks, produced a realistic-appearing miniature.

The Mount Pelee explosion provided an exceptional picture in other ways. "That was the film that a man who had offices in Chicago's McVickers Theatre building colored for us. He had 20 girls, working four weeks, handcoloring the prints of that short film," Spoor later stated.

For a time, Spoor's activities in film turned toward exhibition of motion pictures; he organized a chain of 100 motion picture theatres, but returned to film production in force in 1908, utilizing largely foreign-made equipment, much of which proved inferior.

"A young man, Donald J. Bell, had been an exhibition manager for me in the circuit days," Spoor recounted. "He had a partner, a young fellow named Howell. When they finished work on cameras, per-forators and printing machines for me, they went on to outfit other com-panies. Bell and Howell did very well too!"

Establishing a headquarters and main studio on Argyle Street in downtown Chicago, Spoor, together with a partner who'd made minor successes in vaudeville, set up Essanay, compounding the name from the letters "s" (for Spoor) and "a" for G.M. Anderson, Spoor's partner.

Spoor claimed his partnership with Anderson (Anderson's name was originally Maxwell Aaronson) had been inspired by a visit to a secondhand book store on Chicago's Clark Street where Spoor, brows-ing one evening, found a pile of old "dime novels" which the store was selling at 15 or 20 for a dollar. Spoor bought a bunch, then made his way to see Anderson, an ex-vaudevillian who'd played a bit role in Edison's 1903 one-reeler *The Great Train Robbery*. The resultant partnership with G.M. Anderson produced hundreds upon hundreds of "Broncho" Billy westerns, some of them made from the very novels Spoor found at that bookstore on Clark Street.

None of the "Broncho" Billy pictures ever were made in Chicago, Spoor later said. Instead, Anderson and a small film crew shot the first ones in Colorado, then finally moved to Niles Canyon, California, near Oakland, where a small studio was established. A few of the series of one-reelers were turned out also at Santa Barbara, and another handful in Hollywood. Eventually, though, Anderson and his crew returned to Niles, a tiny town near Niles Canyon. Beginning their studio operations in the rented Oliver barn, Anderson built, nearby, half a dozen modest bungalows to house his personnel. Essanay's western operation, however, eventually outgrew the barn and constructed its own studio.

The town of Niles figured prominently in Essanay history when, for about four years, Broncho Billy was riding the trails of Niles Canyon, Anderson keeping his horses, between films, at the "California Nursery," a well-known plant emporium.

All during its history, Essanay's Chicago studio had been building and maintaining an in-house "stock company" of players, many virtual unknowns when that company hired them. Ben Turpin, Bryant Washburn, Ruth Stonehouse, Rod LaRocque, Marguerite Clayton, Maurice Costello, Gladys Hanson, Taylor Holmes, Lenore Ulric, Wallace Beery—all were to make their starts toward motion picture fame from beginnings at Essanay.

Charlie Chaplin signed on with Essanay in 1915, demanding and getting $1250 per week during the one year that he was there, plus $10,000 to sign his contract.

In that year's time, Chaplin appeared in 14 films, after which he moved on to Harry Aitken's Mutual for a salary of $10,000 weekly plus a $150,000 bonus just for signing his contract.

During the years of its operation, Essanay established several small branch studios, some merely seasonal operations such as the one at Jacksonville, Florida, while the main studio in Chicago continued operating at peak level with stars such as Lewis Stone, Francis X. Bushman, Edward Arnold, and others working at the Essanay lot on Argyle.

Gloria Swanson was one of the players at Essanay who achieved her success from a very modest start at Spoor's studio. "I remember how she broke into pictures," Spoor recalled years later. "Her girlfriend was a telephone operator at Essanay and her boyfriend was Wallace Beery. Between them they finally got Gloria into pictures. The hands around the lot used to kid her. You know the flat tip of her nose? Well, they said she got that from pressing her nose against the door at Essanay, looking in . . . and trying to GET in."

Many cinephiles today believe that Essanay made no feature-length productions. This is not true; George Spoor was fond of recalling some of his studio's lengthy productions, including the five-reel *Graustark,* and the *White Sister.*

Spoor's partner was Maxwell Aaronson, who was born in 1882 in Little Rock, Arkansas. Max's father was a successful cotton broker—a line of endeavor which Max spurned, changing his name to Gilbert M. Anderson and striking out on a career in vaudeville and the legitimate stage.

A dumpy, stocky figure even in his youth, Anderson must have realized he would never be a matinee idol, even if he stayed with the smalltime theatrical groups with which he traveled. In short, there was nothing which would have hinted that he was headed for screen stardom, garnering the adulation of movie audiences the world over.

Quietly, stoically, Anderson fought the odds, and eventually found small roles in such early Edison one-reelers as *Life of an American Fireman* and *The Great Train Robbery;* in the latter he displayed his ineptitude as a horseman by getting on his horse from the wrong side.

No matter that his few screen roles at the Edison company were simply walk-on parts; a few miles from Edison's studios in West Orange, New Jersey, were those of the Vitagraph firm where, by some miracle Anderson rather quickly earned a spot for himself as a film producer.

When George K. Spoor went looking for a partner to join the establishment of a new film studio in Chicago he chose Anderson for the partnership. In 1907 the two organized Essanay Film Manufacturing Company, the trademark unwittingly supplied without cost by the U.S. mint: the stoic profile of an American Indian on the Indian head pennies.

About four years after its founding, Essanay initiated a series of cheap one-reel westerns, the fictional character "Broncho Billy" having been purloined from the pulp magazine writer Peter B. Kyne.

Anderson promptly cast himself in the role of Broncho Billy and began production of the film series near Denver, Colorado.

After a few were completed, Anderson moved his production outfit to California to continue the series already proving immensely popular in shabby but numerous nickelodeon movie houses everywhere.

In 1912, "Broncho Billy" came into the tiny northern California village of Niles, close to San Francisco, with its background of picturesque, rugged Niles Canyon, where natural settings for western films abound.

Although Anderson reputedly was more than comfortably wealthy by the time he came to Niles, it's said that he stood back while townspeople went about the village soliciting funds with which he might lease the large old Oliver barn in order to use it as his first studio. (Anderson carefully noted, it's said, the names of those merchants who contributed to the outpouring of largesse, afterward seeing to it that Essanay personnel traded only with the ones who had contributed to the "startup" fund.)

Anderson possessed numerous peculiarities. Never a fastidious person in appearance, he also proved a slightly uncouth one, a man who, in many ways, was extremely penurious, even in the eyes of that master of stinginess, Charlie Chaplin. Chaplin was quite unprepared for what he found when he came to Niles in early 1915.

Chaplin first met Anderson in Chicago at a time when the former had come there to begin a year's contract with Essanay. His visit to Anderson's somewhat lavish apartment suggested that the movie producer was a person not opposed to the good life for himself, his wife and young daughter. (Oddly, however, Anderson appears to have left wife and child behind when he trekked to California soon afterward.)

At any rate, the opulent style in which Anderson was living in Chicago impressed Chaplin so thoroughly that the comic was only too happy to be offered the chance to share quarters with Anderson when Chaplin transferred from Chicago to Niles to continue his films for Essanay. Chaplin found, however, that Anderson was living like some sharecropper, in a filthy, unkempt hovel in which to flush the toilet one was required to get a jar of water.

But if the townspeople of Niles took any notice of Broncho Billy's idiosyncracies, they probably did not gossip about them: Essanay had brought employment and notoriety to the little town.

The local newspaper printed in its edition of April 6, 1912: "With a payroll of several hundred dollars a week and a company of 52 artists and helpers, the Essanay Film Company of Chicago located in Niles this week and will stay at least three months, coming here to make moving pictures of which this company is one of the best known in the world. . . . Nearly all available vacant rooms, and two or three houses, have been rented to the newcomers, besides a couple barns and a location for their studio. . . . The location of the company before coming here was San Diego and before that it was San Rafael."

Essanay's "Western Division" was to remain in Niles until 1916, four years during which the firm invested a great deal of money constructing a number of modest bungalows for its personnel, and a lengthy one-story masonry building which housed offices, editing rooms, screening rooms and other facilities.

In another portion of that structure were fireproof film storage vaults. Behind this building was a large outdoor stage topped with muslin cloth "scrims" so that the light of the Northern California sun could be modelled into something suitable for lighting ersatz "interiors" for movies.

Along a railroad siding nearby, Essanay's motion picture laboratory, contained in a former baggage car, functioned efficiently, processing the pictures which almost daily were the output of Anderson's entourage. (The "rolling film lab" enabled Anderson to quickly and easily move from place to place, even down to Hollywood where for about six months he and some of his personnel turned out part of the "Broncho Billy" pictures before returning to Niles.)

While he was at Niles, Anderson began spending lavishly (though he continued to stay at sleazy hotels). He began to lose interest in his film activities at Niles, contenting himself in commuting back and forth to San Francisco in his chauffeured, chain-driven Thomas Flyer automobile, while his studio personnel often carried on activities, such as turning out Wallace Beery comedies, or some of the popular

"Snakeville" comedies in which just about all the Essanay acting personnel at Niles were featured.

Chaplin, having appeared in just one comedy at the Chicago studio of Essanay (that film was *The New Janitor*), moved to Niles where in three months, at his contract salary of $1250 weekly, he appeared in five more of the short comedies he was to make while under contract to Essanay in 1915. Four of these were two-reelers, the fifth, a one-reel subject.

Chaplin fans can recite the titles of those comedies: *His Night Out, The Champion* (in which Anderson appears as an extra), *In the Park* (made on location in San Francisco), *A Jitney Elopement* and *The Tramp.*

Chaplin met young Edna Purviance during one of his frequent visits to San Francisco, and, soon after, moved the 19-year-old into his hotel room at the Belvoir in Niles.

Purviance brightened Chaplin's life at Niles but not sufficiently enough to cause him to want to remain there. He and Miss Purviance left, after completion of *The Tramp*, for a climate and surroundings more pleasant, a fact which didn't displease the gentry of Niles, most of whom never liked Chaplin, anyway. Wallace Beery and Ben Turpin, by contrast, were exceedingly popular in the town of Niles.

The "Broncho Billy" series continued in a nearly unbroken stream; eventually the number reached something like 200 to 400 depending upon who was making the enthusiastic report. Fans of the series cared not that the Broncho Billy subjects were exceedingly crude, simplistic in their plotting, and based on a repetitive cluster of basic premises. Few, if any, in the nickelodeon audiences apparently even noticed that their hero lacked not only histrionic abilities, but even skill at horsemanship—at least when he was shown in closeup on his horse. (For medium and long shots, Anderson stepped out of camera range while his double, William Cato, took his place.)

It now appears that Anderson, perhaps not ever an equal partner in Essanay, was forced to rely on his Broncho Billy films and other appearances before the camera to make up the bulk of his income from Essanay.

Such a supposition may cause readers to pity the man. Unfortunately, Anderson appears not to have been the sort of person deserving of one's pity.

"For one thing, actor-producer Broncho Billy Anderson was not exactly a lovable zany and was probably something other than a good and moral influence on the town youth," declares a retrospective newspaper story on Anderson. Continuing: "Compounding what might have been his personal flaws, Broncho Billy 'cleaned up' on the movies he made in Niles. Some of his . . . westerns reportedly earned as much as $50,000 each. They cost only a few hundred dollars to produce."

A decade ago, Hal Angus, said at the time to be the last living actor in the Niles region to have worked regularly in Anderson's films, looked back and said of his years at Essanay: "I'd been enjoying a successful stage career in Oakland when I met a lady named Josephine Rector who'd been with Anderson since late 1907 when he'd made some of his earliest westerns down in San Rafael, California." Miss Rector married Angus, continuing to work as an actress and scenario writer for Anderson, while Angus went to work for Essanay too.

"I never liked him," said Angus, referring to Anderson. "He was disgusting in one way. He couldn't say two words without spitting, and three words without snorting. Besides, he couldn't act."

Angus told some reporters that daily filmmaking was hard on the nerves, because Anderson was a severe taskmaster. "He was a production genius," admitted Angus, "but a rough one to work for. . . . Sometimes he was trying to make two or three movies at a time." Angus and his wife parted company from Anderson before the Essanay operation at Niles was suspended. "When Anderson moved down to Lakeside to make more movies, he asked Mrs. Angus to go along, but she said, 'No, I've had enough of you'," Angus later stated.

At one time the Niles studio of Essanay had as many as a hundred persons on its payroll, though at wages usually amounting to $15 to $40 weekly for a six-day work week. At that time, Anderson himself reputedly was earning $125,000 per year.

Anderson's income derived not only from the "Broncho Billy" films, but from his share of the earnings of Essanay, which, as early as 1912, was employing producer-director Theodore Wharton. During the summers of 1912 and 1913 at Ithaca, New York, his on-location crew and cast included the likes of Francis X. Bushman who appeared in such Essanay two-reelers as *The Hermit of Lonely Gulch* with Beverly Bayne.

Other Essanay subjects made at Ithaca included *Sunlight, For Old Times' Sake,* which featured Bushman with actress Juanita Delmorez, and*The Way Perilous.* (One- and two-reelers made at Ithaca also included *Antoine the Fiddler, The Right of Way* and *Love Lute of Romany.*)

It must be kept in mind that Essanay also operated seasonally at Jacksonville, Florida. The production output of the firm was staggering, the profits secure and certain, though it now appears that George Spoor kept the lion's share.

Just exactly what transpired to cause the hasty end of Essanay isn't exactly clear. One might accept Spoor's version that he bought Anderson out and then proceeded to close the studio so he could devote his fortune to developing such gadgets as 3-D films. Or one can accept the explanation that the firm was financially driven to turn out a dependable program of truly feature-length productions (although Essanay did produce quantities of such films).

Another persistent story has it that Spoor, disgusted with Anderson's style of high living in California, became so incensed that he simply bought out Anderson in order to be rid of him once and for all. Whatever the reasons, Essanay did not close down for lack of profits.

Niles oldtimers recall that the Essanay operation halted abruptly in February 1916 when a telegram reached Anderson from the firm's Chicago headquarters, ordering the immediate shutdown of that operation.

So hastily did that occur, it's said, that one production was never completed at all, while numerous motion picture films—whether negatives or prints has not been established—were left behind in a film vault in the basement of the Essanay branch studio. Sadly, most, if not all, such films were destroyed when local youngsters broke into the deserted studio, set fire to the film or else rolled it playfully and destructively down the hilly streets in the town near which Broncho Billy had once enacted spectacular adventures.

In an extensive interview during 1943, Spoor attempted to explain just why it was that he disbanded Essanay. "I bought out Anderson," he said. "I closed the western branch, and ended Essanay in Chcago."

As he said this, no doubt, Spoor's memories of the studio burned more brightly than before.

After Spoor closed down Essanay, he continued to be active in the film industry, investing considerable time and money in a widefilm innovation called the Spoor-Berggren process.

As for "Broncho Billy" Anderson, he disappeared for a number of years, while rumors circulated that he was dead. Suddenly, however, he was discovered working in some menial industry job. The Academy of Motion Picture Arts and Sciences soon afterward honored him for his contributions to screen history.

As for Spoor and Essanay, well, they were left by the Academy to fade quickly into the dimness of the history of the American motion picture, with the studio at Niles being torn down in 1933.

# First National

Organized as First National Exhibitors by a group of motion picture theatre owners headed by Thomas L. Talley of Los Angeles, First National came into being April 1917 in New York City. Its membership was made up of exhibitors who owned about a hundred theatres across the country.

**The studio of First National, Los Angeles, 1920s. Originally an exhibitor-owned corporation, its directorate eventually bought it away from its exhibitor-founders. The firm eventually was absorbed by Warner Bros.**

Once operative, the new firm first devoted itself to contracting with a nucleus of renowned film stars, rather quickly securing the services of Charles Chaplin (at somewhat more than $1,000,000 for a year), during which Chaplin agreed to turn out eight two-reel comedies under advance payments of $125,000 per picture, said sum to be included with Chaplin's exorbitant salary.

The creation of First National had been triggered by the stranglehold which Adolph Zukor's Paramount had gained on the distribution of major productions and on control of important key theatres throughout the U.S.

First National had no studio during its initial years of operation; instead, it acted as distributors for such production units as those of D.W. Griffith, Louis B. Mayer, Richard Barthelmess, B.P. Schulberg, Charles Ray, and Joseph Schenck, which provided First National for a time with the greatest number of top-quality pictures in the U.S.

One might be led to believe, therefore, that this distribution firm had found a foolproof device for defeating Zukor's Paramount. Such was not the case; many of the major stockholders in First National were heavily in debt on their theatres, so when Zukor threatened to buy or build theatres in the cities in which stockholders in First National operated houses, those exhibitors became frightened. Such fear increased until it reached the infrastructure of First National, a corporation which proceeded to shake severely, for in 1926 the firm had invested in building its own studio at Burbank, California.

Mounting fear, coupled with the expense of installing sound recording equipment for manufacture of talking pictures, discouraged the officials of the studio, which was no longer a co-operative organization and could readily be put on the auction block.

First National thereby was sold to Warner Bros., which continued the First National trademark for a number of years. The firm's studio at Culver City operated as a satellite of Warners for years. Today it is known as the Burbank Studios, serving jointly Columbia Pictures (a Coca-Cola subsidiary) and what remains of the Warner Bros. firm (a Kinney, Inc., division).

# Florida Studios

If some properly progressive leaders from various Florida communities had only played their cards correctly, California might never have found a place in film history.

As it worked out, though, not long after filmmakers from the New York region discovered Florida sunshine for the shiny reflectors and soft scrims of their movie gear, Florida citizenry pulled the welcome mats from under their cinematic visitors.

The movie industry caught Florida fever in 1908, after the Kalem Company of New York had sent a company of players and personnel to Jacksonville, and, investing a mere $400, made a one-reeler, *A Florida Feud*, which was to prove something of a box-office smash at the nickelodeon movie houses of that day.

Kalem officials decided to establish a permanent studio in the Jacksonville region and place that operation in the hands of Kerean Buel, providing him with a stock company of players and a coterie of other personnel, dispatching them once more to Jacksonville, in the fall of 1910.

In those years prior to World War I, the Kalem firm was one of the largest film studios in the United States, so it isn't surprising that its branch studio at Jacksonville was soon to inspire other film organizations to open branches in Florida: Biograph, Edison, Lubin, Thanhouser, Gaumont, Vitagraph, Essanay and other firms had operations in the Jacksonville area by 1913. It is claimed that there were, in

The Miami Studios, which occupied a large tract of land near Hialeah, Florida. This 1922 photo gives evidence of the drainage problem of the region which is so close to the swampy Everglades region of southeast Florida.

the pre–World War I era, some 30 movie production outfits in and around Jacksonville, at that time the largest city in Florida.

The members of Kalem's stock company of players in Florida included Alice Joyce, Anna Neilson, Pauline Frederick, Owen Moore, Victor Moore, Maurice Costello, Clara Kimball Young, Wallace Reid, Tom Moore, Gene Gauntier, Marguerite Courtot and Rise ("Sis Hopkins") Melville; the directorial staff included Sidney Olcott, Robert G. Vignola, and managing director Kerean Buel.

Even obscure film production outfits seemed to prosper in Jacksonville, including one which operated in a studio built at a cost of $40,000 by local architect Henry J. Klutho, in whose studio Briggs Pictures operated. There was also an outfit known as the Norman Studio which functioned in a building in the Arlington section of Jacksonville, making such "all colored cast" films as *The Flying Ace*, a 6-reeler which its makers trumpeted as "the greatest airplane mystery thriller ever produced."

In 1916 Jacksonville mayor J.E.T. Bowden attempted to induce other filmmakers to migrate to Florida; however, the hot summers on those pre–air conditioned days discouraged many Northern filmers from attempting year-round schedules in the Sunshine State.

There was also a growing resentment among the citizenry of

Jacksonville toward the film industry, with its penchant for filming dangerous scenes on downtown streets of Jacksonville, and local scandal, as when nearly 1400 residents, hired for a mob scene, went out of control and completely destroyed a two-story saloon at the corner of Davis and Monroe streets.

Most of the early films made at Jacksonville studios were one- and two-reel subjects, since feature pictures didn't begin to appear in America until the 1912–13 season.

One of the Jacksonville studios, Vim, employed a young, unseasoned actor from Harlem, Georgia, whose name was Oliver Hardy. He usually portrayed villains in pictures made at Vim and at the nearby Lubin lot. Hardy came to Jacksonville in 1913, and remained there for about five years.

It was a Jacksonville barber, an Italian by birth, who supposedly gave Hardy the nickname "Babe" when the barber, patting powder onto Hardy's rotund cheeks, would intone, "Nice-a babe-ee, nice-a babe." The name Babe stayed with Hardy for the remainder of his life.

The world's first Technicolor feature film, the production *The Gulf Between* starring Grace Darmond and Niles Welch, was made in Jacksonville in 1916, the primitive two-color negatives being processed in a rolling laboratory, a railroad coach which was parked on a sidetrack during the filming of the picture.

Probably the most remarkable of the early Kalem features, *From the Manger to the Cross,* was begun in Jacksonville by director Sidney Olcott, who later completed the picture in the Holy Land.

Pathe Freres Southern Studios, based at nearby Saint Augustine, issued to newspapers an interview in which one of its directors is quoted as saying of northeast Florida: "I found every location I needed right here. An expert could not have told me but what [my] pictures were made in the Old World—India, Egypt, Morocco, Persia—instead of the State of Florida." That unnamed official of Pathe may or may not have been correct, for later filmmakers who undertook productions in Florida seemed to agree that the Sunshine State was a good location for island paradise pictures, jungle epics, or sea films, but little else.

For a time, particularly around the late 1910s and early 1920s, various Florida communities became sites of film studios, some successful for a time, others which never got into production. At least one studio of the mid–1920s never got beyond the point where its Hobe Sound locale was surveyed, mapped, and a few of the paved, winding streets constructed; the studio and houses for the movie people never were built. A hurricane in 1926 swept away that dream.

Even before the abortive attempt at studio construction near Hobe Sound, Opelika, near the city of Miami, was the site of ambitious Miami

Studios, a joint effort of the president of the Miami Chamber of Commerce and *Miami Herald* editor Frank Shutts.

Tampa, Palatka, Orlando, Davis Island, and a couple other locations around the state also have been the sites of film studios, yet the dream of turning Florida into a major center for commercial film and TV production has always eluded the state, although some noteworthy pictures have been made in whole or part there. D.W. Griffith made portions of two of his features in Florida. Parts of MGM's *Tarzan Finds a Son* and *The Yearling* were made in Florida as was true of Universal's *Creature from the Black Lagoon,* Warners' *Wind Across the Everglades,* and the Frank Sinatra films *A Hole in the Head* and *Assault on a Queen.*

Among TV offerings, Florida has been featured in such series as *Flipper, Gentle Ben, Cowboy in Africa* and others, but Florida never was to become America's film capital, though history certainly shows it tried.

# Fox—With and Without 20th Century

Brought to America at nine months of age, William Fox could have no recollection of his birthplace at Tulchva, Hungary, where he was born January 1, 1879. As he grew to young, spindly boyhood in the ghettos of New York, he quickly learned that, while America might be the land of opportunity, those chances opened to a poor Jewish lad only if he had capital with which to pave the way.

Beginning as a street peddler of cheap gewgaws, Fox eventually found work as a laborer in a Lower East Side garment shop. It was a job which paid little; yet William Fox gradually, painstakingly accumulated enough savings to enable him to invest in a small coin-machine operation which included a storefront movie theatre.

While Sol Brill and other partners of Fox began going their own financial ways, Fox parlayed his earnings into other movie houses, dozens of them eventually.

With a chain of little theatres under his control, Fox next made his way into a distributorship of motion pictures, a film exchange which proved so successful that he was eventually served with notice by the all-powerful Motion Picture Patents Company commanding him to sell out to that combine or be faced with the prospect of having no films of merit to release in the future.

Fox refused. Instead, he hastily launched his own film studio in an obscure section of New York's Staten Island, the new operation, keeping his theatres and those of his rental accounts with sufficient pictures to stay in profitable operation.

Fox launched his film studio with the making of a dreadful one-reeler titled *Life's Show Window*, a picture so bad, it is said, that even Fox winced when he viewed it.

Dreadful though that initial Fox production was, it made money. Not only did Fox's enterprises produce profits, but they made it possible for him to pursue legal action against Edison, Kleine, Biograph, and the other members of the so-called Motion Picture Trust, resulting in a 1912 decision: the Trust was, indeed, in restraint of trade.

His first court battle having resulted in victory, Fox sheathed his sword while setting out in pursuit of large profits to be earned along cellulose nitrate trails. Gross rentals from the new "feature films" were more than any producer could hope to derive from an entire shelf of one- and two-reel pictures, so by 1917 Fox had not only gone into feature film production, he'd moved his studio operation to Los Angeles, and was frequently starring a young newcomer whose name was Theodosia Goodman (whom Fox publicity had renamed Theda Bara).

Fox didn't stop at making only romantic melodramas. Masculine adventure thrillers, many featuring former stage actor William Farnum, soon were rolling up excellent grosses for the Fox organization.

The studio undertook a series of westerns featuring former Selig player Tom Mix, not long after adding the services of Buck Jones, as Mix's westerns for Fox began grossing $600,000 to $800,000 per picture.

Around 1925, Fox began pouring money into research and experimentation on a system of sound-on-film, employing the services of Theodore W. Case for that project. Case's laboratory used as a basis for its experiments various sound-on-film methods already 10 or 20 years old, and came up with an innovative device which was christened "Movietone." It was used in recording talking newsreels which were, of course, released through Fox exchanges.

As his fortunes continued to burgeon, Fox grew less and less interested in the day-to-day operation of his studio, eventually naming Winfield Sheehan to head the studio operation, a costly mistake for Fox, although he wasn't to realize that until a long time afterward.

With the studio apparently operating smoothly and profitably, Fox decided to buy out the widow of the recently deceased Marcus M. Loew, and thus acquire the holdings of Loew's, Inc., its chain of theatres, and its production wing, Metro-Goldwyn-Mayer.

"The wise heads of the industry," wrote Benjamin Hampton in his book about film history, "did not regard William Fox as a likely contender for the Loew Kingdom." Fox dealt those convictions a severe blow. For a reported $50,000,000 he bought control of Loew's, Inc., and for another $20,000,000 bought an entire circuit of New England movie theatres, thus giving Fox, by the close of 1929, about 500 theatres in the U.S. At the same time, Fox also bought control of the vast Gaumont Theatres chain in Great Britain.

In November 1929, the United States Government, through its Federal Trade Commission, brought suit against William Fox, charging that his acquisition of Loew's constituted a restraint of trade.

To add to Fox's woes, scientist Lee DeForest entered a lawsuit charging that Fox-Movietone devices infringed upon DeForest's patents in the audio field. The entire field of talking pictures soon was clouded by claims and counterclaims, in spite of which the years 1926 and 1927 produced an avalanche of buyers of sound reproduction equipment, the actual legality of which was somewhat questionable!

Fox continued enlarging his empire, obtaining loans amounting to some $30,000,000, largely borrowed from Bell Telephone

William Fox, former cloth sponger, parlayed a 1906 $1000 investment in an arcade and five-cent movie house into an empire.

and the banking-brokerage firm of Halsey, Stuart, and Company. All were short-term loans, set to fall due in the winter the stock market suddenly skidded sickeningly.

Before the financial world collapsed, however, Fox's chauffeured limousine was struck by another vehicle, placing Fox on the brink of death in a Long Island hospital. By the time Fox was released from the hospital, he found himself in a series of disagreements between his bankers, himself, and turncoat Winfield Sheehan, vice president of Fox Film, who sided with the bankers.

Weary, discouraged William Fox thereby sold his interests in Fox Film for $18,000,000 to Harley L. Clarke of Chicago, with the latter succeeding to the presidency of Fox Film Corporation.

**Early views of Fox studios, 1924.**

Before his withdrawal from filmmaking, Fox had opted to purchase a large tract of land in what he less-than-modestly named "Fox Hills," outside Hollywood. There, his "Movietone City" was begun, a 96-acre lot on which were to be stages which had been actually constructed for making "talking pictures," not simply adapted to them.

After William Fox tumbled from his throne as monarch of his film interests, the Fox studios were merged with Twentieth Century, an independent production firm headed by Joseph M. Schenck and former Warner Bros. scriptwriter Darryl F. Zanuck. With Schenck moving into position as chairman of the board of a newly created Twentieth Century–Fox, Zanuck took over the reins as vice president in charge of production at the studios.

After the disastrous failure of the stock market, unemployment

**When Will Rogers was killed in a plane crash in 1935, Fox had only one really money-making star left: Shirley Temple.**

*Top:* The Fox Studio at Western Ave. and Sunset Blvd. William Fox took over this site from Thomas Dixon (see entry on pp. 67–68) in 1917. Two shopping centers occupy the site today. *Bottom:* The Fox Movietone Studio in Fox Hills, West Los Angeles. All Fox productions moved here, leaving the Western Ave. studio as a laboratory and studio annex.

reached an unprecedented peak and movie theatre attendance plum-meted. Every studio, every theatre began to feel reverberations.

It is said that the Fox offerings which featured cowboy-philosopher Will Rogers were about the only profitable item the company was able to turn out, a narrow vein of gold which ended abruptly with Rogers' death in a 1935 plane crash.

It was fortunate for the studio that it still had under contract little blonde Shirley Temple, whose mother had been trying to promote the child's acting abilities around Hollywood for several seasons, with only minimal success.

Low-cost westerns and outdoor action films starring George O'Brien were also more than paying their way at Fox studios, as were actor Warner Oland's works as detective Charlie Chan.

Much of the profits from Fox "B" budget offerings were ploughed back into production of more expensive pictures, some starring Warner Baxter, Ruby Keeler, Dick Powell, Alice Faye, Jack Oakie, and the like.

Like Paramount and other studios, Fox was in receivership for a time, working its corporate way out before the onset of America's par-ticipation in World War II. Enlarging its facilities, the studio began pioneering new presentations of features made in severely gaudy Technicolor which proved strangely appropriate for features which purportedly depicted the Gay '90s, or the turn of the twentieth century.

In those tumultuous years actress Alice Faye, long a great money-maker for the company, began to show her age, so much that even makeup couldn't help. Gradually, then, Fox began to feature a younger female, Betty Grable, and toward the close of the war years, such other newcomers as the studio thought might possess "star magic."

Suddenly, however, a series of events began to work against Hollywood prosperity in general, and that of Fox in particular. A mere decade after World War II ended, Fox had been placed under com-mand of Greek financier Spyros Skouras who, by 1954, decreed that not only was Fox committed to production only of CinemaScope (an ultra widescreen anamorphic lens process) pictures, but that the output of such films would be made with ridiculously expensive and complex magnetic sound tracks. The two systems were calculated to spur a return of customers to movie theatres that were suffering a disastrous decline of box-office revenues owing to the sudden onslaught of television.

Those were years of so-called "blockbuster" pictures, each de-signed to be so astounding, so overwhelming in magnitude that Hollywood felt sure audiences would be again drawn to movie the-atres, which had been reworked to provide gigantic screens, stereophonic speaker systems, enlarged candy counters and inflated ticket prices.

Fox began dumping a cornucopia of CinemaScope feature films onto the public. There were *The Robe, The Egyptian, Beneath the Twelve-Mile Reef, The Gladiator* and a seemingly endless display of other shallow foolishness which did not truly impress anyone. By the end of the ensuing decade, it became clear to Hollywood moguls that mere "gimmickry" was not the answer to the sagging profits of movie theatres.

Zanuck, who had in the meantime been deposed from his position, was brought back to the studio at least long enough to spearhead the overblown, overlength feature *The Longest Day.* An ailing man by that time, Zanuck's second reign at Fox was a short-lived period of further retrenchment by Fox.

The Fox studio began to sell off its "back lot" in order to get a much-needed infusion of cash, and in a like manner began systematic sale of its old feature films and certain of its short subjects. Anything to please the stockholders.

What remains of the Fox studio today devotes most of its space and budgetary requirements to programs for television showings. Productions for big screen presentation are pitifully few in number, and when they are turned out, it's with an eye to just how soon after release they can be offered to pay–TV or to the other television outlets.

# Goldwyn Studios

In 1893, Samuel Goldfisch left the Jewish ghetto of Warsaw, Poland. Although alone and just 11 years old, the lad didn't head directly for America. His journey first took him to an aunt's place in Birmingham, England, where he lived for some two years and accumulated savings sufficient to enable him to purchase passage to America. At Gloversville, New York, the boy found work at Samuel Lehr's glove factory as a sweeper at $3 per week. There, Goldfish (the spelling of his name was altered by an immigration officer) grew to manhood, working as a glove cutter and eventually a glove salesman. Along the way, he met and courted Blanche Lasky, to whom Goldfish seemed to have been attracted, in part at least, because Blanche, together with a brother, Jesse, worked in vaudeville, doing a flashy cornet act.

In 1910, Goldfish became Jesse Lasky's brother-in-law, although Jesse disliked Goldfish intensely, especially when his new in-law moved in with the Laskys. In spite of their animosity, Lasky and Goldfish jointly

*Top:* **Culver City, California, was the site of the Goldwyn Pictures Corp. in 1922. Before that the studio was the home of Triangle, which constructed the glass-enclosed stages.** *Bottom:* **When Mary Pickford and Douglas Fairbanks gave up their studio, it became, at turns, Goldwyn's, and United Artists'.**

backed a Broadway show, *Cheer Up,* on which both men made a substantial profit.

In 1911 Goldfish attended his first motion picture, a western titled *Broncho Billy's Adventures* which, the observant Sam noted, seemed to create a steady flow of coins through the box-office wicket. That night he began to talk to his brother-in-law about investing money in films.

This was one of several of Samuel Goldwyn's World War II entries, popular with civilian and military audiences alike. Who cares that the plot of the film was nebulous? It was fun and it was a great showcase for Danny Kaye's fast-paced comedy.

The next day, Lasky and Goldfish had lunch with a friend of Lasky's named Cecil B. DeMille who, at the time, was heavily in debt from losses incurred in Broadway shows. DeMille, Lasky, and Goldfish formed a partnership choosing to make as their first film *The Squaw Man*, taken from a Broadway hit and featuring its stage star Dustin Farnum.

While Goldfish and Lasky remained in New York, DeMille went to Flagstaff, Arizona, with Farnum and other cast members. Finding Flagstaff not to his liking, DeMille continued westward. Debarking at Los Angeles, the DeMille troup began shooting, on December 29, 1913, the first picture in which Samuel Goldfish was a financial backer.

Reputedly the first feature-length film to be made entirely in Hollywood, *The Squaw Man* was shot in six weeks, upon its release grossing a surprising quarter-million dollars.

The Lasky Feature Film Co. quickly moved into full-scale production, in spite of internal problems, all of which were seemingly due to Goldfish. To quell the storms that soon became almost constant, the other partners bought out Goldwyn for $900,000, enough to enable the former glove salesman to emerge from the fray a millionaire at age 34.

In 1916, advertisements began appearing, announcing the formation of a new firm called Goldwyn Pictures, that compounded from the names Goldfish and Selwyn (the two Selwyn brothers, Archie and Edward, were Broadway producers).

For production of the initial "Goldwyn" pictures, Goldfish leased a greenhouse-type studio at Ft. Lee, New Jersey. Soon afterward he appeared in a New York court where he asked that his last name officially be changed to "Goldwyn," a bit of chicanery in which Sam conveniently "borrowed" the second syllable from the last name of his partners.

In the summer of 1918, the Goldwyn Company, with the Selwyn brothers still participating, moved to California, where the firm leased studio and office space at Triangle studios on Washington Boulevard in Culver City. Built three years earlier by Harry Aitken's Triangle Pictures, the studio was on the brink of bankruptcy at the time Goldwyn moved onto the lot, a fact which made it possible for the Goldwyn firm to buy the studio just eight months later, complete with its 16-acre lot and five glass-enclosed stages, as well as an assortment of offices, workshops, dressing rooms and the like.

Even in those early years of Goldwyn's activities as a motion picture producer, he began to display tendencies toward production of lavish, overblown films which, to his uncouth taste, was artistic and prestigious. At the time, however, he overlooked the fact that what kept his firm solvent were those cheap but profitable pictures that the company turned out along with its "prestige" productions.

Goldwyn began importing expensive stage stars, opera divas and the like — the sort of expensive nonsense which had strangled the earlier Triangle firm.

Utilizing a stylized likeness of a lion as its trademark, this first Goldwyn outfit in 1923 merged with two other firms to form MGM, though Goldwyn himself was not involved in the merger, having by that time accepted $1,000,000 from the Goldwyn firm and gone his own way.

Samuel Goldwyn Productions, Inc., was solely his firm; there were no partners. Leasing offices and studio space at 7200 Santa Monica Boulevard (the Douglas Fairbanks — Mary Pickford studio), Goldwyn made such feature films as *The Eternal City, Potash and Perlmutter,* and early talking films including *Whoopee* (1930) featuring Eddie Cantor, and *Bulldog Drummond* (1929), which introduced American audiences to British actor Ronald Coleman. Turning out a flow of films both good and bad, profitable and unprofitable, Goldwyn in 1938 bought the studio outright. United Artists brought suit against Goldwyn's purchase of the studio and, for a time, the studio carried the U.A. name, though Goldwyn eventually prevailed.

The same mercurial personality traits which Goldwyn displayed in his early business dealing continued to follow him in his relations with the motion picture players he signed to long-term contracts. Eddie Cantor, who appeared in several profitable, top-budget Goldwyn films, grew to hate the producer so much that Cantor bought up his contract from Goldwyn before it expired. Cantor's opinion was doubtless mirrored by another actor, Farley Grainger, who once said, "Goldwyn was a monster."

"When you got a message from Mr. Goldwyn," declared art director Ernest Fegate, "you always knew it meant trouble, always trouble. Never anything nice."

Perhaps author F. Scott Fitzgerald summarized matters best when he stated, "You always knew where you stood with him: nowhere."

Yet in spite of Goldwyn's record for bad relationships, in 1935 he was invited to become a partner in United Artists, the distribution firm founded in 1919 by Mary Pickford, Douglas Fairbanks, Charles Chaplin, and D.W. Griffith. During the 15 years that Goldwyn was part-owner of U.A., he released 40 productions through that outlet, though complaining loudly how, during the same number of years, Chaplin had contributed but five films, Pickford seven, and Fairbanks eight. "I'm the only moneymaking producer in all the U.A. circle," he charged.

His partners took no time in 1939 buying Goldwyn out, the $300,000 paying liberally for his share of U.A., after which Goldwyn rapidly moved into a distribution arrangement with RKO.

In 1943 the back lot at Goldwyn held a sprawling $250,000 set, a concept of a "typical" Russian village as designed by William Cameron Menzies for the film *North Star.* During the latter stages of the production the set was to be set ablaze for a sequence of the picture. On cue, the village went up in flames, accidentally setting afire an adjacent sound stage, burning off the roof of that structure and gutting its interior.

*North Star* didn't merit the trouble it entailed; Goldwyn claimed the picture cost him two million dollars, but it garnered reviews such as in the New York *Mirror,* which said, "Unadulterated Soviet propaganda."

Fires at the Goldwyn studio weren't confined to the back lot. In

1957, after Sam had paid $750,000 for the rights to *Porgy and Bess,* he turned the interior of Stage 8 into a likeness of what he thought resembled Catfish Row, South Carolina. On July 2, 1958, Goldwyn and his wife made a final inspection of the set, pausing to marvel once more at the piles of Irene Sharaff costumes, and the 18 gigantic boxes of Irving Sindler's props to be used in making the picture. That night a fire, later attributed to a smoldering cigarette left on a mattress in one of the "shacks" along the set, razed the entire sound stage and all contents. Fortunately for Goldwyn, his entire loss was covered by insurance, though production of the picture was delayed by eight weeks.

To spare further delays, two complete sound stages were moved from the Eagle Lion lot across the street, although these later were torn down and replaced by three separate new stages.

In March 1969, Samuel Goldwyn was felled by the first of several strokes which left the showman severely paralyzed. Thereafter, his visitors were but few: his family, a barber, a manicurist, and his physicians. He passed away January 31, 1974.

# Grand National

For some curious reason, in spite of the fact that the firm was in existence for just a trifle more than five years, Grand National is today remembered clearly—at least by film enthusiasts!

Even the logo of the firm seems a familiar one today: The art-deco clock tower atop a 1930s style office building, its hands sweeping around the face leaving in its wake either the words "Grand National" or "The End" as suited the position on the print.

Beginning with a releasing schedule of British imports or else U.S. independent productions, the name "Grand National" first cropped up in 1935. These early releases aren't germane to our account; they were merely grist for the distribution mill which was born of the various First Division film exchanges, the chain which had preceded Grand National.

Early in our story, Edward L. Alperson strode egotistically on the Grand National scene, followed by his staff which included Edward Finney, in charge of publicity. In the leased, palatial home of cowboy-actor Tom Mix, Alperson and his entourage established temporary offices in which these entrepreneurs could catch their breath while setting up production schedules for Grand National pictures to be made at RKO-Pathe Studios in Culver City, California.

Possibly the inspiration for the name "Grand National" had come from an older Hollywood outfit, "First National," a firm which Warner Bros. had absorbed. It occurred as a preposterous coincidence that at about the time when Grand National was born, actor James Cagney became involved in a serious quarrel with Warners, culminating in Cagney's departure from that studio and his subsequent contract with Grand national in 1936. Cagney's initial feature, *Great Guy,* a film purported to be an expose of the weights and measures "racket." The film was an auspicious beginning for the new firm, one which would be even more attractive the following year, by which time Grand National had acquired both the financing of Pathe Laboratories and studios at 7250 Santa Monica, Hollywood.

The 1937 lineup of Grand National releases, not all of which were filmed at the Grand National studios, seems alluring, even today.

For one thing, there was continuation of the group of westerns which former publicity chief Edward Finney had launched a year earlier, featuring a new screen cowboy, Tex Ritter. For another, there were independent releases turned out by George Hirliman, and a handful of westerns fashioned by the Alexander brothers, Max and Arthur, featuring an aging but yet appealing Ken Maynard.

A unit which called itself "Criterion Pictures" added to the Grand National release schedule what proved eventually to be a series beginning with *Renfrew of the Royal Mounted,* featuring the rather personable singer James Newill.

About this time, Edward Alperson's biography began to appear in the "Who's Who" section of *International Motion Picture Almanac.* Although not yet 40 when his biography was summarized by that publication, Alperson's story was already studded with many milestones: Beginning as an usher in a theatre in Omaha, Nebraska, he moved to a position as a film shipping clerk, thence to that of film salesman, film exchange manager, and ultimately film buyer for the sprawling corporation Skouras Theatres. In May of 1936, the *Almanac* averred, Alperson was elected president of Grand national Films, the producing and distributing firm financed by Pathé.

The years 1936 and 1937 were to prove the greatest for Grand National, a couple dozen months in which the firm found itself in possession of its own studios, as well as operating the distribution network of film sales offices which Alperson's outfit had fashioned from what had previously been known as First Division.

By the time 1937 reached its mid-point, Grand National had productions in release which included *August Weekend* with Valerie Hobson, *Bridge of Sighs* with Onslow Stevens, the George Hirliman production *Captain Calamity,* which featured singer-actor George Houston, and *Condemned to Live* which featured Ralph Morgan and Maxine Doyle.

When Grand National established its studio, it was acquiring a layout which had its beginnings at the hands of producer Sol Lesser who, in the waning days of the silent film, had employed Jackie Coogan for a series of feature films.

After sound came into being, Lesser had chosen to abandon production of pictures in order to concentrate on his holdings, of a number of West Coast movie houses. That decision had therefore made available Lesser's studio, which was acquired by a flamboyant and garrulous promoter named Earle Hammons who operated a short-subject firm named Educational Pictures.

It was Hammons who sold Grand National the studio on Santa Monica, whereby Hammons moved his production outfit to the East Coast.

From the time of its construction, the studio which Grand National occupied was an exceedingly unattractive place; most film studios are. By the time Sol Lesser unloaded the place, the studio already was becoming distressingly old-fashioned appearing.

After it came under Grand National control, the studio's back lot featured in many productions, including the Stuart Erwin feature *Mr. Boggs Steps Out*, a picture which many film collectors revere for the shot in which the camera truck is clearly evident in the "store windows" reflected on the set.

Erwin appeared in two Grand National features, for both of which he accepted a small salary with the promise that he'd also receive a percentage of the profits of the films. Needless to say, he never realized any of that.

By the end of 1938 Grand National was in immense financial difficulty brought on by the second of two James Cagney films made for the company prior to Cagney's return to the Warners' lot. The picture was the terribly expensive *Something to Sing About*, which Alperson had chosen for production in spite of his having purchased the story *Angels with Dirty Faces* as the next of Cagney's pictures for Grand National. The script for *Angels with Dirty Faces* was sold by Grand National to Warner Bros., the latter firm turning the script into what proved for Warners a most profitable film.

In February 1939, Alperson withdrew from the Grand National firm even as its backers, Pathe, chose to invest no more in the studio.

Earle Hammons of Educational then stepped forward, grandly announcing that he could, and would, save the foundering firm, in spite of the fact that Educational, his own company, was very near bankruptcy.

Another producer, Franklyn Warner, hinted that he could take over Grand National and turn it into a profitable operation. In the final showdown, he too proved inadequate to the task.

Debts of the Grand National firm had grown too immense for

anyone with limited financial backing to shore up the collapsing entity.

The Grand National studio struggled along for a short time as a "rental lot," nearly until the time when America entered World War II; then still another production organization, Producers Pictures Corporation, took over.

# The D.W. Griffith Studio

In October 1919, famous film director D.W. Griffith left Los Angeles with some of his personnel, their ultimate destination a spot called Orienta Point, not far from the town of Mamaroneck, Long Island.

Before they settled down there, the entourage hove to at the Thanhouser Studio in New Rochelle, New York, to do a bit of shooting on the picture *The Greatest Question*. After that the mighty Griffith continued work at the Thanhouser film factory, doing a bit of editing of D.W.'s yet-unreleased feature film *Scarlet Days*.

Griffith was under contract to First National for two more features, *The Idol Dancer* and *The Love Flower*, pictures he chose to shoot on location in southern climes, so on November 17, Griffith departed New Rochelle for Fort Lauderdale, Florida, taking with him Richard Barthelmess, Carol Dempster, Clarine Seymour, and others of his acting company. He left behind Lillian Gish with instructions that she oversee the completion of Griffith's new studio facilities at Orienta Point, while she directed her sister Dorothy in the feature film *Remodelling Her Husband*, a production which was budgeted at $50,000.

As with so much of motion picture history, there are conflicting accounts as to why Miss Gish didn't complete *Remodelling Her Husband* at the new studio, instead transferring production to the Thanhouser facility. Gish herself says it was because the heating plant at the Griffith facility proved inadequate.

Joseph Rigano, a former employee at the Griffith studio, tells it somewhat differently, claiming that there was insufficient voltage to the studio, thus making it impossible to light the sets properly. "They wanted to string a line on Orienta Avenue down to the end of the Flagler Estate," declares Rigano. "But the people down there would not let them."

The Griffith studio at Mamaroneck was completed in 1919, the main building for the studio a former estate of railroad magnate Henry M. Flagler.

**D.W. Griffith and cameraman G.W. "Billy" Bitzer during the filming of *Way Down East*, one of the Griffith feature pictures made at his studio in Mamaroneck, New York.**

In her book *The Movies, Mr. Griffith, and Me,* Lillian Gish writes of the Griffith studio site as "a great peninsula of land jutting into Long Island Sound and surrounded by a seawall of rocks and [with] glorious old trees with branches chained together to withstand the sweeping winter winds."

"Mr. Griffith was a very big spender," Joseph Rigano recalls, explaining that Griffith often employed 100 to 125 men as laborers on the studio. Griffith even had a separate bungalow built for himself, so that he could retire to the privacy and seclusion of that facility whenever he chose.

An outdoor stage also was constructed as well as a studio commissary and other facilities as would be necessitated by some of the massive productions which Griffith was to turn out at his studio.

When Griffith returned from location shooting in Florida, he completed shooting interiors and "pickup shots" at his new studio, cut the negatives of the two features and shipped them to First National. Those tasks finished, the director began to prepare a film version of the Victorian stage melodrama *Way Down East,* in which he cast Lillian Gish and Richard Barthelmess in leading roles, supported by such members of the Griffith stock company as Creighton Hale, Porter Strong, and

Kate Bruce. The creaky anachronism was filmed at the Griffith studio and on locations including White River Junction, Vermont.

All odds appeared to be against the success of the picture: America was moving into what was to become known as the Jazz Age, a period when most strait-laced values were being laughed at in some cases and ignored in others.

It appears that if *Way Down East* had failed as a motion picture, Griffith at that point would have had only his one-fifth ownership of the new United Artists Corporation to sustain him. Rather surprisingly, however, *Way Down East* succeeded in beating the odds.

Favorably reviewed, the picture rolled up astounding ticket sales, enabling D.W. Griffith's studio to quickly become a busy place.

At the depot in the village each work day, Walter S. Webber, who acted as Griffith's chauffeur, would pick up countless "extras" who lived in New York City and drive them out to the studio by bus.

"It was often my duty also to drive to New York City by truck and pick up two hampers of liquor and bring them out to the studios for [Griffith]," Webber recounted during an interview in 1975.

But Griffith was buying things other than liquor during those years. Pouring much of his profits from *Way Down East* into improvements on his studio, he readied his next important production, *Dream Street*, to be made from the same group of short stories which had yielded him the plot for his earlier picture *Broken Blossoms*. Unlike *Broken Blossoms*, however, *Dream Street* proved unprofitable, partly because Griffith poured so much of the budget into making the film a quasisound picture utilizing the Kellum process of synchronizing picture and a musical score. The process proved less than perfect and finally was restricted to its use in a "talkie" prologue and, according to Kellum's son, Terry, to one or more "talkie" short subjects which supposedly accompanied the Griffith feature.

Griffith, by that time, was in a curious position: While he'd already earned himself a position of honor within the panoply of American motion picture pioneers, he was at the same time becoming strangely outdated. His monumental *Birth of a Nation* had established, for all time, his position among important American directors, while his failure to progress beyond old-fashioned morals and mores now made all his work seem dated.

In spite of this, Griffith turned back once again to Victorian melodrama for his next important production at Mamaroneck, purchasing, for $5,000, the screen rights to author Kate Stevenson's hoary American stage melodrama *The Two Orphans*. (Miss Stevenson, when appearing as a stage actress, used the name Kate Claxton.) Had Griffith checked carefully, before buying the story rights he would have found that the Stevenson play was not under copyright, but was in the public domain, subject to no necessity for payment of rights to the author whatever!

These facts were noticed by William Fox, who, quite like his four-legged namesake, hastily managed to secure certain foreign rights to *The Two Orphans* and thus be able to threaten Griffith with lawsuits should he attempt to release his film version of the play abroad.

When the Griffith picture was completed it was retitled *Orphans of the Storm* and the basic storyline infused with many elements lifted from Charles Dickens' novel *A Tale of Two Cities*. Those facts, however, did not prevent William Fox from demanding and obtaining remuneration from Griffith for foreign showings of the picture version.

Almost 14 acres of Mamaroneck had been transformed into the outdoor sets used in making *Orphans of the Storm*. Griffith's master carpenter, Huck Wortman, had filled the area with an immense field of sets which represented Paris in the time of the Revolution, with such collossi of architecture as the Palais Royale, the Bastille, and the Cathedral of Notre Dame (as translated from plans drawn by set designer Charles Kirk). The copies of such landmarks rose among beautifully copied cobblestone streets along which occasionally could be glimpsed, incongruously, a building facade which appeared more a New England piece of architecture, than that of France.

Griffith's vast set drew sightseers from all about Connecticut, New York, and other nearby places. As Lillian and Dorothy Gish wound their tearful ways through the maze of outdoor sets which had been constructed there along the shores of Long Island Sound, Griffith watched most of the profits from *Way Down East* go into bringing the new picture to reality.

*Orphans of the Storm* was not successful with the filmgoing public. It did garner some favorable reviews, however. *Film Daily* purred, "it is a melodramatic spectacle, huge at times." Such reviews heartened Griffith, no doubt.

The small but efficient publicity department at Griffith's studio quickly announced several new projects which D.W. was preparing, including motion pictures to be made for two different South American countries, a new feature film to be filmed in Florida, a filmic version of *Faust*, and a motion picture version of British author H.G. Wells' massive work, *The Outline of History*. Such projects never were undertaken, save for the "Florida-made production."

Instead, the master of the studio at Mamaroneck proceeded to attempt to keep its financial head above water with potboilers such as *One Exciting Night*, and, at least nominally supervising such D.W. Griffith, Incorporated, productions as the 1920 feature *Romance*, which was directed by Chet Whithey, a picture which proved only to lose a great deal of money.

In 1922, Griffith turned out a picture filmed on location in Florida and Louisiana. *The White Rose* was completed and edited at Mamaroneck.

In 1923, Griffith devoted most of his efforts to the production of *America,* an historical-fiction piece, much of which was shot on location at such places as Concord, Massachusetts. He completed the task of editing the picture in January 1924, following which he seemed to have extreme confidence that *America* would become so successful that his studio would suddenly be once again a financial success, enthusiasm which was ill-founded. *America* was to barely pay its costs and then only after years had passed and much "stock footage" from the picture sold to other producers, and considerably after Griffith closed his debtridden studio. Griffith, without funds and discouraged, returned to Hollywood, his directorial career ending with the New York–made feature *The Struggle* (1931), a picture so bad that United Artists withdrew it from distribution soon after its release.

Just about all that remains of Griffith's studio complex at Mamaroneck is the pier where supply boats once moored as they unloaded lumber or other material. A few of the foundation supports for the studio commissary were in evidence as late as 1980, although most of the complex was razed not many years after its completion. A dozen or so houses now dot the restricted peninsula, along which waves lap placidly or wildly as the weather dictates.

# Grossman Pictures Studio

On July 8, 1919, Grossman Pictures Company told newspaper reporters that their firm had leased the Renwick Park property in Ithaca, New York, for a six months' period and was about to produce a "big serial" starring Lillian Walker. Production would commence, announced Grossman officials, before August 1.

As if newspaper readers didn't know the fact, the news story concluded by pointing out that the lease "means the resumption of motion picture film activities in this city on an important scale." Grossman already produced a number of serials by the time the company set up shop in Ithaca, including "Craig Kennedy detective stories" and "the Houdini mystery series," according to the Ithaca newspaper.

The physical move of Grossman Pictures from New York City began on Wednesday, July 8, with two truckloads of motion picture equipment dispatched to Ithaca and arriving four days later.

On July 16 Grossman Pictures, Inc., trumpeted to reporters that the firm would commence work within a week on a "big Pathe serial," with Arthur B. Reeve as a scriptwriter and E. Douglas Bingham as business manager for the firm. The first Grossman serial to be made at Ithaca would be titled *A Thousand Dollars' Reward* with a shooting schedule of fifteen weeks. Grossman pointed out that the firm had turned out the serial *The Carter Case* in just fourteen weeks.

Apparently Grossman Pictures had already decided to extend the short lease it held on Renwick. On July 16 the firm announced that it also would make 20 two-reel pictures in Ithaca, with Marguerite Marsh in the female lead.

Warming to a place in the summer sun at Ithaca, Grossman Pictures' business manager enthusiastically pointed out how his company's "movie colony" would be visited by such stars as Constance Talmadge and her sister Norma — not to mention Ann Pallette, who had appeared in the motion picture version of the Grace Miller White novel *Tess of the Storm Country.* Then, to make his name-dropping activities more complete, the business manager added that Mae Marsh and her sister Margaret, too, would visit Ithaca "at an early date."

With those seeds of publicity planted, Bingham pointed out somewhat less than modestly that it was he who was really responsible for inducing Grossman Pictures, Inc., to come to Ithaca. "We came here," Bingham rounded out the press report by adding, "because of a real advantage of the unexcelled exterior scenery."

By July 18 the title of the new serial to be made by Grossman had become somewhat inflated: *A Thousand Dollars' Reward* had metamorphosed into *A Million Dollars' Reward,* while at the same time, George Lessey of New York and W.G. Williams ("formerly with Cecil B. DeMille forces") were announced as the team of directors for the new serial.

Studio electrician George Connors was named in the press as an important figure, the news story noted, considering how the forthcoming Grossman serial was to entail an elaborately lighted ballroom scene which would be so gigantic overall that the entire west wall of the Renwick Park studio would have to be temporarily removed — "the largest scene ever to be filmed in Ithaca," Grossman stated proudly.

By mid–August one of the earlier Grossman serials, *The Carter Case,* was playing weekly at Ithaca's Star Theatre and drawing larger than usual crowds because in the cast of the film was Louis R. Wolheim, a graduate of the city's Cornell University, class of 1906.

Although by this time Harry Grossman had been a film producer in New York state for quite some time, it wasn't until mid–September 1919 that his firm was granted its charter by the state of New York with authorized capital of $25,000, consisting of shares priced at $100 each. Dreadfully underfinanced, Grossman was depending upon profitable release of its new serial through Pathe Exchanges. At the same time, in another part of Ithaca, Ted Wharton was frantically attempting to complete his 10-chapter serial *The Crooked Dagger,* for which Wharton had highest hopes. Both Grossman and Wharton had pinned the futures of their respective firms upon the tail of the Pathe rooster!

Pathe, however, was extremely particular about the films it distributed, proud of its position in the industry as "The House of Serials." When any producer offered Pathe a chapter play, that producer risked the chance that a reviewing board of Pathe officials would turn thumbs down on any serial which they did not think was up to Pathe's standards, at times rejecting just one or two chapters or, sometimes forcing the producer into expensive remakes.

Just before Thanksgiving, the *Ithaca Journal* announced the fact that both Grossman's and Wharton's new chapter plays had been refused release through Pathe. Wharton immediately threatened to sue Pathe, while Harry Grossman simply was said to have laughed over his predicament, explaining to reporters that he was going to distribute *A Million Dollars' Reward* on a revised basis, offering the serial on the market through "state's rights" distributors.

In explaining the change, Mr. Grossman told newspaper reporters that it was his studio, not the Pathe firm, which had cancelled the contract regarding the new serial. Pathe, said Grossman, sought to make changes in the serial which he would not permit.

As a result of Pathe's rejections of the two Ithaca-made serials, work at the Wharton lot on West State Street halted at once, while Ted Wharton tried to assure all who would listen that the Wharton studio would shortly resume production activities.

On the other hand, production continued at the Grossman Studio, where a seven-reel feature with Marguerite Marsh in the top female role was in production.

Yet, rumors of the imminent collapse of Grossman Pictures were rife not only in Ithaca but throughout the motion picture industry as well. Harry Grossman, in an effort to put a halt to the rumors regarding his firm, announced in early December 1919 that the distribution rights to the serial *A Million Dollars' Reward* had already been sold to several large film distributors ("several large film distributors" implied that each was serving a different part of the country), while Export and Import Film Corporation of New York City purchased the foreign rights.

"We have made a feature . . . *Wits vs. Wits* starring Miss Marguerite Marsh," added the producer, who also indicated that his studio would begin, on December 10, a new feature starring Miss Marsh.

The first episode of the Grossman serial *$1,000,000 Reward* opened at Ithaca's Strand Theatre on January 5, 1920, on a bill which

also included the feature film *When the Clouds Roll By* with Douglas
Fairbanks. Preparatory to that opening, an item appearing in the
January 3 *Ithaca Journal* cited that the new serial had been edited from
about 150,000 feet of negative, the final version of the picture comprising some 31,000 feet, "replete with pep, dash, mystery, and action" the
publicity noted enthusiastically.

Harry Grossman told the news media that *$1,000,000 Reward* had
been budgeted at between $125,000 and $140,000, both figures
doubtless terribly inflated. Even though it was a lengthy 15 chapters, it
probably had cost scarcely $50,000.

Local newspaper reviews of the serial, appearing January 5, were
exceedingly complimentary: "the first episode of which was shown at
the Strand yesterday," the newspaper commented, adding that it was
"one of the best serials ever made in Ithaca . . . [with] . . . one of the
most elaborate settings ever seen in a serial . . . directorship excellent."

The enthusiasm of the reviewer would doubtless have been quite
different had that writer been given access to the news story about to
break in that newspaper just four days later: "Grossman Company to
leave city first of month," a subhead on the story informed readers.
"Ithaca is to lose a motion picture industry, according to an announcement by Grossman Pictures," the text of the story began. "About
February first it will relinquish its lease to the studios at Renwick Park
and will henceforth be located in New York City." The official announcement by the Grossman firm explained it this way: "Due to the
fact that our interests are so closely linked with the City of New York
. . . we find it expedient to make our pictures there. We have twelve
features and three serials to make during the next year. . . . It is
necessary . . . to be handy to get all of the necessary articles such as
props which we cannot get up here. Our production cost[s] for the next
year are three quarters of a million dollars."

The official announcement added that the firm was completing the
feature *Face to Face* starring Marguerite Marsh, Coil Albertson, Joseph
Steward, Mrs. Edna Holman and others.

On February 3, 1920, the *Ithaca Journal* disclosed the true reason
why the Grossman firm had pulled out of Ithaca so hastily: "Grossman
Checks Refused By Banks" read a headline on page seven. "A number
of Ithaca employees of Grossman Pictures, Inc., felt that they had
been given a setback in their efforts to combat the high cost of living
when, yesterday, checks on a New York bank in payment of salaries
which had been tendered them by Harry Grossman, head of the
concern . . . were returned to them . . . with notification of insufficient
funds."

Some of the holders of the bad checks tried to phone Grossman,
one or two actually reaching the producer, who assured them he

expected to deposit sufficient funds in New York City that day to make the checks viable.

If the ex-employees of Grossman Pictures ever received the money which the firm owed them it does seem not to have been recorded anywhere. Whether Harry Grossman ever made good on those checks still is a mystery.

# William S. Hart

"He must eat tons of ham every day," a critic once said of the acting style of William S. Hart. Granted, there was a good deal of Victorianism about Hart's screen portrayals. Like his contemporary D.W. Griffith, he'd come to the motion picture industry after a not-too-lucrative career as a small-time stage actor, where acting styles were, if anything, bravura.

Hart carried over something of that dated acting style to his screen portrayals, as evidenced by any of the many two-reelers he made under the tutelage of Thomas H. Ince (with whom Hart had shared a room in New York City when both were struggling actors).

In spite of the two men's longtime friendship, Ince had to be talked into the idea of casting Hart in westerns, but when the Hart films began appearing in theaters, audiences couldn't seem to get enough of them.

As he developed a sizable audience for his pictures, Hart decided to set up his own studio, and to place his friend Ince on the board of directors, thus allowing Ince to continue sharing in the profits of Hart's fame.

Eventually he located a production facility for lease—the former Mabel Normand Studio in East Hollywood, at Fountain Avenue and Bates Street. An unattractive, factory-like place, it had been built by Mack Sennett for the lady he loved; however, Mabel made just one film there before she left Sennett's entourage for a contract with Sam Goldwyn.

Occupying a cramped, triangular property, Hart's new lot offered little "back lot" space on which outdoor sets might be built, a shortcoming which bothered Hart not at all, who was planning to shoot many portions of his forthcoming features "on location" for the added realism, charm, and authenticity which such backgrounds provided.

The stages at his new studio, he knew, would provide adequate space for shooting any indoor scenes he wished, while also providing space for workers to cut, edit, title, and otherwise prepare his

An Outlaw Believing In No Man, And A Woman Who Trusted Him Together Learn The Real Lesson of Renunciation!

1920

William S. Hart in "The TOLL GATE"

with ANNA Q. NILSSON · JOSEPH SINGLETON · JACK RICHARDSON

directed by Lambert Hillyer

*The Toll Gate* was one of many feature films turned out while Hart occupied his own studio.

productions. The new quarters offered space for offices, a screening room, and such other facilities as might prove necessary, all under the guidance of E.H. Allen, studio manager.

The beginning of 1918 saw the first of the Hart studio's productions entered for copyright. *Wolves of the Rail*, distributed through Adolph Zukor's Artcraft, was directed by Hart, as were several of the ensuing films from the Hart studio. Those eight pictures represented the entirety of the 1918 output—*Blue Blazes Rawden, The Tiger Man, Selfish Yates, Shark Monroe, Riddle Gawne, The Border Wireless*, and *Branding Broadway* being the remaining seven.

At the start of 1919, Hart contracted with 26-year-old Lambert Hillyer to assume duties as director with the Hart studio. Hillyer, who was to enjoy a long career as a motion picture director, faced a formidable task in undertaking work with Hart's studio, for much of the filming was to take place "on location," some of it at considerable distances from Los Angeles, and all to be accomplished within budgetary restrictions, of course!

In the hope of rekindling her love for him, Mack Sennett built this studio for Mabel Normand, who made one film there before leaving Sennett's employ for a contract with Goldwyn. William S. Hart thereby leased it. This photo was made in 1916.

The total costs of the Hart productions of this World War I era now seem ridiculously low (although not nearly so low as his 1915 2-reeler *The Disciple*, budgeted at a mere $8,000 including overhead!). Yet, they were in no way cheap, hastily made pictures. Hart was fond of authenticity and scenic allure in his pictures, and he seemed not to mind taking his production crews and casts to the Grand Canyon, to New York City, to Chicago, San Francisco, or elsewhere when the screenplays called for such locations.

Many who recall Hart's westerns seem to recall that his little paint horse "Fritz" appeared in most of them, but in truth, the actor did not utilize the animal consistently, at one point doing 15 consecutive films in which Hart rode other mounts.

*Breed of Men*, on which preparation and shooting actually began in late 1918, was ready for distribution by Adolph Zukor's Artcraft division in early 1919 and marked the first of Hart's productions to be directed by Lambert Hillyer, much of it filmed on location in Chicago, around the infamous stockyards which had been so thoroughly exposed in an Upton Sinclair novel, *The Jungle*, some years earlier.

*The Poppy Girl's Husband,* copyrighted only about two months after Hart's previous film, again took Hart, cast, and crew on extensive "location shooting," involving sequences shot in and around San Francisco and neighboring Oakland.

*The Money Corral, Square Deal Sanderson, Wagon Tracks, John Petticoats,* and *Sand* were the remainder of Hart's productions for 1919. During that year distribution of his films was transferred to the Paramount label, although his contract with Zukor remained under terms similar to those he'd been bound by under the Artcraft distribution setup. *John Petticoats* marked the last of Hart's productions to be labelled with a credit to Thomas H. Ince; in September 1919 Hart organized his exclusively owned firm, continuing operations at the Sennett/Normand studio, as before.

*The Toll Gate,* copyrighted 1920, was the first of the Hart productions made that year, a 12-month period which saw four pictures from Hart. *Cradle of Courage* and *The Testing Block* were both rather unimportant, though the final 1920 production, *O'Malley of the Mounted,* fashioned from an original story by Hart, was an outstanding one of Hart's entire filmography and a good enough story and script so that it was remade by Fox in 1936 with George O'Brien in the Hart role.

*The Toll Gate* was shot largely on location, the actor to remember such location work as long as he lived; he nearly lost his life while working on that film.

About 16 miles from Sonora, scenes were being shot in a swiftly flowing river which burrowed its way through a mountain, creating a tunnel about 100 yards in length. This watery tomb was being used in the picture to represent a "bandit's cave" into which hero and horse Fritz were to boldly plunge. Before the scene was shot, the depths of the stream were probed, one spot proving to be too deep for accurate sounding. Shooting began just seconds later with director Lambert Hillyer and other personnel standing by, helplessly watching in horror as Hart and his pony were driven by the current into the center of the unsounded area of the underground river! Hart and his horse came close to their deaths, the actor later declaring that the Almighty had intervened at that heartstopping moment, sparing horse and rider from their deaths.

Costly and troublesome location sequences weren't the only extra expenses which Hart saw fit to budget into many of his films. Even after he no longer had his own studio, Hart displayed an almost reckless abandon for rather expensive devices with which to add to the appeal of his pictures. For his picture *Singer Jim McKee,* for example, an elaborate "dummy horse" was used in one sequence. At the Lasky studio, a copy of the horse Fritz was constructed by a couple of the model and special effects men, the resulting bronco being, in Hart's words, "a horse that was as nearly like Fritz as it would be possible for anything to be," every joint on springs, the head swinging to and fro in a natural, lifelike manner.

The dummy horse was utilized in this manner: "I brought Fritz at a gallop and threw him," Hart later was to recall. "Then the dummy horse was fixed up with the same outfit we used on Fritz and held in upright position by piano wires so I could mount." When the camera again rolled, the piano wires were severed "and down we went," Hart plunging over a cliff.

If only that sort of imaginative approach had been applied by Hart to diversification of the production at his own studio, perhaps his name might have endured longer on motion picture screens, if not as a star, at least as a producer.

Perhaps if Hart had chosen to diversify the program of films he was making by 1921, he might have made his production unit a lastingly profitable one, but his notions of what his studio should produce did not, unfortunately, go beyond churning out William S. Hart pictures.

Thus, his studio plunged blindly ahead, supplying for Paramount release a quartet of now nearly forgotten features: *The Whistle, Travelin' On, White Oak* and *Three Word Brand.*

While the titles of these 1921 pictures seem trivial, one of them, *White Oak,* involved costly location shooting on the Sacramento River and, in the cases of the desert scenes, an area near Chatsworth, California.

*Three Word Brand* marked the last of the William S. Hart films to be made through his own studio. In the spring of 1921, trucks hauled away the final remnants of Hart's production unit, leaving the Mabel Normand Studio vacant once more.

Hart appeared in nine more films, all of them using the facilities of Famous Players–Lasky Studio, these including *Wild Bill Hickok* and *Singer Jim McKee.*

When his career closed, it was with the feature *Tumbleweeds* (1925), directed by King Baggott and distributed theatrically by United Artists.

The era of accuracy in western films by then was past. The cowboy of the silver screen by that time was of the flashy, tent-show variety, exemplified by Tom Mix, Ken Maynard, and Buck Jones.

William S. Hart's day was gone.

# The Haworth Studio

Though racial prejudice was rampant in the United States at the period around World War I (for example, publisher William Randolph Hearst was, at about that time, seeing to it that his chain of newspapers was freely larded with items screaming of the "Yellow Peril" which accused Orientals, particularly the Japanese, of plotting against America), a Japanese citizen became a sudden screen success here.

Born in Chiba, Japan, Sessue Hayakawa came to the United States in 1911, entering the University of Chicago and undertaking courses in political science. During a vacation to Los Angeles he organized a group of actors and presented *The Typhoon,* a play he'd written.

Thomas H. Ince, then a renowned Hollywood producer-director, saw the play and was so entranced by Hayakawa's acting and the play itself that he offered the youth a six-month, $500-a-week contract. During the six months, Ince transferred *The Typhoon* to the motion picture screen, where both actor and story were immediate successes.

His college studies put aside, Hayakawa stayed on in Hollywood, signing a Paramount contract which, from 1915 to 1918, brought him a salary which eventually reached $6,000 per week.

During the summer of 1918, Hayakawa organized a studio of his own which he christened Haworth Film Corporation. He established a studio at 4500 Sunset Boulevard, naming George W. Stout, former general manager of the Keystone Comedies lot, to manage it. Space at the Haworth lot was sufficiently large so that rental accounts could be accommodated; actor-producer Carter de Haven was one who occupied such facilities.

Starting production quickly after his firm was organized, the Oriental actor produced the feature *The Birthright,* following it soon after with *Shadows,* the latter distributed through Samuel Goldwyn.

In 1919 Haworth entered six more films for contract, among them *The Tong Man,* in which Hayakawa cast opposite himself actress Helen Jerome Eddy.

Each of the Sessue Hayakawa productions was budgeted at $350,000, of which amount Hayakawa himself received a $200,000 salary. Such largesse allowed Hayakawa a life of unimaginable luxury. He built a residence, "Greystone Castle," at the corner of Franklin and

These remarkable pictures show a set for a Sessue Hayakawa film, both as it appeared to persons on the set itself *(opposite, top)* and to the theatre audiences *(bottom).* Note how entire set is sunlighted, utilizing muslin, a tentlike structure that softens the light.

Argyle in Hollywood, a lavish dream palace where weekly luncheons for up to 500 guests were held. Banquets frequently accommodated as many as 900 people, who were entertained by three orchestras.

Hayakawa's gold-plated Pierce Arrow limousine was the talk of the film colony, even long after, in a moment of pique, Hayakawa gave away the car to the Long Island Fire Department after the actor learned that Roscoe "Fatty" Arbuckle had a copy of the automobile.

The busiest year for the Haworth studio was 1920 when nine pictures were turned out, quickly saturating theatres with so many Hayakawa dramas that the public gradually tired of them. Robertson-Cole distributed such 1920 Haworth productions as *The House of Intrigue, The Devil's Claim,* and *Moon Madness.*

By 1921, Hayakawa had shut down his studio, departing for England where he made a picture, returning to the United States at what was to prove an unhappy time for the world, a cataclysmic period which was triggered by the United States stock market collapse of 1929, that virtually wiped out his fortune.

After that occurred, Sessue Hayakawa, in considerably reduced financial circumstances, moved to France where fortunately for him he found considerable work as an actor.

He eventually returned to the United States where he made occasional film appearances, most notably as the cruel prison camp commandant in *Bridge on the River Kwai* (1957).


# The Thomas Ince Studio


Considerably less than 40 at the time of his death in 1924, Thomas Harper Ince had entered motion pictures before his thirtieth birthday. His initial film work was as an actor at New York's Imp Pictures, a small outfit owned by Carl Laemmle who later was to be an organizer of Universal.

When Mary Pickford and Owen Moore signed on with Imp, Ince directed *Their First Misunderstanding,* the initial picture Pickford and Moore made for that organization.

Ince proved himself a skilled organizer and an extremely competent director; these abilities were honed to exceeding keenness by Ince's background as a stage player born of a theatrical family.

While employed at Imp, the actor-turned-director called on Adam Kessel, a partner in the New York Motion Picture Company. That firm, Ince had learned, was seeking a director and was willing to pay top salary, providing the right person happened along. Ince borrowed a

The Ince studio's pictures were released for a time by Artcraft, a branch of Paramount. This 1920 feature was released when Charles Ray was yet at the peak of his popularity.

diamond ring of more than modest size, and flashed the opulent jewel at Kessel while he talked his way into the directorial position with a Kessel and Bauman production group. The group was supposed to set up in a ramshackle studio at Edendale, a suburb of Los Angeles, but soon moved out to Santa Yñez Canyon, a few miles from Santa Monica, California.

As his new "Inceville" encampment grew in size and importance, Ince added his stock company of players. William S. Hart, whom Ince had known when they were both smalltime stage actors, came to Inceville, straddled a horse and soon rode to top stardom in westerns. Sessue Hayakawa, Charles Ray and many others also achieved stardom at Ince's hands.

When Kessel and Bauman cast their lot with ill-fated Triangle Pictures, it quickly became clear to Ince that it would be well for him to set out on his own, where he could control the stakes of the game. Upon the collapse of Triangle, Ince selected property fronting on

Washington Boulevard in Culver City, California, not far from the studios of Triangle. The real estate which Ince chose, it is said, was given to him by the promoters of the new Culver City, although ultimately, Ince purchased additional adjacent acreage in order to enlarge his new studio.

Choosing a timeless and tasteful Southern Colonial design for the administration building of his new studio, Ince created a structure which strongly resembles George Washington's "Mt. Vernon" in Virginia. In the 1930s the facade of this building became the screen logo for Selznick International Pictures.

In keeping with the then-current practice of design for motion picture stages, those at the new Ince lot were of the "greenhouse" variety, enabling sunlight itself to be the major light source for even those pictures produced indoors.

Employing numerous directors to fashion films made from detailed, tightly controlled shooting scripts, Ince was able to pour forth from his studio productions which bore the unmistakable, craftsman-like touch of Ince himself.

Even after moving into the new studio in Culver City, Ince retained "Inceville" at Santa Yñez Canyon, where a great deal of the location shooting for his pictures was accomplished.

Following the establishment of the Ince production facility, William S. Hart, Charles Ray and other players went out on their own, although Ince's pictures continued to be top attractions at the box office, netting for Paramount, the distributor of the Ince films, immense profits.

There have been many film historians, professional and otherwise, who have claimed that Thomas Ince was as creative a filmmaker as D.W. Griffith. Such pictures as Ince's *Civilization* (1915) seem to lend considerable credence to those claims. Possibly if there had not been such widespread publicity of his assembly-line production of films, and of Ince's own propensity to claim credit for much that others created, he well might be ranked alongside Griffith.

In 1924, while on a weekend cruise aboard the yacht of William Randolph Hearst, Thomas Ince became very ill with a severe intestinal ailment, whereupon the Hearst party set Ince ashore below Los Angeles, where he stayed at a hotel until his personal physician could be summoned from Los Angeles.

*Opposite, top:* **The facade of the Thomas Ince Studio on Washington Boulevard, Culver City, California. The photo was made at the time when the lot was being used for production of Selznick's *Gone with the Wind*. At turns, this was the PDC studio, among others. *Bottom:* The Thomas Ince Studios at Culver City, California. Today, much enlarged, this lot still is in operation, although it is primarily used as a rental operation.**

Ince died soon after his return from the cruise, and his "mysterious" death produced ugly rumors and screaming headlines. Radio reports made the facts of the case sadly inadequate to quash the false rumors, some of which implied that publisher Hearst had somehow poisoned the studio magnate as a result of a love triangle. Even the physician's assertion that Ince had a long record of severe stomach ulcers (as a result of eating foods he shouldn't have, causing his death), failed to end the rumors.

Following Ince's death, the studio passed into the hands of William C. DeMille (Producers Distributing), then to Pathe (which firm merged with RKO to make the studio RKO-Pathe). In the 1930s the studio was known as Selznick International, which filmed there the immensely profitable film *Gone with the Wind,* as well as such features as *Since You Went Away* and *Duel in the Sun.*

As theatrical film production slowed in the era following World War II, what had once been the Thomas Ince Studio was sold to Desilu Productions (then jointly owned by Lucille Ball and her husband Desi Arnaz). Presently it operates as Laird International, a studio rental facility.

# Kalem

There were many American film studios prior to World War I which were both ambitious and profitable, but because of one reason or another ceased operation before the next decade; one was the New York firm of Kalem.

Kalem's history spanned little more than a dozen years, but during that brief time it established several studios more than halfway around the globe.

The firm had been established in 1907, its founders George Kleine (formerly of Kleine Optical Company), Samuel Long and Frank Marion (the latter two formerly with Biograph). The initials of the three, K, L, and M, formed the backbone of the synthetic name "Kalem."

Soon after its inception, the firm concentrated upon turning out cheaply made films of one or two reels, distributed to the seemingly countless "nickelodeon" movie houses (in New York City alone there were hundreds of such); Kalem's New York offices were in a loft building on 21st Street.

Kalem did not even trouble to copyright its productions, except for a multi-reel film titled *From the Manger to the Cross* (1913), part of which was photographed in Jacksonville, Florida, at a time when the firm was pioneering the making of motion pictures in that state, and when Sidney Olcott, a man who was to contribute much to film history, was director of the biblical epic. The filming started in Jacksonville, as has been noted, but completed a season or so afterward in the Holy Land.

Soon after the inception of Kalem, the company dispatched only a small group of players and personnel to Florida each winter, beginning in 1908. That was early enough in motion picture history to give the firm pioneer status with regard to the Sunshine State.

In 1908, Kalem had made a one-reeler near Jacksonville which it titled *A Florida Feud,* a successful film at the box offices of nickel theatres everywhere. It was not, however, a production calculated to win accolades with the citizenry of the budding city of Jacksonville, most of whom disliked the way the "poor whites" of their area were depicted in that film.

Local reaction to *A Florida Feud* may well have planted one of the seeds for eventual death of the film industry in and around Jacksonville. Yet, how could any permanent settler of that region be less than enthusiastic about a winter industry which brought such unforeseen funds as the $400 which *A Florida Feud* had cost to produce?

Not only did Kalem invest in its productions which were made in Florida, a partner in the firm bought or built a large house for himself along the St. Johns River in Jacksonville, while the company invested several thousand dollars in a studio along the waterfront, enriching a hotel owner and a boarding house operator as Kalem casts and crews wintered in that city.

The Jacksonville operation of Kalem, seasonal though it was, continued to exist for a number of winters, but was gradually phased out by the company as its several California locations proved again and again to provide more advantages.

Kalem's studio operation had started in Glendale, California, in 1909. A company of Kalem players and personnel came to that small town looking for an inexpensive site at which to make films. The Glendale "studio" at first was located at the northeast corner of Orange Street and Broadway (it amounted to a no more ambitious operation than a large open backyard for the crude, handpainted "drops" to be flown, with boardinghouse facilities close at hand for Kalem employees).

That setup proved only temporary; about a year later a Kalem director named Kerean Buel began moving the operation to what appeared would become a permanent lot, a spot in Syracuse Canyon two miles east from Verdugo and Chevy Chase. The lot became known locally as "the airdrome," for the manner in which scenery was simply hung on a group of poles, seemingly placed haphazardly about the field, so as to

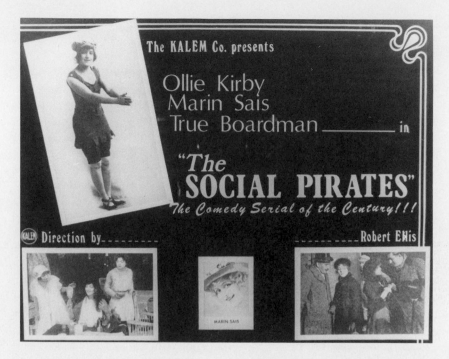

**The Kalem Company filmed this "comedy serial" at its studio at Glendale, California, one of several locations which the firm occupied during its brief history.**

expose the canvas "drops" to the sunlight while the cameras recorded the players as they moved about while miming rudimentary stories. Such a crude arrangement sufficed only for a short time, following which it was replaced, under guidance of Frank E. Montgomery, an early Kalem studio manager.

Sometime after 1918, James W. Horne was to pause, in his ascendency toward fame as an outstanding Hollywood director, to recall his early days of work at Kalem's Glendale lot, saying nostalgically, "I joined the company in August, 1912 . . . [when] we had offices in the building housing the First National Bank, and a studio out beyond Verdugo Park. Later that year we moved down Verdugo Road to George Woodbury's [ranch] . . . where we stayed until the firm dissolved. The first studio, however, was . . . in 1911 or 1912 . . . what was [behind] a drug store at Orange and Broadway."

Kalem employed a stock company of players at Glendale, including an ingenue named Esther Ralston, a youthful Carlyle Blackwell and a good many other luminaries of the films made prior to World War I. Newspaper writers, looking back upon the Kalem years later, were to stretch the list of players which, one time or another, appeared at the Kalem lot to include Wallace Reid, Eugene Pallette and Mabel Normand.

Kalem is responsible for one of the earliest—and most lengthy—serials ever made: *The Hazards of Helen* starring Helen Holmes and directed by J.P. MacGowan, which came to a 119-chapter picture! When MacGowan, in company with Miss Holmes, left Kalem abruptly, Helen Gibson, who looked so much like Miss Holmes that it is said even film fans couldn't tell the two apart, then appeared in the same role. *The Hazards of Helen* was filmed in part at the Glendale studios of Kalem, but chiefly at points along the route of the San Pedro, Los Angeles and Salt Lake Railroad.

During its years of growth, Kalem also started studio operations at East Hollywood and Santa Monica, but by 1916 these were phased out, and all California productions by the firm made thereafter at Glendale.

By 1915 a series of *Ham and Bud* short comedies were being filmed there, as was the serial *Social Pirates* (1916) which featured True Boardman and Marin Sais (and which was directed by James W. Horne). One particular chapter of that serial was considered by Kalem's publicity department to be newsworthy, for a then-unique type stage set which news releases described as a "floating stage." It was on rockers so that stage hands could rock the set and players before the camera, simulating a ship's cabin in a storm. (Such an effect can be more readily obtained by mounting the motion picture camera itself on a rocking platform.)

In 1913 Kalem announced that one of its directors, George Melford, was at work on a vast new three-reel "feature" (i.e., a film approximately 40–45 minutes in length) titled *The Invaders*. By early autumn of that year the picture had been shot, edited and released, with initial showings made at Clune's Broadway Theatre in Los Angeles. Enthusiastically described by one reviewer as "decidedly pretentious," the picture had been based upon a novel about cattle rustlers of the infamous "Hole in the Wall" area of Wyoming in about 1892. Carlyle Blackwell and Marin Sais were the featured players.

Just a couple months following release of *The Invaders*, director Melford was again at work, this time on an abbreviated feature about Africa's Boer War, in which Kalem claimed it was employing 300 in the cast. The claim was very likely true; the firm utilized all 250 of the members of the First Battalion, Seventh Infantry, Troop 3 of the Second Cavalry. The picture, which carried the pallid title *Ladysmith*, featured a relative newcomer to the screen, Larry Peyton.

In its anniversary issue of 1914, the famous newspaper *Christian Science Monitor* wrote enthusiastically about Kalem at Glendale: "The plant employs three companies of players, besides a band of Indians," and pointed out that "before Kalem had tried nearly every corner of the world," but found Glendale the "most desirable base of operations . . . from several points of view." The *Monitor* cited the desirable spots around Glendale for "location" scenes, including the nearby ocean, mountains, mission-style structures, the deserts, snow regions and so on.

When 1917 began, Kalem was a financially strong operation, surely able to fund feature film production, yet its owners made few such pictures.

At the time of the death of Samuel Long, president of Kalem, in 1915, partner Frank Marion declared, "long pictures . . . tie up a lot of money. . . . We will keep Kalem going [only] as long as short pictures last, and then we'll quit."

The Cliffside, New Jersey, studio of Kalem became nothing more than a rental operation long before Vitagraph, in 1919, purchased all the scenario properties of Kalem. In July of that year Creation Films, Inc., purchased the Cliffside studio and in November the Artco Company acquired the studio in its entirety.

In various trade journals of December 1921, it was announced that the Cliffside studio (of the former Kalem firm) had burned completely to the ground that month.


# Kinemacolor


Kinemacolor is not a widely known name nowadays, although it was the earliest of the "natural color" motion picture processes.

Unlike Technicolor, which operates no studio, the Kinemacolor firm once had a studio in Hollywood as well as in the Eastern United States.

Kinemacolor was a process developed in England by a former American, Charles Urban, working in collaboration first with a British photographer, and later with an English chemist, perfecting the color process just prior to the outbreak of World War I. (There had been handpainted color films as early as 1894 when the Thomas A. Edison company offered them.)

A two-color system, Kinemacolor could be shown only on motion picture machines which had been altered so as to operate at 32 frames per second, and which had a special set of shutter blades fitted with colored gelatins. The cameras with which Kinemacolor subjects were photographed had the same sort of colored "gels" on the shutters.

Renowned Hollywood cameraman Karl Brown once recounted

Even today this photo, made in connection with the Kinemacolor feature *The Klansman*, looks ominous. Due to legal difficulties involving the author of the novel (Thomas Dixon) from which this film was made, this version was never released.

how he'd first come to Hollywood as an employee of Kinemacolor, though he was a beginner at photography. Brown states that Kinemacolor, while a trifle overly bright on the screen, was quite satisfactory.

The first of the Kinemacolor subjects shown theatrically in the United States was filmed by British crews, using English-made Moy motion picture cameras modified for the process, covering the durbar in India held in commemoration of accession to the throne by England's George V. A good many in Britain felt it almost a patriotic duty to see the film of this event; the choice of the subject matter was therefore a wise one for Urban and his Warwick crew.

Encouraged by box-office returns from his film, the American-born Urban next took some examples of the new motion picture color process to exhibit in America, though when he returned to England, Urban felt sure he'd failed utterly: no backers had come forward to finance exploitation of Kinemacolor in the United States.

Urban learned soon after sailing from New York City that his color process had found a couple of enthusiasts in America. What's more, the pair followed quickly after Urban, and soon after reaching Great Britain, signed an agreement allowing the new Kinemacolor process to be exploited in the United States.

A short time later the American firm of Kinemacolor set up

**Charles Urban assigned the rights to his Kinemacolor film process to the American firm which utilized the Kinemacolor name and process, the first successful method for producing color motion pictures photographically.**

operations in New York (at Whitestone Landing, Long Island) and in Hollywood, acquiring a motion picture studio at 4500 Sunset Boulevard (previously occupied by Revier Labortories).

The office of the Hollywood operation was manned by a person named Wiener who is yet recalled with affection by former Kinemacolor employees for the fact that he had carefully paid them in full when Kinemacolor collapsed in 1913, even offering to pay their return transportation back East if they'd been recruited for its Hollywood contingent from that region.

In the years that Kinemacolor existed, the American firm turned out numerous films, mostly one-reel subjects wherein color was exploited chiefly for color's sake. A hospital fire, and a motion picture made from a Nathaniel Hawthorne tale in which a fat golden pumpkin turned into a man, were typical Kinemacolor subjects.

Technically the color process appeared to be a successful one; however, motion picture theatres of the time failed to respond in large numbers to Kinemacolor's lure, because, to utilize the film, theatres had to equip themselves with at least one special projection machine to handle the color film. Even in Los Angeles, there was only one theatre ever equipped to show Kinemacolor: California Theatre, Ninth and Main in downtown L.A. All across the nation theatre owners remained as disinterested as their counterparts in the City of Angels.

Despite its failure to achieve a wide market for its product, Kinemacolor promoters in the United States chose to gamble on production of a full-length feature film in the new color process, selecting for their initial production *The Clansman,* a popular novel written by a clergyman named Thomas Dixon.

For its picturization, Kinemacolor sent cameras and crew to Louisiana where services of a stock company of travelling actors had been secured.

Claims are that this version of *The Clansman* actually was completed. The finished production never was shown, some film historians maintaining that copyright disputes between Kinemacolor and the Reverend Dixon prevented the release of the film. So it remained for D.W. Griffith to resurrect the plot for *The Clansman,* which Griffith photographed in black and white film, later tinted. The picture, soon after its premiere in Los Angeles, was retitled *The Birth of a Nation.*

The American and British Kinemacolor firms expired peacefully, swiftly in 1913. Many of the former cameramen for the Hollywood operation chose not to leave the area, several of them going on to illustrious careers as famous directors of photography for other studios. That number included not only Karl Brown but Gerald MacKenzie, Alfred G. Gosden and Marcel Le Picard.

With Kinemacolor's death, its Hollywood studio was taken over and renamed the Fine Arts–Griffith lot. It was here, along with a back lot just across the street, that D.W. Griffith was to turn out his film *Intolerance.*

When Griffith and his associates moved on, the old studio became a rental lot for independent filmmakers who occupied the premises until 1943, when the place was purchased by Columbia Pictures for use as a branch studio. A disastrous fire razed the buildings in the early 1960s.

Subsequent to the fire, a wrecking crew tore down what remained of the place, destroying the last vestiges of what once had been Kinemacolor.

When the Jesse Lasky Feature Film Co. arrived in Hollywood they rented this barn, part of the Harry Revier "studios" which occupied an orange grove on Sunset Boulevard, 1913.

# The Jesse Lasky Company

Harry Revier chose not to buy the property; he leased the land from a farmer named Jacob Stern, who was owner of several large tracts in the area. Revier selected an open area within Stern's well-established citrus grove along Vine Street, between Sunset and Selma. There Revier authorized construction of a 40' x 60' outdoor stage, six dressing rooms, and a modest film processing laboratory. The unimpressive layout looked even shabbier because Revier rented the carriage house on the premises to serve as his offices.

Cecil B. DeMille, Samuel Goldfish and Jesse Lasky came to this ramshackle "studio" in 1913 and, finding Revier to be between productions at the moment, rented the place while they filmed on the open, outdoor platform "interior" scenes for their first motion picture, *The Squaw Man.*

*The Squaw Man* was already a successful Broadway play, so it is not surprising that the film, too, was a financial bonanza — so successful that the Jesse Lasky Company was able to purchase all the north half of the block occupied by Revier and, subsequently, that entire block, paying Stern more than $100,000, a price which included an additional block immediately to the east.

**At Selma and Vine streets, Los Angeles, this was the Harry Revier lot as it appeared in 1916 when it was in the possession of the Jesse L. Lasky Co.**

While DeMille was later to claim he had directed the initial film version of *The Squaw Man,* in truth the director was Oscar Apfel. Apfel, having an inordinate fear of snakes, protected his legs by means of heavy leather puttees, a practice DeMille adopted before directing his first picture, *The Rose of the Rancho* (1914).

By the time the Lasky Company got around to buying what had been the Revier studio, Harry Revier moved elsewhere in Hollywood, continuing work as a film director and later was owner of a large film laboratory.

As for Jacob Stern, he profited so from his dealings in Hollywood real estate that prior to the onset of the Great Depression in the 1930s, he built the new Plaza Hotel which he leased out, moving on to new enterprises.

The Jesse L. Lasky Feature Play Company by that time had merged with Adolph Zukor's famous firm, only to be absorbed into Paramount. Paramount, in turn, eventually acquired the property which had originally been the Revier operation.

During those years all Hollywood had undergone change. The citrus groves had disappeared and so had the pepper trees which once lined the streets of that community. In a decade and a half, Hollywood had metamorphosed from an agricultural center into a place where thoroughfares abounded with 1920s automobiles and trucks.

The film industry, less than 30 years old, had transformed Los

Angeles into a city where ecstatic real estate salesmen were able to sell postage stamp–size residential lots for as much as $500 apiece.

Only about a year after Cecil B. DeMille's arrival there, the showman had been followed by his brother William C., author of such stage successes as *The Woman* and *The Warrens of Virginia*. William DeMille rapidly carved out a Hollywood career for himself, working as a director, producer or sometimes both, his films released through Metro, Pathe, and Paramount.

Both DeMilles became associated with a firm known as Producers Distributing; however, the brothers rather quickly parted company, Cecil turning to making in 1931 a talking-picture version of *The Squaw Man* with a cast including Warren Baxter, Lupe Velez, and Roland Young. It was, after all, a chance for DeMille to rightfully claim directorial honors for such a film. Distributed by MGM, the later version of the picture drew audiences not largely cognizant of the fact that a silent version of that film ever existed.

After all, 17 years had passed; 6,200 days of motion picture history had intervened. Something of a legend by then, C.B. DeMille had publicized himself well, making some extremely profitable pictures as he did so.


# *Lubin*


When Siegmund Lubin died he was a wealthy and respected resident of Philadelphia. Just one part of his empire, a chain of motion picture theatres, had been bought by the Stanley Corporation and already was proving the nucleus of Stanley Mastbaum's profitable conglomerate. Yet the Lubin theatres had been only a small part of the Siegmund Lubin money machine.

We first glimpse Lubin in the mid–1890s, when he was but one of the hordes of immigrants in the Land of Opportunity. The newly arrived emigrant of Germany frequently trudged the streets of New Orleans, vending cheap eyeglasses, novelties and patient, pleasant sales talk.

Somewhere along his route through Louisiana Lubin encountered a genuine motion picture magnate, one William T. Rock who, with two partners, had founded a new motion picture "studio" atop New York's Morse office building. The three called their firm "Vitagraph," a name and a growing reputation which utterly fascinated Lubin. What "Pop" Rock had done, Lubin reasoned, he could duplicate, perhaps even more profitably, since Lubin proposed to be the sole owner of his empire.

Just how successful Siegmund Lubin was in aping the success of

Siegmund Lubin, the Philadelphia filmmaker, optical shop owner, and founder of the chain of Lubin theatres (the latter enterprise later absorbed by the giant Stanley Corporation).

"Pop" Rock is evidenced by the fact that Lubin supposedly grossed about half a million dollars each of the 20 years that he was active in the motion picture business.

His entry into motion pictures started in 1896 with an optical and film business in Philadelphia, where he gradually had equipped a small plant with equipment largely designed by film pioneer C. Francis Jenkins. By 1897 he already was turning out short motion picture films and beginning to show himself as an imaginative promoter, such as when the Corbett-Fitzsimmons prize fight of 1897 occurred. That was when the wily Lubin filmed a duplicate of that ring event, using a couple of freight handlers from the Pennsylvania terminal as "ringers" for Corbett and Fitzsimmons. It was simple enough to recreate the battle, practically blow by blow: a "prompter" stood just out of camera range, reading a newspaper's detailed account of the fight as Lubin's actors went through the identical fisticuffs for the Lubin camera.

Lubin had hardly gotten his film activities profitably working when on January 10, 1898, lawyers of Thomas A. Edison sought to enjoin Lubin from making his film productions with equipment made by Jenkins, and Edison laid claim to ownership of Jenkins' designs.

Faced with an expensive and probably nasty court battle with Edison, Lubin hastily withdrew from production of films and from the United States. His stay in his native Germany was but a brief one, however. After all, there was too much money to be made off "nickelodeon movies."

A new and enlarged flow of Lubin motion pictures soon began to emerge, the first made at a crude "rooftop studio" where sunlight was the medium of photographic illumination and where the crude "sets" were placed so as to take advantage of the light, though often catching disturbing gusts of wind which caused the sets (which often were rented or borrowed from local vaudeville houses) to weave back and forth disturbingly. "Props" were scanty on Lubin's "sets" of this time.

Almost from the beginning of his career as a motion picture producer, Lubin was somewhat of a rascal in his practices. Strong rumors soon swept the infant film industry to the effect that "Pop" Lubin was not above pirating illegal copies of films made by others, and of lifting the stories for Lubin productions from competitors' productions whenever those ideas had proved profitable.

When Edwin S. Porter turned out the extremely profitable one-reeler *The Great Train Robbery* (1904), it was only a short time afterward that Lubin countered with his very similar tale, *The Bold Bank Robbery*.

The famous *Passion Play* which originated in the German village of Oberammergau was translated into a motion picture, which was filmed on a rooftop in New York City during what has been called the third year of motion picture history, 1896.

Released in January 1898, this film spurred the opportunistic Lubin to rush into production an exceedingly crudely made version of *The Passion Play*, Lubin filming his version of the film on a rough wooden stage in a back yard in Philadelphia. Players and personnel were nonentities, all lacking utterly in any seriousness of purpose or reverence toward their subject. During production, the player who portrayed Judas Iscariot went off on a drunk, while other players proved nearly as profligate. In spite of such problems and those of cheap sets which parted occasionally in the wind and thus revealed very Philadelphia-type houses behind the sets, Lubin's *Passion Play* was completed and when released was financially successful.

As Lubin's picture productions increased in number, the witty, smiling entrepreneur expanded his activities connected with film. He began selling stamped-metal fronts for movie theatres, and a line of cheap, cardboard ones for use by travelling showmen who wanted to "put up a bold, colorful front" for their temporary shows.

Lubin headquarters at 23 South Eighth Street, Philadelphia, poured forth large numbers of 35mm theatre projection equipment, too. As he equipped countless showmen with projectors, theatre facades, films and the like, Lubin was planning and constructing elaborate theatres of his own including "movie palaces" in such cities as Philadelphia, Richmond, Cincinnati, Norfolk, Baltimore and others, each one with a balcony for bargain-seeking five-cent patrons. And though many of his critics predicted his financial finish when he dared to lease one theatre at a whopping $50,000 annually, Lubin not only went on rolling up profits but continued enlarging his business activities.

Dealing in high finance, Lubin seemed also to recognize that the basis of any fortune frequently was that of dealing successfully with a lot of very small accounts. In one of Lubin's many advertisements, he offered complete motion picture exhibition outfits at $99, the offer including a projector, a group of Lubin's "Cineophone" pictures, an amplified model of the Victor floor-type phonograph and a handful of exclusive "Cineophone" records so that showmen wouldn't have to run their movies in deadly silence.

During the process of building his motion picture empire, Lubin (whose first name often was shown as "Sigmund") acquired a number of United States patents. Most were not inventions which were products of Lubin's brain, but rather were those by other men who'd simply assigned their patent claims to Lubin to do with as he saw fit. Probably he paid little for the devices, since he, as assignee, paid most, if not all, costs of patenting the devices.

Lubin's patents amounted to but a handful, perhaps earliest of which was an optical prism-plate on which the patent was granted April 4, 1899. An inventor named John J. Frawley next came along, assigning to Lubin a very crude drawing and rough description of a motion picture projection machine on which patent was granted March 27, 1900. On September 11 of that year, Lubin claimed patent no. 657,555 on an improved 35 mm "Kinetographic film" which he claimed to have dreamed up by himself, though it appears that inventor John J. Frawley actually had conceived the new film format, and assigned the concept to Lubin. At any rate it was an invention, or more properly an "innovation" of rather questionable value, since it was based upon manufacture of commercial quantities of 35mm film stock which were so shaped as to be thicker along the sprockethole areas of the film than it was in the picture portions of the strip. Such a filmstock, of course, would be expensive and troublesome to manufacture.

On March 27, 1900, Lubin also was assigned patent no. 645,949 for a "projection apparatus" designed by John J. Frawley. It was so poorly described and pictured in the patent papers that the crude machine seems almost childish in concept. Certainly it was not sufficiently worked out to yield a device of useful and usable capacity.

Lubin and an inventor named Frederick Darcy patented on December 17, 1907, a rather complex "illusion apparatus for amusement," which was designed so as to provide an audience with the illusion of being in a free balloon as it drifted dreamily above the earth — the illusion being created partly by means of the projection of aerial views of earth. It probably was never built and tried.

On June 25, 1907, Lubin was assignee of patent no. 857,697 for a "life motion picture projecting machine" conceived by Orville T. Weiser. While crude and simplistic in concept, the machine seems now to have roughly set forth the general layout of the Lubin projectors which followed into production.

The 1912 patents for motion picture machines to which Lubin was assignee seem unnecessarily complex in design, but proved so eminently workable and enviably sturdy that production models eventually made the name Lubin rather a formidable one in projector manufacture.

On December 18, 1908, Edison was instrumental in calling together most of the important filmmakers of the period in order to pool their expertise, power and patents in what was intended to be an all-powerful syndicate. Edison's lawyers and cohorts saw fit to invite Siegmund Lubin to join them, along with Biograph, Kleine, Vitagraph, Selig, Essanay, Pathe, Kalem and Melies. The Motion Picture Patents Company resulted from that holiday-period meeting.

For more than a half-dozen years, the Patents Company was to prove "an octopus, holding the rest of the motion picture industry in its slimy tentacles" as one observer was to term it. Even when its power had been broken by United States government intervention, the Patents group continued to function in reduced power and with a low profile, its film distribution arm, General Film, a failure to the extent that a group of Patents Company members formed their own distribution network, V.L.S.E. The initials stand for Vitagraph, Lubin, Selig and Essanay.

During this period, Lubin had been at work expanding his activities in the motion picture industry. In 1912, he established a small studio in Jacksonville, Florida, at a time when that city was burgeoning into a film production center.

Rooftop studios were being phased out when Lubin joined the trend toward creation of permanent greenhouse-type studios. While he commanded as many as 20 locations for his production empire, Lubin remained faithful to his Philadelphia headquarters, directing construction at his base of operations of a vast glassed-in studio of such size that it could accommodate several good-sized sets simultaneously, and enough electrical lighting devices to supply "full light" on the scenes whenever the Philadelphia sunlight happened to prove uncooperative.

As his film studio facilities were enlarged and refined, Lubin proceeded to build a stock company of actors and production personnel, among whom was Fred J. Balshofer, a cameraman who learned his craft at Lubin studios so well that when Kessel and Bauman organized their New York Motion Picture Company, they had the good sense to hire him as their director of photography.

Most of the names of Lubin players are forgotten today, although many of them were stage and motion picture favorites of the pre–World War I era, who had started with the Lubin firm in the days when all productions had been nothing more than one-reelers (running time each about 15 minutes), but who had remained through the transitional period in American film production when serials were in vogue, and when the making of full-length feature films became standard.

Lubin failed to make the transition not because he failed to read the handwriting on the wall of cinema history; he simply was unable to successfully bridge the gap between short nickelodeon-type films of the 1895 to 1912 period and the longer, more expensive productions which had come to dominate film output by the time of World War I.

Lubin closed his production of motion pictures by turning out such full-length feature pictures as *Dollars and the Woman, Souls in Bondage, Those Who Toil, The Evangelist, Flames of Johannis, Light at Dusk* and *Love's Toll.*

During his time, Lubin also managed a couple serials and series — offerings such as the Patsy Bolivar series and a 14-chapter serial titled

*Road o' Strife,* the latter a picture so bad that even some of its production personnel referred to it as "Load o' Tripe"!

"Pop" Lubin then gathered the small fortune he'd accumulated from the motion pictures and, giving his onyx-headed walking stick a devil-may-care rap on the floor of his office, retired comfortably to count his money and review his experiences, the latter of which had assured him a part in American film history.

# Majestic-Reliance

Harry Aitken, a former film exchange operator, became a film production official back in the days when really "big money" for some stars needed be no greater than $275 weekly. At least, that's the figure at which Aitken landed the services of Mary Pickford and her then-husband Owen Moore—a total of $550 weekly for both players.

With Pickford's and Moore's names scarcely dry on their contracts, Aitken hastily set about buying a group of film rental exchanges from Kessel and Bauman, and soon after that, the acquisition of the old Reliance Studios, 515 E. 21st Street, New York City.

The latter purchase gave Aitken the use of the Reliance name, which he hyphenated with that of Majestic and brazenly set out to do financial battle with the rest of the U.S. film production powers.

Those intents and purposes aroused the ire of many, principally that of Carl Laemmle, who had once employed Miss Pickford and Mr. Moore and was considerably less than happy they had left him.

Reliance had been in existence at the time Aitken entered the production end of the film industry, but its studios had been inactive. J.V. Ritchey, in fact, had taken over that studio, pressing it into service as a lithograph plant, which obliged Aitken to rent a loft building on 18th Street, New York City, whenever he needed studios in which to film interior scenes for his pictures.

Somewhere about this point, Aitken became acquainted with Biograph director David W. Griffith. Aitken reasoned quickly that Griffith was Biograph's one real asset. Signing Griffith to a Reliance-Majestic contract, therefore, would be all that Aitken needed to turn his enterprise into a surefire winner.

Events were shaping up quickly for Aitken: He was readily able to contract with Griffith, but was threatened with having no "raw stock" (camera film) for Griffith's cameras! Carl Laemmle threatened to cut off Aitken's supply of film from Jules Brulator, distributor for Eastman Kodak.

The junction of Hollywood and Sunset boulevards has been the site of countless historic studios. Here it is shown as it was when the Fine Arts operation occupied it. Before that, Majestic-Reliance, and earlier, Kinemacolor, were there. Later Tiffany studios occupied the property.

In an effort to protect his firm from such a problem, Aitken countered by totally reorganizing his firm, making Majestic-Reliance into a sales organization which came to include American "Flying A," Gaumont, Great Northern, Solax and other firms. Aitken named the resulting conglomerate "Film Supply Company of America, Inc."

While all these changes were taking place, the Los Angeles studio of Kinemacolor fell dark, the pioneer color film organization a victim of exhibitor apathy toward buying the expensive equipment needed for exhibition of such film. The Kinemacolor lot became Aitken's.

Griffith was permitted to make two independent pictures per year under the terms of his contract with Majestic-Reliance, his Aitken product to be released through Mutual. These terms agreed upon, Griffith left Biograph in the fall of 1913 to join Aitken.

Aitken had gone ahead and bought the Clara Morris estate on Long Island as a studio and also rented the loft studios in New York City, both otensibly for the use of Griffith. When his new director-genius declined to accept facilities in the East, Aitken shrugged, permitting Griffith to bring his entourage to Los Angeles.

There, the Reliance-Majestic lot, like most film studios, was not at all an attractive place, existing as it did when many were yet calling such operations "film factories." Beginning in 1916 however, a once vacant field directly across from Reliance commanded much attention: D.W. Griffith there erected the sprawling "Babylon" set for his expensive fiasco *Intolerance*, the set looming over the tawdry California bungalows in the neighborhood for literally years after the picture was completed.

As for the Reliance-Majestic studio itself, the lot consisted of a complexity of frame structures at the corner of Hollywood and Sunset—low-roofed, painted drably, its one- and two-story structures trimmed around windows and eaves with unimaginative white, its various offices, laboratories, editing rooms, projection rooms and storage vaults crowded together along the front, its stages at the rear of the complex.

By early December, 1913, Aitken leased the Kinemacolor lot at 4500 Sunset Boulevard, Hollywood. All these rental contracts and purchase agreements cost Aitken a great deal, probably a fact which prompted him to promote his own Reliance-Majestic at a level which others concerned with the Mutual firm came to regard as unfair to them.

When D.W. Griffith announced that he was about to make a film version of the Reverend Thomas Dixon's novel *The Clansman* (later to be retitled *Birth of a Nation*), it was to be made as a Reliance-Majestic picture, budgeted at around $40,000 and utilizing both the studios which Aitken had rented and the "ranch" which later became Universal City.

Mutual's officials other than Aitken refused to back the project, leaving it strictly to Aitken and his director, so Aitken paid off the investment by Majestic-Reliance in that feature film and formed Epoch Films with D.W. Griffith.

These moves placed Griffith's monumental Civil War drama outside our continuing story of both Mutual and of Reliance-Majestic.

The internal explosion which destroyed Mutual, though not immediately apparent to those outside the organization, occurred when Aitken was ousted from the presidency of the firm. His departure caused him to discontinue the names Majestic and Reliance (though both names were used by later Hollywood production setups which had no connection with Aitken).

In casting about for a new name for his production unit and the studio it was to occupy, Aitken chose "Fine Arts," his personal operation, the output of which was fed to Triangle for distribution under the latter firm's logo.

Like Mutual, Triangle was a short-lived firm, its name and its memories nearly completely erased by the time the First World War ended.

# MGM

For some curious reason, MGM still is considered by many to have been the greatest film studio ever spawned. Recitations of the

*Top:* 1325 Eleanor, Hollywood, was the address of Metro studios, a place also occupied by Buster Keaton. *Bottom:* MGM's main entrance, 1937.

roster of film stars and many of their most memorable films at Metro come readily to the minds and lips of just about all film historians and hobbyists.

   Yet, Metro's lot was no more well designed, its sound stages no better, its recording and photography departments no more complete than its competitors'. And, certainly, the beginnings of the company were as

Multi-tiered "wedding cake" sets such as this one in the 1936 MGM production *The Great Ziegfeld* have long been favorites with filmgoers; so too have been multiple keyboards and pianists.

humble as those of even the Poverty Row studios—Monogram and the rest.

The history of MGM traces back to a man named Al Lichtman and a day in 1914, when, cast off from his job as the sales manager for Famous Players–Lasky, he came up with his own sales organization, named for syllables obtained from his first and last name: Alco Pictures

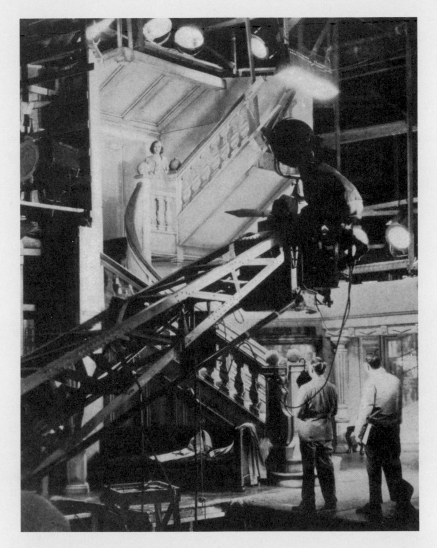

At MGM, director Richard Boleslavski directs a scene for the 1934 Greta Garbo film *The Painted Veil.*

Corporation. Lichtman's avowed purpose was to have his firm tie up with leading theatres in key cities, especially in the eastern and middlewestern United States, backed by powerful men in the field of motion picture exhibition and distribution: William Sievers of St. Louis, Richard Rowland of Pittsburgh, and James B. Clark of Philadelphia. A little man named Louis B. Mayer, who was an exhibitor in and around Boston, decided to become part of the firm as well. Alco was to have a franchise for all Paramount distribution in the Boston area.

Unfortunately, Alco developed a fatal case of internal dissension soon after its organization and slid into the hands of receivers; even that startling and disappointing affair failed to dissuade Lichtman from his designs on the world of celluloid. Together with certain other stockholders from Alco, he reorganized as "Metro," a name conveniently lifted from that of an Eastern lithographing firm.

Unlike Paramount, which had put Lichtman out of his job at Famous Players, Metro was not organized simply as a film distribution outfit. With Max Karger in charge of production, Richard Rowland as president, Joseph Engel as treasurer, and Louis B. Mayer as secretary, Metro Pictures Corporation was soon grinding out two dozen films a year, distributing features made by outside producers including Tiffany, Buster Keaton, and a production unit headed by Louis B. Mayer.

Metro began making a strong showing; its first "star," the fabled Petrova, signed her Metro deal just prior to the company's acquisition of a young movie actress who had first called herself Juliet Shelby, but who changed her name to Mary Miles Minter. The repetition of the letter "m" echoed the same letter in "Metro."

A number of factors began working against the Metro firm, only about three years in existence at the time that the United States found itself catapulted into World War I. While our nation's participation in the conflict brought the movie audiences of America healthy pay envelopes out of which to indulge themselves in the movies, it sharply changed the tastes of the audiences. Suddenly, pacifist-oriented pictures such as producer Thomas Ince's *Civilization* were no longer shown in theatres, demand during the final years of the war being upon films promoting patriotism; every studio, every production unit pumped out war pictures.

Alas, for Hollywood, the war came to a sudden end before all these war films were distributed. The end of the hostilities in Europe meant that no one would spend a nickel to see a war picture.

Even before Hollywood studios could realign their production output to fit such changing audience whims, a terrible influenza plague struck the nation. Theatres in many cities were closed by order of public health authorities, though even where the law didn't close movie houses, common sense kept audiences from assembling at places where they might contract the flu.

Metro appeared to be preparing for its final moments prior to bankruptcy, when the ultimate decision was made to produce the feature film from the Ibanez novel *The Four Horsemen of the Apocalypse*, the screen rights for which Metro president Richard Rowland recklessly bid $190,000. "Just another war story," many asserted gloomily.

Under the guidance of Rowland, Metro placed the feature *The Four Horsemen of the Apocalypse* into the hands of June Mathis for production. It was Miss Mathis' casting of a bit player named Rudolph Valentino in an important role in the picture which undoubtedly made the film the immense moneymaker it proved to be. The release of that picture occurred long after Metro's financial coffers were drained and the company taken over by Eastern theatre magnate Marcus Loew. Loew bought into the Metro firm at exactly the right time: the company's investment in the war picture returned such profits that Loew quickly recouped all his investment in the firm. By that time Metro was featuring such players as Mae Murray, John Gilbert and Lon Chaney, the star roster being enlarged when, in 1924, Metro and the Goldwyn studios merged, followed soon after by the addition of the Louis M. Mayer production facility, and resulting in the tripartite name Metro-Goldwyn-Mayer.

Then it was that a youth named Irving Thalberg, who had been with the Louis B. Mayer outfit (after serving at Universal for a time), climbed aboard the MGM bandwagon garnering the title of supervisor of production for that organization.

By late 1924, MGM was organized into what basically would be the studio as it was to exist into its sunset years, Louis B. Mayer as head of studio operations, Loew's, Incorporated, the controlling head of the overall operation.

Production facilities were concentrated by 1925 at the former Goldwyn lot in Culver City, California, earlier the old Triangle studio.

As MGM continued its almost lightning-like rise to permanence in Hollywood history, its contract players came to embrace Joan Crawford, Norma Shearer, Ramon Novarro, Lillian Gish, Lewis Stone, Lionel Barrymore, Wallace Beery, Marie Dressler, Antonio Moreno, and—at a somewhat later date—Mickey Rooney, Judy Garland, Greta Garbo, Robert Taylor, Robert Young, and others.

Before that roster had fully materialized, the day of the silent picture had slipped soundlessly into history, although Metro for a time seemed unwilling to accept that fact. When MGM entered into production of talking pictures, it was with a "B" budget offering, *Alias Jimmy Valentine*, starring William Haines. (His career for all purposes came to an end when he admitted he was a homosexual.)

It wasn't until 1929 that Metro's second talkie, *Broadway Melody* starring Charles King, Bessie Love, and Anita Page, was released, an "A" budget picture and ultimately an Academy Award winner.

The MGM facilities on the West Coast were controlled by a firm which came to be headed by Nicholas Schenck, a Russian-born Jewish immigrant who had made his way into film production by way of amusement parks and early movie theatres which he and his brother Joseph had operated in the East.

In the spring of 1949, MGM celebrated its Silver Anniversary, an event looking back triumphantly upon such releases as *The Big House, The Big Parade, Trader Horn, Grand Hotel, David Copperfield, Madame Curie, Wizard of Oz, Camille, The Champ, Ben Hur, The Good Earth,* and many other great box-office champions.

After World War II, attendance at movie houses quickly plummeted, hurried by the emergence of television receivers. By 1973, MGM ceased distributing pictures, instead licensing distribution of its very limited production output through United Artists where domestic releases were concerned and through C.I.C. for all foreign rentals. By 1980, MGM released only half a dozen or so features per year, some of which were made at the Culver City lot, others made elsewhere though financed by Metro, the golden era of Hollywood by then lying behind.

# Monogram

Hollywood Boulevard and Hoover Street is the site of what, less than 40 years ago, was Monogram Pictures Studio, although today it is occupied by a PBS television outlet, KCET. Many early film studios occupied that corner, including Kalem, Essanay, the Charles Ray Studio, Willis and Inglis Studios, and Ralph Like's International Sound Recording.

By the time W. Ray Johnston and his associates took over the property in the late 1930s, the place had been enclosed behind a forbidding-looking brick wall which caused the establishment to look as if it might be a National Guard Armory.

In 1930, nearly ten years before Monogram established itself on Hoover Street (earlier called Fleming), Johnston had founded the firm, although for years it had no studio of its own. (Neither had Johnston's earlier production/distribution firm, Rayart Pictures, organized in 1924.)

Like many other firms' names, the name Monogram had seen service before; as early as 1924 there was another Monogram Pictures, releasing a brief flurry of feature films through F.B.O.

Johnston's firm, for more than the first four years of existence, utilized as a trademark a drawing of a city of the future, its skyline crisscrossed by a pair of elevated tracks on which two trains appeared, towing the words which together spelled out, "Monogram Pictures Corporation."

Late in 1934 the Monogram firm merged with Mascot, Liberty, and

**We practically owned Monogram, said Huntz Hall (second from left) in recounting just how important the "East Side Kids" (later known as the "Bowery Boys") were to the fortunes of Monogram. Needless to say actor Leo Gorcey (third from right), Sam Katzman and Jan Grippo, alternate producers, profited as well.**

Supreme to form a new firm, Republic Pictures, but Johnston and his associates remained with the new firm only a short time. By 1936 Monogram was reorganized, its output of features and westerns quickly reaching 50 pictures per year; the firm, however, was never to rise above the production of "B" films. Indeed, it could not readily have marketed products budgeted higher, for the type of theatres playing Monogram films chose also to book major pictures with more famous players than Johnston could afford. Monogram pictures were made specifically for a market which could obtain all the "A" pictures it wished through major studios.

Profits from each Monogram picture were relatively modest for the corporation, in some cases amounting to only a few thousand dollars. Although the overall market for its pictures was small, and this factor seemed to be exceedingly limiting, it must be remembered that it was invariably a dependable one. Small, steady profits garnered through a worldwide network of film exchanges were the rule.

By the late 1930s Monogram had 30 film exchanges handling its product in the United States, a half dozen more in Canada, with British distribution handled by Pathe Pictures, Ltd., of London.

The studio itself had established executive and production areas which included Norton V. Ritchey, foreign sales department, and George W. Weeks in domestic sales. Leon Fromkess (a few years later, he was to be in charge of production at the studios of PRC) was the firm's treasurer.

For the 1938–39 season, Monogram announced a production schedule of 26 features and 16 westerns, that number being the same as the previous year. Not all of these were produced by the firm; many were the work of such independent production units as headed by Sam Katzman, Paul Malvern, and others.

In the two decades following the revival of the Monogram label, the studio continued to release around 50 features and westerns annually, and with such "B" picture casts as Jack Randall, ice skater "Belita," Peter Cookson, Warren Hull, Jean Parker, Boris Karloff, Johnny Sheffield, the Bowery Boys (earlier known as the East Side Kids), Bela Lugosi, Anne Nagel, Tom Keene and Frankie Darro.

While the screenplays for Monogram pictures were uniformly wretched, the studio productions and those of its independent producers usually called upon experienced directors such as Spencer Gordon Bennet, Howard Bretherton, William Beaudine, and Jean Yarbrough, who often managed to get quite creditable films out of shabby material.

In November 1945, Steve Broidy, who had formerly been Monogram sales manager, was elected president of the firm, while former president W. Ray Johnston moved into the position of chairman of the board. In November 1946, Allied Artists Productions, Inc., was formed as a wholly owned subsidiary of Monogram, but on November 12, 1953, replaced the earlier name entirely. At that juncture, Stratford Pictures Corporation, organized four years earlier, was Allied Artists' distribution channel within the United States for various foreign-made "prestige" films.

In 1953 the corporation began production of films for television, in so doing organizing Interstate Television Corporation, which in 1970 was changed to the name Allied Artists Television Corporation.

Some of the Allied Artists releases are memorable: *Friendly Persuasion* (1956) with Gary Cooper and Dorothy McGuire is a beautiful and unpretentious color feature; *A Man and a Woman* (1956), *The Man Outside* (1969), *Gold* (1974) with Roger Moore and Susannah York, *Al Capone* (1959) with Rod Steiger, and *Billy Budd* (1962) with Peter Ustinov and Robert Ryan; all were well reviewed.

In 1968 the firm resumed production of pictures, following a four-year hiatus, co-producing *Cabaret* (1972) and *Papillon*, though these were to prove its swan song.

# Nestor: The First Studio in Hollywood

The powerful steam locomotive, pulling its lengthy passenger train through miles of deep ravines and across vast plains, clawed its way toward California.

"Mr. David Horsley?"

The young Englishman nodded wearily.

"My name is Murray Steele," the stranger explained. "I'm a businessman from Los Angeles, and I've been given to understand that you and your brother are going to transfer your moving picture company from Bayonne, New Jersey, to our California region."

Horsley again nodded.

"Have you chosen the place where you're going to set up your operation?"

That was probably about how the conversation went that day. As recorded, Steele proved eager to advise Horsley, who was enroute to Los Angeles with about 40 of his personnel from the New Jersey operation. Horsley had first operated a studio he called Centaur, at 900 Broadway, Bayonne, New Jersey, where the operation primarily turned out westerns and rural-type melodramas. As early as 1907 Centaur, occupying a 22' x 52' storefront building, was an independent filmmaker.

Now, with the train rumbling toward the sunset, Steele mentioned a Los Angeles photographer, Frank Hoover, who Steele declared was a good man for Horsley to look up when he reached L.A., because Hoover was a person familiar with photographic conditions throughout California. Only hours after reaching the City of Angels, he looked up Hoover, who urged the newcomer to set up shop in a suburb of Los Angeles known as Hollywood. The date: October 27, 1911.

Other motion picture companies, spearheaded by a bogus colonel named William Selig, had already filmed one- and two-reel pictures in and about L.A., but none had given a thought to Hollywood, a suburb which was still outgrowing its previous predilections for ranching and citrus growing.

At the northwest corner of what soon would become Sunset Boulevard and Gower Street, Horsley succeeded in leasing a small cluster of structures which not long before had been known as Blondeau's Tavern, and also as Cahuenga House. The lease called for a monthly rental of $30, which included use of the entire quadrangle

**Nestor used this to advertise its early stock company. Dorothy Davenport (whose first name is misspelled on the ad) became Mrs. Wallace Reid.**

of shabby frame structures comprising tavern, stables, and carriage house.

Operating on what today is known as a "tight budget," the Horsley operation found it necessary to take photographic advantage of the California sunlight almost as soon as they'd unpacked. Hastily, they built an outdoor stage—a crude, raised platform about 40 feet square, above which they placed an array of muslin cloth suspended upon a network of wires in such a way as to allow the muslin to be slid quickly about as diffusers, depending on how much sunlight it was desirable to filter.

Each week the Horsley operation, which called itself "Nestor Films," was scheduled to ship to New Jersey one western and one non-western film subject, both of which were hastily edited, titled, printed, and released at the company headquarters in Bayonne.

There were three directors employed by David Horsley: William

Hollywood's first studio was the home of Nestor, a firm from Bayonne, New Jersey. The studio is shown here after Nestor had been absorbed by Universal.

H. Fahrney, who directed the Nestor westerns; Thomas Rickett, the dramas; Al E. Christie, who was responsible for the comedies (the same Al Christie who, with his brother, later formed the Christie Comedy Company, which eventually took over the original Nestor lot).

Nestor production appeared to go smoothly right from the start. A one-reeler titled *Law of the Range* was quickly followed by a drama, *Her Indian Lover;* and then by the first of what became a series of Mutt and Jeff comedies; as well as the original entry in a series titled *Desperate Desmond.*

About a year and a half after feverish output of productions began for Horsley, a diminutive German-Jewish ex-clothier and penny arcade operator named Carl Laemmle came on the Hollywood scene. On May 20, 1912, David Horsley merged his company with a new one which Laemmle and some partners had just formed: Universal. For a time, David Horsley remained with Universal and, some historians claim, helped his brother to design Universal City. Possibly the claim is accurate, for it was not until 1915 that David Horsley established a new studio for himself, this one in Bostock's Arena and Jungle, an animal farm at the corners of Washington and 18th Street in Los Angeles (former site of Chutes Park).

David Horsley continued to produce films and, during World War I, turned out comedies and short melodramas, releasing some under his name, others under a short-lived setup called Piedmont Pictures Corporation.

**Centaur Film, Bayonne, N.J. This was the Horsley motion picture operation which led to the founding of Nestor Films, the first studio in Hollywood.**

Around 1914–15, brother William Horsley supposedly superintended the construction of Universal City, but by 1918, had narrowed his activities to the operation of William Horsley Laboratories on Sunset Boulevard between Gower and Beachwood.

Once the William Horsley Laboratories were in operation, a steady flow of lab work for small, independent producers began. The problem of collecting from many of the customers often led Horsley to take rather severe legal measures. In 1925, for example, Horsley found it necessary to seize the negatives of the serials *The Power God* and *The Mystery Box* for lab bills owed him by Davis Distributing. He had the prints released through his own choice of distributors in order to get the money owed him!

By 1924, William Horsley began to turn much of his laboratory work to narrow gauge 16mm film, and still later to activities involving the recording and processing of 33⅓ rpm discs used in sound-on-disc "talkies." The latter work was short-lived, however; sound-on-film quickly supplanted the disc method.

When the great economic depression fell upon the world, William Horsley managed to continue in the film industry with his Hollywood Film Enterprises, operating in the same Los Angeles suburb where, in 1911, he and his brother David had brought Hollywood its very earliest motion picture studio.

# The New York Motion Picture Company

They were typical racetrack touts, Adam Kessel and his pal Charles Bauman, dressed in what might best be described as "overdone chic"; their sartorial splendor announcing to any astute observer that the partners hadn't truly shaken off all evidences of their former occupation.

The generally accepted story as to what led the pair into the film industry usually reads like this: Adam Kessel loaned $2,500 to an acquaintance; his money not being returned promptly, Kessel paid a call on the recalcitrant debtor who, it turned out, disclosed that the proceeds of the loan had been invested in 35mm motion picture films which were being rented to nickelodeon movie houses. So intrigued was Kessel, it is said, that he acquired the exchange, called in his friend Charley Bauman, and established a discount film rental house.

The operation prospered, so much so that film producers soon sought to cut off the supply of new pictures to the two ex-bookies, who were undercutting prices. The threat forced the partners to go into film production; their initial picture, a one-reeler, was *Disinherited Son's Loyalty*. The stars? Kessel and Bauman.

Their cameraman, Fred Balshofer, was owner of his own camera, a fact which prompted his being asked to become a partner. The camera was an outlawed one, a type on which Edison's all-powerful Patents Company held exclusive rights. Undeterred, the former bookies, accustomed to gambling, told Balshofer to go ahead and crank up his illegal camera, this time turning out *Davy Crockett in Hearts United*.

On the box-office strength of that pair of films, Bauman, Kessel, Balshofer and an attorney named Louis Burston formed a corporation, its trademark the bison, the same one shown on the buffalo head nickel. The partners named their enterprise Bison Life Motion Pictures and launched a busy production schedule, beginning with a film titled *A True Indian's Heart*, filming it on location at Coytesville, New Jersey, with Charles French in the leading role.

Early productions from Bison were crude almost to a degree of ludicrousness. The fledgling producers once borrowed a bearskin from an obliging taxidermist, while a hapless actor concealed himself under it long enough to give a semblance of life to the thing.

By 1913, the New York Motion Picture Company, already promoting its new Keystone Comedies, had established offices in New York's famous Putnam Building. That was about the time when Adam Kessel discovered that vaudeville audiences in New York were crazy over a low comic who had shown up on United States shores in the

**When Mack Sennett Comedies was a branch of the New York Motion Picture Co., this was its headquarters at 1712 Allesandro, Los Angeles, as it appeared in around 1916.**

company of a Fred Karno theatrical group from England, currently appearing at New York's Hammerstein Theatre.

Kessel and Bauman watched a performance of the Knockabout act, afterward hiring Charlie Chaplin at $150 a week to appear in their Keystone Comedies, a production enterprise under the leadership of ex–Biograph employee Mack Sennett.

In 1909, the firm moved its production activities to the West Coast, establishing early offices and studios in an abandoned grocery store building at Edendale, on the outskirts of Los Angeles.

In 1912, NYMPC moved its Bison unit to Santa Yñez Canyon, near the town of Santa Monica, that transfer making it possible for the Keystone Comedies unit to occupy the Edendale lot.

Producer-director Thomas Ince, in charge of the Bison unit, now had untold space for filming his continuing stream of outdoor pictures.

Once he'd established himself at Santa Yñez Canyon, Ince made an interesting discovery: A good portion of the Miller Bros. 101 Ranch Show was wintering nearby. Ince quickly wired Kessel and Bauman in New York, announcing that he could obtain the services of the ranch show for the coming winter months at a weekly stipend of $2,100. The former bookmakers agreed to the price, enabling Ince to proceed soon after on production of the two-reel western *Across the Plains*, in which cowboys of the show were featured.

In his autobiography, actor William S. Hart repeatedly refers to Inceville as "the camp," as that sprawling layout in the canyon may have seemed in 1913 when he came to work at Inceville.

During the time that Hart was employed there, other members of the stock company of players included Frank Borzage, Charles Ray, Sessue Hayakawa, Dick Stanton, and Walter Edwards; the leading ladies included Clara Williams, Gladys Rockwell, Enid Markey, Louise Glaum, and Gretchen Lederer.

The regular directorial staff at Inceville in those days comprised Reginald Barker, Raymond B. West, Scott Sidney, Charles Giblyn, and others.

By early 1915, Hart avers, he'd appeared in more than 20 two-reel pictures made for Bison label. (That was the year Kessel and Bauman ended their distribution arrangement with Mutual, and followed entrepreneur Harry Aitken into the latter's new Triangle Pictures.)

New York Motion Picture Company appeared to be a prosperous firm, the progress of which appeared unstoppable, although it must have seemed to the partners that the rest of the film production and distribution circle was made up of claim-jumpers who made the Alaskan variety appear tame by comparison! After releasing Bison products through Universal, for instance, Kessel and Bauman became embroiled in a drawn-out, costly court suit with Universal which ended with Universal's being granted ownership of the Bison name and trademark. Later, the racetrack touts watched their Keystone Comedies trademark pass into hands of Paramount. "Affairs like that," said Bauman, "sickened Kessel and me against further activities in film."

Not all of the partners' troubles came from the outside, the pair showing little willingness to produce anything longer than two- or three-reelers. By the time Adolph Zukor imported the foreign-made feature film *Queen Elizabeth*, such short films were passé. Many other firms other than Kessel and Bauman's disappeared at this time. Biograph, Edison, Kalem, Essanay and others preferred to cease production rather than to invest heavily in multi-reel productions.

Before the end of World War I, the two former bookies gathered their winnings from the motion picture game and closed the doors on participation in that sort of gambling. In 1916 the partners divested themselves of their production holdings, selling out at a net of about $1,000,000, which in those days before the federal income tax, wasn't exactly a small sum. The price included countless negatives and other pre-print materials of productions which the partners had spearheaded. By January 31, 1917, the firm was no more.

Sennett went his way, founding his own Mack Sennett Comedies. Thomas Ince organized his own outfit, for a time utilizing the old Inceville lot near Santa Monica as well as Ince's new lot in Culver City. Chaplin, of course, was long gone from the K and B organization. Even the Japanese actor Sessue Hayakawa, who'd found early screen fame at the hands of the two racetrack touts, had gone on to greater screen success and, ultimately, ownership of his own studio, as had William S. Hart and Charles Ray.

# The George V. Osmond Studio

The state of Utah, famous for its Mormon Tabernacle, Great Salt Lake, and Monument Valley, possesses one huge motion picture–TV studio, which was originally called the George V. Osmond Studio at the time of its dedication by a Mormon Church leader on November 1, 1977.

The studio was born of the financial largesse of a large Mormon family of which Donny and Marie Osmond are probably the best known. The dream was first visited upon 22-year-old Merrill Osmond in 1976.

The site chosen was at Orem, Utah, a 28-acre lot never owned by the Osmond family, but rather obtained by them on a 2.2 million dollar, 50-year lease. In the mid–1970s, the Osmonds were reaping a harvest of wealth as entertainers, their pure and unsullied reputations quickly having built their family act into what amounted to a musical dynasty.

Reputedly the family poured in $6,000,000 for construction of only the 104,000 square-foot sound stage at the lot, a figure which included editing facilities, a recording studio, rehearsal hall, carpenter shops, makeup and dressing rooms, and offices.

When it first started operation, the new studio enjoyed considerable financial success, especially as long as the Osmonds held a large contract to turn out TV shows for one of the networks. When the show failed to be renewed, times became difficult for the gargantuan studio, which was rumored to have lost $2,000,000 in one disastrous year. Payroll checks were being returned, stamped "Insufficient funds," the Osmond dream having turned to bitter gall.

No clientele could be found who would rent studio space so far from large film centers, and where it was a truly great distance to bring actors, personnel, and equipment.

In February 1983, Paul Jensen, said to be a multimillionaire from Dallas, purchased the studio for $6,000,000, but in just two yers Jensen had declared bankruptcy, placing the former Osmond Studio once more on the market, the asking price $8,000,000.

# The Pacific Studios and Others in Northern California

Following World War I, many predicted the San Francisco area would become an important filmmaking center. Accordingly, near the city of San Mateo an ambitious studio construction project was begun, spearheaded by such figures as W.W. Hodkinson, Dudley Field Malone, and Thomas Dixon, the latter the author of the novel *The Clansman*, which had been the basis for D.W. Griffith's film *Birth of a Nation.*

The new Pacific Studios, designed by John Jasper of Hollywood Studio, included enclosed stages, motion picture laboratories, dozens of dressing rooms, scenery docks, countless offices, and warehouses for storage of such things as properties and costumes. The processing lab would provide overnight service, permitting next-day screening of "rushes."

Occupying more than 100 acres along the south side of Peninsula Avenue, the studio structures were primarily of the popular Spanish style, with stucco walls, arched windows, and tile roofs. Studio designer Jasper had done his work exceedingly well. Many of the dressing rooms had private baths. There were two gigantic stages, each built on a steel frame more than 40 feet high, with a 60' x 120' floor area, fitted with 50 banks of powerful twin-arcs, at that time a lighting engineer's dream.

Alongside the processing laboratory was the film printing department in which 14,000 feet of film could be printed per hour, next to which were editing rooms and fire-resistant film vaults. Other buildings comprised studio carpentry and plaster shops, property departments and screening rooms.

By the time the Pacific Studios were ready to begin operation near the end of 1920, the original heads of the project, Hodkinson, Dixon, and Malone, no longer were connected with the firm.

Functioning as a "rental stage" the studio was opened to outside producers, one of the first of whom was Hobart Bosworth, the talented actor, producer, and writer whose initial picture at Pacific was *The Sea Lion* (1921), directed by Rowland V. Lee. The cast of that film was impressive: besides Bosworth there were Bessie Love, Emory Johnson, Carol Holloway and Charles Clary. A major picture, *The Sea Lion* was distributed by the young giant First National.

The same month that *The Sea Lion* was released, Bosworth Productions delivered two additional pictures (both made at Pacific Studios) to his distributor, *Blind Hearts* and *White Hands*.

*Blind Hearts*, like the Bosworth film which preceded it, was directed by Rowland V. Lee and had Bosworth heading a cast which this time included Madge Bellamy, Robert McKim, and Calette Forbes.

Bosworth's third feature, completed in December 1921, also was directed by Lambert Hillyer and again had Bosworth in the leading role, the supporting cast including Elinor Fair, Freeman Wood, Robert McKim and a youthful George O'Brien. Unlike the initial two releases, *White Hands* was distributed by FBO.

Early in 1922, Bosworth returned to the Pacific Studios, this time for *The Man Alone*, made for distribution through Anchor Films.

Other producers besides Bosworth figured in the history of the Pacific Studios. Max Graf, for instance, organized his own film production outfit after serving as production manager for Bosworth. Graf proved a good client of Pacific Studios. *The Forgotten Law* (1922), featuring Milton Sills, Cleo Ridgeley, and Jack Mulhall, was only the first of his pictures at Pacific.

Graf continued leasing space at the Pacific Studios for such later films as *The Fog* (1923), *Half a Dollar Bill* (1924), *Wandering Footsteps* (1925) and, after a two-year hiatus, the knockabout farce *Finnegan's Ball* (1927).

Although Pacific Studios reorganized in 1924 (at which time it was renamed Peninsula Studios), it never could seem to attract enough film producers to continue operation.

Before "talking picture fever" had spread across the world in the late 1920s, both the names Pacific Studios and Peninsula Studios were forgotten, the city of San Francisco losing forever its bid to defeat Los Angeles as the leading United States film production center.

A Londoner by birth, Paul Gerson had been trained for a career as a stage actor, coming to America and achieving success on the New York stage, where he appeared in a role in *Ben Hur*, and with actress Minnie Maddern Fiske in her stage production *Becky Sharp*.

Gerson felt his stage career fitted him to teach drama, so in two cities, Chicago and San Francisco, he set up dramatic schools, and soon both were drawing well from among would-be thespians, one of whom was a youthful girl named Marjorie Rambeau.

The Gerson Dramatic School soon began supplying screen talent, first to the California Motion Picture Corporation, and later to Gerson's own studio.

As his film enterprise burgeoned, Gerson tried using as screenplays solid period stories such as Charles Dickens' *Cricket on the Hearth*, only to find that moviehouse habitués were much more receptive to what later were called action pictures, often made on bargain budgets. The titles of some of Gerson's later pictures disclosed types which fitted this mold: *Waterfront Wolves* (1924), *Three Days to Live* (1924), and *Pride of the Force* (1925). The cast of such films often included Tom Santschi, Ora Carew, Rex Lease, Maurice Costell, Dorothy Dwan, Cullen Landis, and Theodore von Eltz, all of whom featured in one or more pictures made by Gerson.

As with most independent studios, Gerson's was frequently used by outside production units. In 1921, *The Heart of the North* with Roy Stewart, Louis Lovely, and George O'Brien was filmed at the Gerson lot, as was the 1922 feature *Life's Greatest Question*, another Roy Stewart–Louis Lovely picture, *The Broadway Madonna* and *The Flying Dutchman* also were made at the Gerson facility.

Primarily, however, the studio operated for the purpose of churning out its own productions, many of which were little more than "B" budget features, as evidenced by titles such as *Getting Her Man* (1924), *Ten Days* (1924), *Too Much Youth* (1925), *The Canvas Kisser* (1925), and *Goin' the Limit* (1925).

There were also such Gerson pictures as *In Search of a Hero, The Waster, The Reckless Mollycoddle* (all 1926) and a final one, *The Boaster* (1927), after which the studio went dark for the last time.

In scrambling toward profitability, Gerson Pictures proved to rely too much on a group of films starring screen newcomer Richard Holt, a youth who tried to emulate then-popular Douglas Fairbanks. In pictures such as *Ten Days, Too Much Youth,* and *Easy Going Gordon* (1924–1927), Holt often was depicted in scenes of reckless courage and high-speed auto chases involving sporty Marmon cars, or flashy, open Hudson roadsters. Many Gerson films were craftsman-like productions, frequently making good use of the breathtaking scenery of the San Francisco area. But as with many other film studios, Gerson simply could not find wide enough distribution for its pictures, or audiences which would pay money to see a Richard Holt instead of a Douglas Fairbanks film. Such problems proved insurmountable.

# Paramount

William W. Hodkinson, operating a couple of independent film exchanges in Western United States, encountered considerable difficulties obtaining for his customers an unbroken stream of up-to-date, high-quality feature films.

In New York, Adolph Zukor, a former furrier who'd turned film exhibitor, was also upset about the general shortage of films.

So when the two got together during the winter of 1913–14, a solution to their problem was agreed upon.

Having bought and released in the U.S. the foreign-made feature film *Queen Elizabeth,* Zukor had garnered enough profits so that he was seriously considering establishing his own film studio, proving he could be assured of national distribution for all the pictures he'd make.

Hodkinson arrived at Zukor's door at that propitious moment. Operating film exchanges in such key cities as San Francisco and Los Angeles, Hodkinson was confident that he possessed the nucleus of a nationwide system of exchanges, and convinced that he could do so, Hodkinson settled upon the name "Paramount" and a logo consisting of a distant view of a snowcapped mountain—both usurped, it's often said, off the side of a laundry truck!

While Hodkinson was engaged in organizing his Paramount system of exchanges, Zukor was preparing to produce his initial feature film, *The Prisoner of Zenda,* for which the Broadway star James K. Hackett had been engaged. Zukor named his outfit "Famous Players" and signed up as his chief of production Edwin S. Porter who, in 1903, had directed the Edison Company's landmark one-reeler *The Great Train Robbery.*

By the time the filmed version of *The Prisoner of Zenda* was completed, the picture had cost $20,000, but was to prove so profitable that Zukor was quickly able to enter full-scale, quantity production of other feature films—a feature per month as it proved.

In 1913 there was no single place in the United States which could be considered the movie production center of the country. There were large, busy studios in New York City, Chicago, Philadelphia, Jacksonville, Florida, and even a few as far west as Los Angeles.

The Jesse L. Lasky Feature Play Company was organized in the eastern United States, although Lasky and his partners quickly hied themselves, along with their fledgling organization, to a suburb of Los Angeles called Hollywood. They were told by a man named Brunton that there was a barn, part of which Brunton felt certain could be rented cheaply, ideal for use as a movie studio. As a result, Lasky's entourage, which included his brother-in-law Samuel Goldfish (later known as

The Paramount Studios, viewed from Marathon Street, 1933. Built as the Brunton studio, it was first the United Studio and then Famous Players–Lasky studios before finally becoming Paramount.

"Goldwyn"), a stage director named Cecil B. DeMille and their lawyer Arthur Friend, in company with stage actor Dustin Farnum and a film script of a Broadway show, *The Squaw Man*, went to see Harry Revier, who had leased the barn from its owner, Jacob Stern.

How well the Lasky group soon fared may readily be gleaned from the fact that soon after the release of its first film, the company was able to buy something like nine or ten acres abutting the corners of Sunset and Vine, and a sizable ranch just across the mountains from Hollywood.

Adolph Zukor, soon to become a major United States producer of feature films, placed his Famous Players, also, into the Paramount "pool"; Zukor receiving a contract for 25 years under which Paramount agreed to advance to Zukor $20,000 to $25,000 per five-reel negative, providing the producer agreed to distribute his features only through Paramount during the life of the contract. The Lasky-Goldfish-DeMille organization, also, was under a 25-year contract at similar terms.

Hobart Bosworth, an ex-stage actor who'd come into films via some early Selig one-reelers, had formed his own production outfit, financed largely by Los Angeles capitalist Frank C. Garbutt. Bosworth and his financial "angel" had set up at least three film production units including Pallas, Morosco, and one called Bosworth, Inc. Bosworth's groups, like Zukor's and Lasky's, entered into a 25-year contract with Paramount, thus assuring Paramount an unbroken string of brand new feature films all around the calendar.

At this point, there was no Paramount motion picture studio, the firm being only a distribution operation during those first years.

Mary Pickford was under contract to Adolph Zukor's Famous Players when Paramount was formed. It wasn't long, though, before Mary and her mother were dissatisfied with the paltry $1,000 a week salary which Mary was drawing from Zukor. Approached on the matter, the wily Zukor dumped the problem with Hodkinson who, at the time, was head of Paramount. Hodkinson decided to raise Paramount's advance payments to Zukor on all Pickford films thereafter, passing along that extra cost to theatres in the form of increased rentals on Pickford films.

On January 15, 1915, Pickford signed a new contract with Famous Players, calling for her to make 10 films a year, receiving a salary of $2,000 weekly, plus half of the profits from her films. For a time, that seemed to settle things, and "Little Mary" went on smiling for Zukor's cameras.

By such compromises, it appears that Hodkinson's plan for Paramount might have continued being successful, save that Zukor and Hodkinson commenced quarreling more and more, Hodkinson being an absolute believer that Paramount should remain simply a distributor, Zukor countering that the basic plan was all wrong and that Paramount should operate its own studio.

Eventually, Zukor prevailed; moreover, he succeeded in ousting Hodkinson from Paramount, thereby winning the top position for himself. Soon Paramount studio was established (it was the Famous Players–Lasky lot which had earlier still been United and before that Brunton).

Under Zukor's aegis, half the most popular United States film stars soon were under contract to Paramount, suddenly the largest producer and distributor of feature films in the world. For years thereafter, Zukor remained in command even during those transitional years when "talking pictures" came into vogue.

During those stages of Paramount studio history, Zukor kept a thin-lipped smile as he undertook the acquisition, starting in 1919, of a gigantic chain of motion picture theatres, some acquired by questionable, very nearly "strong arm" methods, it's said.

Yet, when Jesse L. Lasky left the firm in 1932, Paramount appeared to be a sinking vessel. Three years later, the bankrupt firm submitted a reorganization plan to the courts, which the bankruptcy advisers approved. The following year, 1936, theatre magnate Barney Balaban became president of Paramount. The firm had long since bought into the famous Ufa studio in Germany, and by 1939, revealed that it also owned Allan B. DuMont Laboratories, a firm deeply committed to the development of television. By the time war clouds had begun raining death on much of Europe, Paramount had managed to pull itself out of bankruptcy, as diversification of its annual output of feature picture releases enabled the studio to offer a program of films for just about all motion picture audiences.

Features released in 1939, for example, ranged from "B" budget offerings such as *Ambush* with Lloyd Nolan, *Arrest Bulldog Drummond* with John Howard and Heather Angel, and several of the Hopalong Cassidy series produced for Paramount by Harry Sherman Productions. On up the budgetary scale could be found *The Great Victor Herbert* in which Allan Jones and Mary Martin starred, *Typhoon*, a Technicolored swashbuckler with Dorothy Lamour and Robert Preston; and Cecil B. DeMille's *Northwest Mounted Police* in which Gary Cooper and Paulette Goddard shared screen honors with Madeleine Carroll and Robert Preston.

There have been hundreds of stars and supporting players under contract during the years since the firm began releasing films. It would serve little purpose to cite all of them; it is sufficient only to recall that Bing Crosby, Mae West, Bob Hope, W.C. Fields, Ronald Coleman, Martha Raye, Hedy LaMarr, Betty Hutton, and even the likes of Elvis Presley, Bob Burns, and others all have appeared as stars at Paramount during its history.

For many of its feature films, Paramount allowed the construction of dreadfully costly sets, some of which have been described as being the "dazzling white frosting on tall, tiered wedding cakes." Sets for some of Cecil B. DeMille's productions, spectacular when presented on the motion picture screen, were nearly as impressive when viewed by someone standing on a stage at Paramount.

A single set for the Bob Hope comedy *Casanova's Big Night* (1954) not only required the entire interior of the studio's largest sound stage, but continued on outdoors, a portion of it beneath a gigantic, canvas-topped tent so that a comic "Casanova" could glide by gondola along a lengthy reproduction of a Venetian "canal," filled with water tinted rich Technicolor blue in order to conceal the shallowness of the immense plastic "trough." Flanking the sides of this ersatz canal were scores of facades of Italian-style buildings, in many of which were lights, and on which there occurred countless realistic-appearing balconies, some of which actually were full-sized and usable. The expensive set was typical of the overall lavishness of any number of other sets built for Paramount extravaganzas since back in the days of voiceless movies.

Such lavishness must not have always been financially easy. Like that of nearly all other film studios, the history of Paramount has often been beset with financial problems. Yet Paramount endures, although it has become little more than "another milk cow in a herd driven by a giant conglomerate," as an economist described it.

But as the motion picture industry has changed, retrenched, regrouped, the most visible aspect of what remains of Paramount is its immense studio, for many years symbolized by that ludicrously ornate entrance gate alongside narrow, shoddy Marathon Street in L.A.

# *Pathé*

The massive ocean liner from the port of LeHavre, France, tied off at a pier in New York Harbor and began disgorging freight and pasengers. Among the latter was Sigmund Poppert, whose demeanor disclosed that he had not been sent to America as an idle tourist. He had a mission — that of ascertaining just how large the U.S. market might be for the French-made photographic products of Pathé Frères.

He went about his tasks without undue delay, quickly establishing an office in New York City and a warehouse-studio in an abandoned cash register factory at Bound Brook, New Jersey. The New Jersey operation provided adequate space for the storage of chemicals, unexposed motion picture film, even for the installation of a complete film laboratory and, as it later proved, a place to actually film motion pictures. The Pathé plant began operation in April 1910, soon after which it began assembling an American stock company of players under the directorship of Louis Gasnier who had been sent to the United States from Paris along with J.A. Berst, the manager of the studio at Bound Brook.

That same year, American Pathé began production of a weekly newsreel, an equivalent of its earlier French news film Pathé Gazette, the American counterpart being called simply Pathé News.

When Thomas Edison and other holders of United States patents on motion pictures established a joint patent trust in January 1909, Pathé was a charter member, claiming several patents relating to film.

As Pathé enlarged its operations in the United States the firm built a two-story laboratory and office building with glassed-in studios on both floors of the structure at 1 Congress Street, Jersey City, New Jersey. This was where many scenes for Pearl White's 1914 serial *The Perils of Pauline* were made, including sequences involving an indoor set in which swirling waters were shown rising ominously about trapped, helpless Pearl. That scene, filmed by cameraman Arthur Miller and directed by Donald MacKenzie, involved the camera magic of dipping the entire set into the 30' x 40' swimming pool in the studio, the camera being "deceived" by the water level in the "room" apparently growing deeper, when in reality the set was being plunged deeper into the pool.

Because the first and second floors of the studio were offset from one another, both could have not only glass walls on the stages, but glassed-in "greenhouse" ceilings as well, thus requiring a minimum of artificial light provided by Cooper-Hewitt, Aristos, or other similar, primitive electric studio lighting gear.

The Pathé brothers, Charles, Emile, Jacques, and Théophile, had rapidly built Pathé Frères into a giant organization.

By the time America became mired in the slaughter known as World War I, the Pathés had determined that, profitable though their American branch was, they should sell their film production facilities there. Accordingly, in 1917, the American Pathé producing company was acquired by the U.S. investment firm Merrill Lynch Company.

While American Pathé (the name is correctly pronounced "pa-TAY," the "h" silent) was yet under control of the French, it had begun producing serials, a type of picture not only continued under the Merrill Lynch ownership but expanded considerably. Chapter plays had proved highly profitable, as evidenced by such Pathé offerings as *Adventures of Ruth* (1919), *Daredevil Jack* (1920), *Hurricane Hutch* (1921), and many more, continuing as late as 1928.

As its list of stars, directors, and cameramen grew so too did Pathé Frères; a southern studio operation was begun, cameraman Arthur Miller states, near the north Florida city of St. Augustine. (Miller stated that it was to this studio he was called to replace another cameraman on *Perils of Pauline.*)

By the beginning of 1912 Pathé also had established its first studio on the West Coast of the United States, at 1807 Allesandro (now Glendale Boulevard) in Los Angeles.

After U.S. Pathé had passed into the hands of Merrill Lynch, other larger studios were purchased such as the former facility of Thomas H. Ince at 9336 Washington Boulevard, Culver City, California.

The lot was a large one, its numerous stages having been for the most part built in the era when studio designers favored the glassed-in design. The Ince lot, however, consisted of large stages wherein most daylight was filtered onto the sets by means of clerestories set atop the roofs of the stages. All the windows eventually were painted an opaque color, it having been found that artificial light was more dependable and much more readily controlled.

"Baby Marie" Osborne was a favorite of World War I motion picture audiences. Many of her films were produced by Diando Film Co. (the name is misspelled on the poster) and distributed by Pathé.

There was the prevailing idea at Pathé that whenever possible its productions be independently made, the Pathé rooster merely crowing onto the screen serials, features, and short subjects made by "outside" producers. (Whenever it was necessary to create a production unit of its own, Pathé established one, as it did with "Eclectic.")

Firms such as Hal Roach, Balboa, Harold Lloyd Productions and numerous others enjoyed the distribution facilities, the prestige, and advertising benefits of Pathé, as well as, in many cases, its guidance and financial aid, while being totally independent of the Pathé Exchange, Incorporated.

Conversely there was a benefit for Pathé itself: When production units such as the Whartons and Balboa got into financial difficulties which wiped them out entirely, Pathé, which had distributed pictures from these studios, bore none of the stigma attached to these bankruptcies.

In 1921, when Associated underwent reorganization and an infusion of $3,000,000 in new capital, that firm announced it would thereafter handle distribution of all Pathé feature films, while Pathé

**Warner Oland and Pearl White appearing in a scene for the Pathé/Eclectic serial *The Perils of Pauline* (1914), for most of which serial Arthur Miller, shown here with his Pathé camera, was cameraman.**

Film exchanges would carry only the Pathé short subjects. It was to prove an arrangement which did not endure; eventually Pathé assumed distribution of its features and its short product, while also carrying the releases of Associated Exhibitors.

By the late 1920s, when talking pictures suddenly triumphed over voiceless ones, officials of Pathé hurried to equip their lot at Culver City (And Pathé newsreel facilities as well) with the cumbersome and complex gear with which to give the Pathé rooster a voice.

Throughout the industry there was a rush to create new equipment and innovations which would make the "talkies" from each studio compete well against all others on the market. Cameras which had been built to operate usually at 16 frames of film per second, were revamped to a "normal" speed of 24 pictures per second, and the noise of the camera mechanisms muffled in order to prevent the camera from being "picked up" by the microphone.

Warners utilized large, immovable booths in which the cameras and operators were imprisoned while filming, while engineers at Pathé studios developed a camera "blimp case" which, while bulky and exceedingly unattractive, could manage to restore a measure of mobility to the camera.

The Pathé Studio continued turning out feature films well into the era of talking pictures, having by that time long ceased to make serials.

In 1931, largely through the merger guidance of Joseph P. Kennedy, the Boston financial promoter, Pathé and Film Booking Offices (F.B.O.) merged with RKO Radio, a firm newly established by Radio Corporation of America, Albee Vaudeville, and Keith-Orpheum.

In January 1931, soon after RKO had purchased the production facilities of Pathé, it named Lee Marcus as president of the Pathé lot and Charles R. Rogers as chief of production there, producing very ordinary, often deplorably dull feature films including *The Big Gamble* with William Boyd (at that time a contract player of Pathé), and *Born to Love*, which featured Constance Bennett and Helen Twelvetrees (both of whom also were contract players at Pathé).

When RKO entered an economic slump, however, it found it more economical to cease operating the Pathé lot completely separately and thereafter operated it simply as an auxiliary facility.

The name Pathé continued to be applied to the studio at Culver City; the Pathé newsreel continued in production, though before its final years it was sold by RKO to Warner Bros.

In 1957 both the RKO lot on Gower Street in Hollywood and the old Pathé studio in Culver City were sold to Desilu Productions, thus erasing forever the Pathé name in American film production.

The rooster survived as an American bird only to identify the United States film laboratories of the Pathé name, although they too have now disappeared, as did the Pathé newsreel.

# The Pickford-Fairbanks Studio

Designed and built in 1919 by Jesse Durham Hampton and purchased by Douglas Fairbanks and his wife, Mary Pickford, the studio along the west side of Santa Monica Boulevard was Pickford's first venture into studio ownership. It was not Fairbanks'; in 1916, he'd taken an option on what once had been the Clune Studio on Melrose Avenue, an operation which was operated by Doug's brother Jack, with another brother, Robert, acting as production manager. Bennie F. Zeidman, who in later years was to become an independent producer, was publicity chief of the Fairbanks operation.

The studio, operated as Douglas Fairbanks Pictures Corporation, where the swashbuckling extrovert made such films as *In Again, Out Again* (1917), which entailed a great deal of shooting "on location" in the

**Mary Pickford and her husband (in this admittedly poor photo) are joyfully oblivious to the fact that they are nailing the entrance sign to the wrong side of the posts to mark the opening of their own studio.**

East. The story itself spun from fibers of an actual news event of sabotage in factories and on docks in New Jersey.

Fairbanks turned out four other films during his first year on the Melrose lot: *Wild and Wooly, Down to Earth, The Man from Painted Post* and *Reaching for the Moon,* the last-named filmed largely in New York City.

Always an exuberant friend and a lavish gift-giver, Douglas had bought a lively Malamute dog to give to a friend. The dog was fine, the friend said in returning it to Fairbanks, except that, wolf-like, it howled loudly and endlessly on moonlit nights. Fairbanks, unwilling to keep the dog at his home, made it a sort of mascot and watchdog at the studio, where it quickly became a regular part of the studio personnel, though a noisy one whenever the moon was full.

In the second year of operation of his studio, while Fairbanks was busy preparing forthcoming production schedules, his wife Beth's lawyers handed him legal documents indicating that the lady was divorcing Fairbanks, giving him his marital freedom in return for a settlement amounting to about half a million dollars. During the year of his divorce he headed into a schedule of films which included *Mr. Fixit; A*

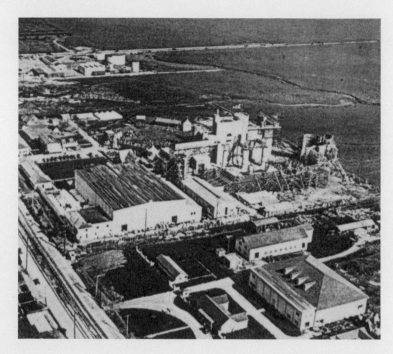

**The Samuel Goldwyn lot, earlier the United Artists studio, and before that the Pickford-Fairbanks Studio, to mention only part of its past.**

*Modern Musketeer; Headin' South; Say, Young Fellow; Bound in Morocco, He Comes Up Smiling;* and *Arizona.*

That was also the year when Fairbanks purchased property with a hunting lodge on it in Beverly Hills. The property became the site of "Pickfair," the lavish two-story house which Doug built for Mary Pickford when they were wed.

In 1919, Fairbanks had joined Chaplin, Pickford, Griffith, and others in the organization of United Artists, a distribution outfit which was suggested to the principals by B.P. Schulberg. The firm was officially organized on February 5 of that year.

Just after Fairbanks turned out his sumptuous feature *The Three Musketeers,* he and his wife purchased their own studio in 1922. The Pickford-Fairbanks Studio on Santa Monica Boulevard was next door to Vidor Village, operated by King Vidor, where Vidor made *The Sky Pilot* (1921). There they built a five-room bungalow at one end of the lot around which there was nearly a full acre of lawn.

Doug, at the same time, had his domain at the other end of the property with private office, dressing rooms, swimming pool, Turkish bath, gymnasium, and other amenities.

Laboring amid these glamorous surroundings, Doug undertook his first production at the new studio, a tremendously lavish picturization of the fanciful legend of Robin Hood. Utilizing the motion picture screen as a vast canvas on which to paint eyefilling scenes, Fairbanks turned *Robin Hood* into what many historians rate as Doug's finest film.

Financing such a high-budget picture was somewhat difficult: Motion pictures were suddenly doing poorly at the box offices of the world. With outside finances difficult to obtain, Fairbanks determined to meet all production costs from his own resources.

As an example of just how lavish a production *Robin Hood* was, Fairbanks commissioned the construction on a good part of the five-acre "back lot," a ludicrously expensive medieval-style castle, 450 feet in length, 90 feet in height.

Fairbanks is said to have been away from the studio at the time the set was under construction. When he returned and saw how overwhelmingly huge it was, he suddenly was afraid to use it in the picture.

Director Allan Dwan is said to have argued convincingly that, large as that set was, it could not possibly dwarf the screen hero of Robin Hood as portrayed by the ebullient Douglas Fairbanks.

Doug was not hard to convince; besides, he'd guessed that film audiences were craving extravaganzas.

Fairbanks' next film was *The Thief of Bagdad;* his wife Mary turned out *Dorothy Vernon of Haddan Hall,* which was far from a commercial success. In truth, at this period of their careers the Fairbanks films were more popular than Mary's.

*The Thief of Bagdad* proved to be vastly expensive but an impressively popular film, the sets designed by William Cameron Menzies, one of which was an imaginative likeness of the city of Bagdad, but built around a vast plaza. The concrete was painted black, then waxed and polished repeatedly until it shone with nearly a galactic sparkle.

As for the "city," it was like something seen in a dream, and had tastefully wrought mosques, minarets, stairways and bazaars.

The script, transformed into pure celluloid adventure by director Raoul Walsh, was packed with screen figures of genuine interest. Thieves looked like thieves, and no wonder! Walsh had recruited a lot of his extras from the sleaziest dives in Los Angeles. Photographed by veteran cameraman Arthur Edeson, *The Thief of Bagdad* provided outdoor "standing sets" which were still in evidence fully a decade after the film itself was made.

*Don Q., Son of Zorro* followed next on the Fairbanks production schedule, a film in which the actor co-starred with Mary Astor, and was backed by a fine supporting cast which included Donald Crisp who was also director of the picture, as well as Warner Oland and Jean Hersholt.

In 1926, Fairbanks decided to employ the nearly 10-year-old color process Technicolor, at that time a two-strip color system. Fairbanks used it for the picture *The Black Pirate*, written by "Elton Thomas," the pseudonym of Fairbanks. Fairbanks also copyrighted many of his films under the name "The Elton Corporation."

*The Gaucho* (1927) allowed Fairbanks to introduce U.S. film audiences to the Argentinian cowboy and to his use of "boleadoras" or "bolas," a device with three leather thongs tied together in a "Y" pattern, at the ends of each of which was a stone or metal ball.

Just as the sets for *The Gaucho* were under construction, late in 1926 Doug's older brother John passed away leaving Doug grief-stricken, for John had always been a sort of quasi-father to Doug.

As *The Gaucho* was in production, Mary was engaged elsewhere on the lot on the feature *My Best Girl* in which she co-starred with rising young star "Buddy" Rogers. It is probable that Pickford fell in love with Rogers at this time; Doug, who visited a set for *My Best Girl*, said afterward, "It's more than jealousy. I suddenly felt afraid." After all, Fairbanks by then was 44 years old.

*The Gaucho* was a silent film, released about the same time as Al Jolson's part-talkie *The Jazz Singer*.

Fairbanks allowed one more of his films, *The Iron Mask*, to be filmed as a silent. Mary Pickford, however, turned quickly to production of talkies, her first being *Coquette*, for which she won an Academy Award.

Fairbanks' initial talkie was *The Taming of the Shrew* in which he co-starred with his wife, both Fairbanks and Pickford being appallingly miscast in the Shakespearian comedy.

The picture received a disastrous public reception, probably made less palatable to film audiences which were becoming aware that all was not well between Fairbanks and his wife. The Hollywood "dream marriage" had begun to fall apart.

After a solo visit to Europe, Doug returned to Hollywood to begin preparations for *Reaching for the Moon*, a satire on business tycoons, filmed on location in New York. This was followed quickly by another vapid offering, *Around the World in 80 Minutes with Douglas Fairbanks*, and shortly thereafter, *Mr. Robinson Crusoe*. All three were mediocre films, although the third is somewhat entertaining.

When Fairbanks and his wife divorced their film studio became, at turns, the United Artists Studio and finally the Samuel Goldwyn Studio, Goldwyn having obtained the lot through court proceedings.

# Powers

The inferno consumed the frame building at 241st Street and Richarson Avenue, Bronx, New York, while an official of Powers Picture Plays (also known as Powers Stock Company) cranked away at the Pathe cameras, recording on primitive orthochromatic stock the graphic story of this devastating, costly event in the life of the firm.

It was June 5, 1911—early afternoon; several young women in the film finishing room on the second floor of the frame building had suddenly faced the first terrors of the fire. Minutes after the outbreak the blaze burst through the roof of the leased structure which but four years earlier had been the city's police department horse-training stable.

Even as flames leaped upward on the building, the treasurer of Powers was telling reporters that no lives had been lost but that monetarily the loss would total at least $300,000. A good part of it was represented by unreleased productions, some of which had been undergoing titling and sub-titling procedures at the patient hands of women who put together such productions in the assembly rooms.

"We will reopen tomorrow," said treasurer Thomas W. Evans, "at our other facility—241st at White Plains Avenue."

It was an optimistic, seemingly implausible announcement. After all, the fire had destroyed the motion picture laboratory, many cameras, costumes, sets, indoor stages and what the Mt. Vernon newspaper, *The Argus,* was to describe in its edition of June 6, 1911, as "all kinds of paraphernalia valued at many thousand dollars."

In making announcements to the press, Evans added, "And there is not a penny of insurance on anything."

The matter of his failure to insure the Powers firm against fire losses was probably the only oversight which Patrick Anthony Powers had ever made.

Even as a boy he had displayed amazing talent toward operation of business enterprises. Growing up in Buffalo, New York, Powers, when yet a young man, met and entered partnership with Joseph Schuchert, Sr., in what eventually became forty stores, dealing in Edison and Victor phonographs.

In 1907 the partners became intrigued by the profits which could be made from buying prints of motion picture films, then renting them to nickelodeon movie houses in and around Buffalo, so the partners launched a new firm, Buffalo Film Exchange, 13 Genesee Street.

In 1909, his cash and assets from film and phonographs considerable, Powers moved from Buffalo to New York City, soon after his arrival setting up a motion picture studio in the Bronx. It was a time

**Mary Miles Minter, who first was known to screen audiences as Juliet Shelby, made her first screen appearance for P.A. Powers. A still from that picture, *The Nurse*.**

**Pearl White, whose name is synonymous with that of the silent film, entered movies through Powers Picture Plays, continuing with star roles for Crystal, Pathe, Lubin, Wharton and other studios.**

when New York City had many studios such as Biograph, Vitagraph, Rex, IMP, and Fox. The competition did not trouble Powers and his new partner, Irving Cummings, who established their studio near Mt. Vernon, in the Bronx. There, film director Joseph Golden and cameraman Ludwig Erb quickly began grinding out a seemingly endless supply of pictures, some only of split-reel length wherein two such productions would be combined onto one 1000-foot reel.

Early in 1912, Mary Miles Minter, whose real name was Juliet Shelby, made her first screen appearance in a Powers production titled *The Nurse.*

Miss Minter's debut at the Powers lot must have occurred about the time that studio introduced Pearl White to screen audiences, if one relies upon statements which Miss White made while recording her none-too-accurate autobiography.

The Powers studio was created during the troubled historical period of U.S. film when the industry had divided into two camps, one allied with Edison's Motion Picture Patents Company, the other group the poorly organized but amazingly lively firms usually referred to as "independents." Powers was one of the latter. Universal was soon to be another.

When initially organized, Universal comprised several partners, among them Powers, Laemmle, Robert Cochrane, and Mark Dintenfass.

For a time after Universal began operations, Powers continued producing pictures, releasing them through the Universal firm, of course, but after a long series of quarrels involving primarily Powers and Laemmle, affairs were settled when Powers sold his share of Universal to Laemmle and got out.

Powers then turned his interests to the development, manufacture and sale of equipment for recording and playback of "talking pictures," and became an early source of such devices as the Powers Cinephone sound attachments for conversion to sound of silent projection equipment in theatres.

As "talking pictures" swept into prominence, Powers became associated with Walt Disney in the making of early "talkie" animated films and a trifle later, two series of cartoons made by Ub Iwerks and released by MGM: *Willie Whopper* and *Flip the Frog*.

All this led Powers to organize an animated film outfit which he named "Celebrity Productions." Powers' brother was the "front man." Celebrity, for a time in the 1930s, produced what were called "Comi Color" cartoons.

By then Powers had drifted away from studio ownership; at the time the '30s ended, he was becoming less and less active in the film industry, eventually keeping his name alive in film circles only through his occasional imports of British feature films.

Before 1940, he withdrew entirely from activities within the motion picture industry, moving back to the eastern United States, where he operated for about a decade the well-known Westport Country Club, Westport, Connecticut, an activity in which he was still involved at the time of his death at age 75 on July 31, 1948.

# Producers Releasing Corporation

In 1939 Ben Judell, operator of film exchanges in Chicago and Milwaukee, having failed with a production entity called "Progressive Pictures," tried his luck again, this time with a pair of firms, Producers Pictures Corporation and Producers Distributing Corporation, naming himself president of both. In announcing his plans, Judell indicated that the first year's output by the new company would amount to 36 feature films and 24 westerns, to be produced at a total of $1,000,000, which is to say about $15–16,000 per picture.

Before 1940 had ended, however, Judell withdrew, having completed but a handful of films among which were *Torture Ship*, *The Sagebrush Family Trails West* (completed at a small studio Judell had set up in Prescott, Arizona, but which closed down after making only a couple of pictures), and an exploitation feature, *Hitler, Beast of Berlin*.

Under Judell's aegis, Sigmund Neufeld had been an executive producer; he remained when, in December 1940, control of the firm's assets was taken over by the Pathe Corporation (part of the Allegheny Corporation). Pathe, then controlled by international financiers Robert, Kenneth, and John Young, named O. Henry Briggs president of what was then named Producers Releasing Corporation.

In March 1941 production by Producers Releasing came to a halt for lack of operating capital, at which time Consolidated Film Laboratories (which controlled Republic Pictures) agreed to advance $1,000,000 in return for a guarantee by Producers Releasing that its negatives and prints would thereafter be processed in Consolidated laboratories.

In those days, one could not study the lists of players in PRC films without a feeling of nostalgia, since players who possessed any sort of box-office value were for the most part those whose appeal had peaked a dozen years earlier at least.

Henry Armetta, Harry Langdon, Anna Mae Wong, Neil Hamilton, James Dunn, Bryant Washburn, Clara Kimball Young, and scores of other has-beens managed to find employment at PRC, their screen appearances made even more pitiful by the lack of production values and the poor stories and scripts which the studio and its producers thrust upon them.

Shabby and slipshod though most PRC films were, they found a market, particularly away from the large U.S. cities or at least the downtown theatres in cities.

The western picture, little more than an action-filled morality play, seems one type of film that could not be so badly made as to produce sheer boredom for audiences, yet PRC managed that, while its non-western offerings were as bad, sometimes worse. The list of the studio's many, many disgracefully poor films is too lengthy to bear recitation. Mere examination of Harry Langdon in *Misbehaving Husbands*, Ralph Byrd in *S.O.S. Clipper*, Henry Armetta in *Boss Foreman*, or the John Litel feature *Submarine Base* illustrates how poor scripts and general lack of production values were the rule more often than the exception among PRC offerings.

Only occasionally was a creditable picture released by the firm. In 1944, the company surprised exhibitors and audiences alike when it came forth with *Minstrel Man*, a modest but satisfactory musical-drama in which Benny Fields and Gladys George were starred. In 1945, a PRC picture in Cinecolor, *Enchanted Forest*, appeared, the Jack Schwarz production offering audiences a sort of Walt Disney forest film come-to-life. Two sound stages were opened up to provide one very large stage on which an ambitious "green set" was constructed, a likeness of a dense forest in which Harry Davenport, cast as a likeable hermit, lived in what passed for a giant hollow tree of a sort which might have intrigued even John Muir. Edmund Lowe, Brenda Joyce, and John Litel headed the cast in the picture which was guided by director Lew Landers.

If only there had been more offerings from PRC which were on a par with *Enchanted Forest*, the firm might well have survived far longer than it did.

A handful of mildly interesting PRC offerings were turned out, however. *Detour* with Tom Neal and Ann Savage is a satisfactory "B" feature, as is the John Carradine offering *Bluebeard* (although the latter film suffers badly from sets which were designed with forced perspective in an effort to disguise their small size).

During its first years, PRC as well as the Judell operation before it, produced its pictures either on location or at rental studios such as Argyle or, later, at Talisman. In September 1942, PRC purchased from a subsidiary of Western Electric the former studios of Grand National, which it outfitted with equipment bought from the old Chadwick Studio. Cost of the Grand National lot came to $305,000.

By the time World War II ended PRC had succeeded in improving the overall quality of its pictures. Features such as *Fog Island* with George Zucco, *Strange Illusion* with James Lydon, and the Martin Mooney production *Crime Inc.*, were as well made and interesting as "B" films issuing from even major production entities.

When British film magnate J. Arthur Rank decided to enlarge his worldwide firm, Eagle Lion, he turned to financier Robert J. Young. In December 1945, the pair signed an agreement to form a U.S. corporate entity under the name Eagle Lion.

Bryan Foy, who was thereby appointed a vice president, immediately changed the name of the PRC Studios to that of Eagle Lion. On August 8, 1947, trade journals announced that Robert Young was "considering" merging PRC with Eagle Lion. By month's end the transition was complete.

Only a short time after the merger, Eagle Lion itself became part of United Artists.

The Hollywood lot which was PRC's was razed some years ago, most of it later becoming a parking lot, a supermarket, and similar shopping facilities.

# Charles Ray Studios

When the boyish-appearing Charles Ray showed up at Inceville, a motion picture lot near Santa Monica, California, he'd been with smalltime repertoire companies which travelled the western towns presenting a mixed bag of stage plays. These were from a tried-and-true catalog of light entertainment which generally delighted audiences of an unsophisticated type.

Ray first commuted to Inceville by trolley car; the year was 1912. Ince placed Ray in parts of gradually increasing importance, culminating in starring roles in short films and, finally, in feature pictures.

In a 1915 Thomas Ince Civil War drama, *The Coward*, Ray reached full-fledged stardom, his sudden screen fame proving to be something which Ray could not handle gracefully, for by the time Ince had begun release of his feature productions through Paramount, Charles Ray had become, according to Paramount chieftain Adolph Zukor, something of a prima donna.

Matters weren't helped by Ray's wife, who encouraged her husband to squander his income recklessly, investing foolishly in gold doorknobs and other equally tasteless decorations in the couple's Hollywood house. By 1921 Ray left Thomas Ince, striking out on his own.

In 1921 Ray set up his own motion picture studio. Initially, Ray's self-produced pictures were well received, the future of his Charles Ray Studios seemingly assured. Even the motion picture reviewers seemed on his side.

In early 1921, when Ray's *The Old Swimmin' Hole* went into release, a *New York Times* review cheered the picture as one "all can enjoy . . . as moral as the most careful, conventional censor could wish."

**Charles Ray and his dog replete with a new raceabout at Mercury (DeMille) Aviation, 1920.**

After that, Ray's perception of just what the movie-going public wanted of him changed sharply, his studio undertaking a historical romance titled *The Courtship of Myles Standish* (correcting the spelling of the surname "Myles," which the poet Longfellow had misspelled in his poem).

At the time Ray assembled his production organization, he was an important Hollywood star, so brilliantly burning in the firmament that it was a matter of condescension on Ray's part when he chose to release his productions through First National, a relatively new force on the Hollywood scene.

Ray's affiliation with First National, however, came to an abrupt end in 1923, just before the hapless actor-producer's feature *The Courtship of Myles Standish* was ready for release.

It was not that the Myles Standish film was a bad picture. It was, in fact, called his "greatest film effort" by the *New York Times* which in December 1923 judged the film an excellent one. But it was too far afield from the types of films in which Ray had previously appeared.

For Ray had commissioned the construction of a full-scale copy of a vessel which, supposedly, was an exact replica of that one which had

This building, photographed in 1920, was part of Charles Ray Productions, where the expensive and ill-fated *The Courtship of Myles Standish* was made.

borne Myles and his followers from Europe to the New World. Alas, that ship, which could be seen for long distances from Ray's studio, was destined to become a long-lived monument to the sad fall of Charles Ray, whose credit and accumulated wealth both were destroyed by the one picture — 120 minutes of running time which led Ray to a pauper's world. From an $11,000 weekly salary during his late Thomas Ince years Charles Ray had fallen to an income of zero!

While his credit held out, Ray managed some further productions, although it probably was apparent to him that his days as owner of his own studio were over.

Ultimately, plagued by creditors, his studio gone, Ray left the West Coast for a time, trying to establish himself as an author, a playwright, and a stage actor, none of these endeavors but were successful.

A leading role cropped up for him in a Spoor-Berggren wide-screen release titled *The Flagmaker* (1927). Directed by J. Stuart Blackton, one of the founders of Vitagraph, the film was fashioned from a script by Blackton's wife, Marion Constance Blackton, and was claimed to be from a story originally concocted by Theodore Roosevelt which had turned into a short story, "The American," by Jewel Spencer.

Showings of the picture were limited, since a great deal of special projection equipment was required by the wide-screen process.

The failure was unfortunate for Ray's career, because he had just completed an MGM film, *The Fire Brigade,* which seemed to suggest he might be near to a comeback.

Fans loyal to Ray had frequent chances to see their idol on screen after the debacle of *Myles Standish. Dynamite Smith* directly followed the Standish epic, featuring Ray and a capable supporting cast.

*Percy* (1925), *Some Punkins* (1925), and *Bright Lights* (1925) all re-introduced Charles Ray to his role as the country bumpkin, a role in which he continued to be cast in *Sweet Adeline* (1926) and *The Auction Block* (1926).

By the 1930s, the Charles Ray studios was forgotten, and its namesake nearly so. Ray cropped up in bit roles in a handful of features of the 1930s, and even managed to find one leading part in *Just My Luck* (1935), a cheap feature made by Corona Pictures.

An infected tooth led to Ray's death at Cedars of Lebanon Hospital, Hollywood, in 1943.

# Reliable Pictures

The Great Depression fell on America in October 1929. Six years later, our economic fortunes still hadn't turned around. Many film studios had passed behind the veil, and many which remained in business were on the verge of bankruptcy or, like Paramount, were operating in receivership.

Portents notwithstanding, in 1934 a new outfit, Reliable Pictures, set up operations at Sunset Boulevard and Beachwood Drive, behind the Columbia Pictures' lot on Gower.

The corporation was headed by Bernard B. Ray and Harry S. Webb, neither of whom was a newcomer to the film industry.

Ray had started his career in motion pictures in 1911 as a film laboratory technician employed at the Biograph Company. In 1917 he became laboratory supervisor. When Griffith left Biograph for Triangle, Ray followed, functioning as a cameraman. Later he became supervisor of a Hollywood laboratory and went on to eventual work on miniatures and special effects for several studios.

Webb, Ray's partner in the Reliable firm, was a longtime director and, briefly, a sort of partner of Nat Levine when in 1926 Levine was just getting established as "Serial King" in Hollywood.

Because B.B. Ray was the titular head of the new studio and a

**A lobby card for a Reliable picture from the studio's western series. Bob Custer played in another such series made by this studio.**

major shareholder, it required real diplomacy to talk him out of his initial plan to spell the firm name "Rayliable," arguments against which often included the fact that such a move might lead to confusion: there had already been a "Rayart" firm. Fortunately, good sense prevailed. The name chosen was "Reliable Pictures Corporation."

There were no mad dreams around Reliable of producing any but action films—cheaply budgeted, assembly-line productions, devoid even of music on the sound tracks, except for its use in connection with beginning and end titles, or in sequences where dialogue and effects did not occur. (*The Test*, one of Reliable's 1935 pictures which featured Rin-Tin-Tin, Jr., eschews the use of music even where there are prolonged sequences of little other than the sounds of men's footsteps in the snow.)

Dick Talmadge, whose real last name was Mazetti, had found his earliest work in Hollywood as a stuntman for Douglas Fairbanks, Sr. Eventually, he'd moved into a few leading roles in action features.

By the 1930s, Talmadge had established himself in featured parts in the low-budget films Reliable poured forth. Like Bob Custer, who was also a star in Reliable offerings, Talmadge was an inept actor, handicapped further by his excessively thin, nasal voice, and heavy,

An artist's sketch of the Reliable studio, used as the letterhead of the firm. Note how the artist included many details not generally painted on the outside of any building—the telephone number of the firm, for instance.

foreign-sounding accent. Talmadge at times claimed he was born in southern Switzerland, close to the Italian border, but at other times declared he was born of Italian parents who had migrated to New York City from Italy!

Still another star of Reliable products was the dog called Rin-Tin-Tin, Jr., an animal which may or may not have been an actual scion of the original Rinty. Lee Duncan, trainer and owner, let it be known he had brought back from France the dog he named Rin-Tin-Tin, an appellation derived, he said, from the simulation in French of the sound of machine guns—the equivalent of the American "rat-tat-tat."

The elder Rinty had proven wonderfully profitable at the box office when the animal starred in a long string of quite well-made features produced by a financially troubled Warner Bros. studio, just about when silent pictures were soon to be replaced by the "talkies."

Rinty, Jr., was a performer in numerous independent pictures, both serials and features. Trainer Duncan shuttled the animal from Mascot Productions to Reliable studios and later from Metropolitan Pictures to Eagle-Lion. For years the dog was in evidence around Hollywood although often the onlookers had seen one of Duncan's several other "look-alikes" who performed stunts which the real Rin-Tin-Tin, Jr., either could not or would not do. During the brief history of Reliable, the German shepherd appeared in several pictures for that studio, the first ones *Timber Patrol* and *Skull and Crown,* completed by mid-winter 1935. As Reliable studios carried on through 1936 and part of 1937, the dog appeared in *Caryl of the Mountains, The Silver Trail, Outlaw River,* and *Vengeance of Rannah,* all of which were fashioned from original stories by famed writer James Oliver Curwood, who gained his livelihood primarily from fictional tales of the frozen North. However, that author spent most of his productive years no farther north than his residence at Owosso, Michigan, where "Curwood's

Castle," as it was called, became something of a tourist attraction.

Most westerns made by Reliable *(Ridin' On, Fast Bullets, Roamin' Wild,* and so on) featured Tom Tyler, a screen cowboy of Polish extraction who was born in New York City. (Of the many screen cowboys, only a few were actually born in a western state.)

One of the chief reasons for the paucity of historical coverage of Reliable probably lies in the fact that its pictures were distributed by territorial film distributors. Obviously, that system called for each of the 30 or more film exchange centers to have an independent film exchange which would carry Reliable productions, and thus rent such films to theatres within each area. Unfortunately for Reliable, it never proved possible to achieve total coverage of all exchange areas.

Sputtering uncertainly into production in the latter part of 1935, the firm marketed its early efforts: *Skull and Crown* with Regis Toomey, Molly O'Day, and Rin-Tin-Tin, Jr., *The Midnight Phantom* (which the studio classified as an "exploitation" picture) and the Dick Talmadge action feature *Never Too Late.* (The feature *Step on It,* a 1936 film, was Talmadge's final one for Reliable.)

The following two years the studio managed to turn out such Tom Tyler westerns as *Fast Bullets* and *Roamin' Wild.* A couple other Tyler westerns, including one titled *Trigger Tom,* were announced by Reliable but appear never to have gone before the cameras.

There were also Rin-Tin-Tin, Jr., features advertised by Reliable which apparently never were made, including *Mystery of the Seven Chests* and *Speck on the Wall.* Rinty was starred in a group of other Reliable offerings, however, possibly the one shown most widely being *The Test* in which the canine was in pursuit of Monte Blue, while Grant Withers tagged along behind, in search of Rinty.

Ray and Webb claimed later that their company turned out 21 pictures in 1934 and more than 30 in 1935. Oddly, there is not a single Reliable picture which was copyrighted—an understandably convenient omission where the original stories used had already been copyrighted, but hardly explainable with other features made by the studio!

In the years after Reliable vacated its studio the place was temporarily the home of Monogram, during the period when that firm was negotiating for a studio of its own.

Upon Monogram's departure, brothers Max and Arthur Alexander occupied the premises while the two spearheaded a few inexpensive westerns.

Columbia was next in line, renting the lot for production of short subjects.

The place still is in use, but its output of theatrical films has ceased.

# Rental Stages and "Locations"

Many of the dazzlingly fancy trademarks, especially those found at the opening of "B" budget feature films, were simply very bold banners of filmmakers who had no studios of their own. Melody, Ambassador-Conn, Lippert, Cameo, Screen Guild, Chesterfield, Invincible and many more outfits never possessed studios of their own. It was nothing to be ashamed of; the practice wasn't restricted to producers whose offices might only be a phone booth on Gower Street. Even Howard Hughes' expensive production *Hell's Angels* (1930) was made at a rental lot. So were Harold Lloyd's pictures, as well as several early Douglas Fairbanks features.

Seldom well-known outside the immediate geographic region where each such operation was based, extremely huge, well-equipped rental studios were once to be found in large numbers around Los Angeles, and to a lesser degree in places such as New York City, Fort Lee, New Jersey, Miami, Chicago and elsewhere.

In the Los Angeles area the ever-changing number of "rental stages" has included such names as United Studio, Talisman, Tec-Art, Bryan Foy, Clune, Darmour, and scores of others.

Even nowadays such operations exist, though few are as profitable as once would have been possible. Should one care to produce a show, a TV or theatrical firm might choose to obtain space at the huge Osmond Studio up in Utah.

Some of Hollywood's rental lots once were the general offices of independent producing outfits. One such lot, Talisman Studios at 4516 Sunset Boulevard, leased office space to such producers as Argus Pictures, Cameo, Monogram, Boots & Saddles Productions, Crescent Pictures, Arthur Dreifuss Productions, George Randol, Sherwill, Bennie F. Zeidman and a good many others.

Over at 5300 Melrose Avenue was one of the most active Hollywood rental stages. Tec-Art, a New York firm, obtained the studio years after its establishment by William Clune who, by 1915, was employing actor-director Donald Crisp as manager of his studio.

By the coming of the 1920s Tec-Art had, like "Topsy" the famous fictional character, "just growed," encompassing a jumble of stages, offices, shops, storage barns and other disparate buildings.

Nat Levine, one of the most charming and the busiest of film producers from the late 1920s through the late 1930s, produced many of his earliest "Magest" pictures at the Tec-Art lot. In the years following Tec-Art, that studio, at turns, was renamed "Prudential," "California Studio" and "Producers Studio."

*Top:* At 5300 Melrose, the studios which were called, successively, the Tec-Art, Prudential, California, and Producers lots, in Hollywood. *Bottom:* The Tec-Art Studio at 5360 Melrose Ave., Los Angeles, where many independent productions were shot, including some of the earliest Mascot Pictures. Later the studio was called Producer Studios.

**1040 Las Palmas Ave., Los Angeles. This studio has been known as the Hollywood Studios, Metropolitan Studios, and General Services Studios. Numerous Harold Lloyd pictures were made here.**

Another well-equipped motion picture rental lot was the one known in the silent era as the Hollywood Studios. In 1926 it was the headquarters of Harold Lloyd Productions and later of Howard Hughes Productions.

General Services Studios, Inc., by the mid–1930s operated rental lots on both coasts, its eastern one on 35th Avenue in Long Island City, its western studio at 6625 Romaine Street near downtown Hollywood. The parent firm by that time was also supervising such other rental stages as Metropolitan on Las Palmas, and the Educational lot at 7250 Santa Monica, Los Angeles.

On Washington Boulevard in Culver City, close to the MGM studios, the RKO-Pathe lot rented studio space and offices to Liberty Pictures and still later to producer David O. Selznick and some others. Selznick for years utilized the "Southern mansion" facade of the Culver City lot as his impressive-appearing logo.

What is now the Paramount Studio once was the world's largest rental lot, an immense place then called the United Studio and jointly owned by the manager. Before it became the United Studio it was the Brunton Studio, named for the man who designed the facility.

In addition to the many rental studios, there invariably were "locations" for rent or lease to filmmakers. Such locations might consist of one building, an entire ranch, or anywhere else that a producer might wish to use in a picture. Locations such as Iverson's Ranch, Vasquez

Once the Principal Pictures lot of Sol Lesser, this place became the Educational studio in 1922. Pictured here are comic "Ham" Hamilton and others of the studio staff.

Rocks, Corriganville, Chatsworth and many other places could be rented in whole or part. Most of the places frequented by producers of western movies possessed permanent sets which consisted mostly of dummy "fronts" of buildings, but also included roofed four-walled barns, blacksmith shops, as well as buildings which afforded facilities for motion picture players and personnel to "overnight" while a production was in progress.

Nat Levine began his filmmaking career by the use of rental studios and locations; he recalls how convenient and well-equipped many of the rental facilities were. "Many had quantities of props for dressing the sets. Some afforded us buggies, trucks, covered wagons . . . all on hand at short notice."

And of course, rental lots possessed facilities for background projection, as well as for screening rushes, editing, edge-numbering footage, even of conducting research for historical pictures to insure accuracy.

There were also many independent productions made at the major studios. Facilities of MGM, RKO, Universal and others have been used for the production of pictures which may or may not have been released through these studios.

Lippert pictures were made at the Republic lot, a facility which Ken Murray rented for making his Academy Award feature *Bill and Coo.* This picture was also distributed through Republic.

Many of the rental studios have been torn down as urban sprawl drives upward the value of the property on which many studios were built. The Klutho studio at Jacksonville, Florida, was destroyed years ago. So was the venerable and *never used* rental studio at Sun City, Florida. The Miami Studios (actually situated not in Miami but in Opa Locka), after serving as a roller rink, and an emergency shelter, was torn down. None of the several rental studios which once existed in Ft. Lee, New Jersey, remain except one which has metamorphosed into a drab factory with offices.

One still operates, the former Thomas Ince lot at Culver City, California, where *Gone with the Wind* was in large part photographed. It is now looking decrepit and forlorn, though still in use.

What originally were major studios now are mostly rental stages; Fox, MGM, the combined Warner-Columbia lots, all offer space to independent film and TV producers, the film industry being as it is nowadays.

# *Republic Pictures*

Herbert John Yates, a former executive of American Tobacco, entered the film industry in 1916 by way of Hedwig Film Laboratories. Brooklyn-born, he was 36 when two years afterward, he established his Republic Film Laboratories, based originally in the East.

Establishing a film laboratory was not difficult in those years of the motion picture when even the largest and best equipped relied solely upon variations of the simple rack-and-tank method of processing motion picture negatives and prints, and when few laboratories were equipped to process anything but black-and-white film of the primitive orthochromatic type, along with toning and tinting occasional prints.

A year after he organized his film laboratory, Yates established the Allied Film Laboratories Association and, in 1922, he named his firm Consolidated Film Industries.

From its very founding, Consolidated was making the theatrical release prints for countless film production organizations who went to Yates' laboratory in Los Angeles for their processing work. Many were small, precariously financed firms, some of which Yates watched

Soon after its establishment, Republic Pictures began to turn out chapter plays in a steady stream. Pictured are Charles Middleton and Ralph Byrd in a 1938 offering.

carefully as they struggled along, sometimes not even able to pay the laboratory bills which they had run up with his outfit. Out of the welter of such customers, the former tobacco executive observed a few whose output appeared somewhat profitable, such as Mascot, Monogram, Liberty, and Supreme.

Of these, unquestionably hard-driving Nat Levine's Mascot afforded the most valuable assets to Yates. While Monogram, Supreme, and Liberty had no studios — turning out what films they made at rental lots — Levine had recently leased the studio which Mack Sennett had built in North Hollywood in 1927, and could have bought it at the time for $190,000.

Moreover, Levine had purchased some acreage adjacent to the former Sennett lot for future enlargement of Mascot facilities; in addition, he held contracts for screen newcomers Gene Autry and Smiley Burnette, and story rights to western novels by William Colt McDonald, a series featuring a trio of fictional cowboys that McDonald had dubbed "The Three Mesquiteers."

Yates' new studio was named "Republic" after one of his earlier film laboratories. W. Ray Johnston and Trem Carr were placed in top posts

**The sound stages of Republic in the 1940s. This studio, built in 1927, was originally the Mack Sennett Studio. When Sennett fell into bankruptcy, the studio was leased by Nat Levine's Mascot Pictures.**

at Republic, along with Nat Levine who was designated as chairman of the board for all Republic companies. A short time afterward, Johnston and Carr revived their former Monogram firm.

In 1935, Republic began operation, its earliest releases consisting primarily of unreleased productions of Mascot and Monogram. To the outsider, even one who claimed wide knowledge of Hollywood, Republic was securely launched and headed for a place at the top of the independent studios of Hollywood.

Less than a year after Republic was organized, however, serious internal troubles occurred, problems which later were identified by executive Nat Levine as "severe personality clashes." Whatever the causes, both Johnston and Carr withdrew hastily, and Levine succeeded to the post of head of Republic studios.

When Nat Levine had moved his Mascot Pictures firm onto the lot which Republic acquired, he was acquiring some of the finest equipment and stages ever to be controlled by an independent film production firm. Sound recording equipment was modern RCA type, the stages themselves built along relatively recent designs in which the greenhouse-type of structure was eschewed in favor of those designed exclusively for controlled artificial lighting.

In separate buildings, toward the rear of the lot, there was plenty of space for set construction, where two talented, skillful brothers, Ted and Howard Lydecker, working at the rear of the lot, operated the effects and miniatures department. The Lydeckers learned much of their skills from their father, an imaginative craftsman and builder of motion picture sets who had worked for Douglas Fairbanks and for Charles Ray at their studios.

At the beginning the firm had no individualized trademark, so, just after it started production, it adopted an idealized likeness of the attractive Independence Hall in Philadelphia (for reasons unknown). That trademark was abandoned around the close of World War II for the less original one, which wags quickly were to dub "the eagle on a dung heap," a somber rendering of the national symbol, its wings poised as if in flight from some ill-chosen resting place.

Much has been made by film buffs over the fact that, once Republic got under way, it set up an impressive music department, employing its own orchestra, arrangers, music copyists, and conductors to score musical bridges, backgrounds, and title music for all Republic pictures.

In truth, however, the audiences for most Republic productions were unaware of the difference between specially created musical scores and the "canned music" employed by virtually every other small independent studio extant.

As it geared up for a full production schedule, Republic possessed Gene Autry as well as John Wayne; the latter had been utilized for a series of Paul Malvern westerns for Monogram and three chapter plays produced by Nat Levine at Mascot.

Autry and actress Ann Rutherford were both screen discoveries of Nat Levine, Autry entering movies by way of success in radio and phonograph recordings.

Contracted to Nat Levine, Autry had appeared in a Mascot serial which starred cantankerous star Ken Maynard and also as a sort of "guest artist" doing a couple or three western songs in Maynard's western feature *In Old Santa Fe,* both pictures released only a short time before Mascot merged into the new Republic organization. Maynard would have probably been acquired by Republic then except that Levine had suddenly decided not to use Maynard in one of the final Mascot serials, *Phantom Empire,* and quickly substituted his new cowboy, Autry, in the Maynard role.

When Levine elected to become part of Republic, the producer brought along very nearly all the personnel of Mascot: Terry Kellum, who had headed Mascot's sound recording department; the brothers Lydecker; writers and producers such as Armand Schaeffer, Barney Sarecky; and cameramen Ernest Miller and William Nobles.

While the Monogram branch of the new Republic organization at first appeared to be the largest contributing factor to Republic's initial organization, it rather soon became apparent that it was Nat Levine who had unwittingly given Republic very nearly all its initial momentum.

The golden years of Republic began in 1937 and ended about a decade afterward, when most, if not all, Hollywood began its roller-coaster plunge which ended under skies of America splattered with television antennas, just as England's were years before.

This was a world predicted long before Republic Pictures came into being, yet comparatively few of those who were in Hollywood in the 1930s and 1940s foresaw the day when the nation's motion picture industry would be crippled by a new type medium of home entertainment which was more powerful than radio ever had been.

But Yates and the other officials at Republic should have worried about television and changing audience tastes, for Republic was a studio built squarely on "B" pictures, its system of film distribution (both United States and foreign) geared strictly for markets which welcomed, profited from, and utilized quantities of pictures best described as definitely not for elite audiences, although Republic made fine pictures of the types they produced.

As the competition from television became severe, the firm managed to forestall the inevitable by "classing up" their westerns through the use of two different color processes, both dubbed "Trucolor," while also marketing a handful of "Class A" feature films in Technicolor (as with such Republic offerings as *MacBeth* and John Ford's magnificent production *The Quiet Man* with John Wayne, Victor McLaglen, and Maureen O'Hara).

One Republic release, produced for the firm by entertainer Ken Murray, won a special Academy Award: *Bill and Coo* featured a cast consisting entirely of love birds.

Prestigious films might have turned the tide for the ailing production branch of Yates' Consolidated Film Industries, but unfortunately Yates no longer seemed interested in the studio or its precarious future. Marrying Vera Hruba Ralston, the ice skater on whom Yates had squandered a fortune in a vain effort to make her a profitable star, he seemingly then turned his back on Republic, its personnel and its future.

When the studio closed its doors, its parent company, Consolidated, endured, and is one of the Los Angeles area's busiest motion picture laboratories. The Republic lot was idle for but a short time when CBS purchased it, christening the place "CBS Television City."

# RKO and Its Predecessors

While America participated in World War I, Robertson-Cole, British exporters of U.S. pictures, announced that in 1918 they would set

**Hollywood at its most glamorous. This lavish soundstage set was built for use in the Fred Astaire–Ginger Rogers picture *Top Hat* (1936).**

up an American film production outfit and would distribute films both abroad and in the United States.

Accordingly, in 1919 the firm announced plans to establish film exchanges in various sections of the United States, a plan which the firm implemented in 1920 by the acquisition of the entire Hallmark Exchange system. The following year, Robertson-Cole was reorganized and the name changed to R-C Pictures Corporation.

A year prior to the reorganization, another film organization had cropped up: Film Booking Offices of America, which shortly after changed its name to F.B.O. This new firm took over the R-C exchange system, and relegated R-C to a role as a supplier of occasional new product which it copyrighted in the R-C name, but turned over to F.B.O. for release. In 1927, R-C was completely absorbed by F.B.O.

While R-C had attempted to offer a well-balanced program of features and short subjects, F.B.O. was to prove little other than a "western factory," turning out pictures of several types, but showing a preference for those of the sagebrush-and-saddle variety.

Accordingly, when Tom Mix no longer was a highly desirable property at Fox he received a welcome at F.B.O., signing on there for his first "talkies," *King Cowboy* and *Son of the Golden West* (both 1928).

**The RKO studios, Gower and Melrose, 1946. RKO's nextdoor neighbors were the Paramount Studios.**

Continuing at F.B.O., Mix appeared in such pictures as *The Drifter, Outlawed,* and *The Big Diamond Robbery* (all 1929). At F.B.O. also were Buzz Barton, Bob Steele, Tom Tyler, Harry Carey, and Jack Perrin, all of whom contributed large numbers of westerns to the list of releases by that studio.

There were but few exceptions to the output of westerns: In 1928 there was *Hit of the Show* starring Joe E. Brown, 1929 features *Jazz Age* with Douglas Fairbanks, Jr., and *Love in the Desert* with Olive Borden, Hugh Trevor and Noah Beery. F.B.O. even attempted to revive the Valentino legend, using Rudolph's brother in a couple pictures.

At about the time that Tarzan was busily swinging before F.B.O. cameras, an ex-United States ambassador, Joseph P. Kennedy, came into control of the studio, having also taken control of the production facilities of Pathe, enabling himself to draw salaries from both firms as he debated how he could merge the two, collect a handsome profit, and get out of the film business.

While movies gained in popularity worldwide, vaudeville had hit on extremely hard times, an event which was to aid Kennedy. In the sudden decline in the fortunes of vaudeville, two of the greatest of the vaudeville chains elected to merge interests and form a film production outfit, causing the B.F. Keith and Orpheum circuits to eventually come together with RCA, forming an outfit called Radio-Keith-Orpheum, or RKO as it was finally christened. Naturally, it was preferable for the new firm to buy out older, established film producers and distributors. F.B.O. and Pathe answered that need!

When the dust cleared, Kennedy was counting profits from the sales, while Pathe and F.B.O. became part of the RKO conglomerate.

RKO thus found itself in possession of not one, but two complete studios—the former F.B.O. lot in Hollywood, and an older one which had been Pathe's lot at Culver City. For a time the latter was renamed RKO-Pathe, and since RKO was continuing to turn out the so-called "Pathe Newsreel" (though later selling that name to Warners), the firm tried to keep the Pathe name a viable one.

There was widespread public confusion at this time regarding the Pathe name, as it applied to film production as opposed to its use in connection with Pathe Laboratories. Actually, there was no longer a connection between the photographic labs and the production firm (the two had separated some years before).

At the time RKO acquired the Pathe lot it attempted to keep both its studios busy, though as things worked out, it found itself having to help pay the cost of operating the Culver City lot by renting out stages, offices, and editing facilities.

When RKO began operation it hit the market with films which in part had been made by Pathe and F.B.O. before the merger, the backlog of pictures enabling the RKO chieftains to decide on some sort of profitable output of films for the future market. Gradually, westerns were downplayed, allowing a series of George O'Brien offerings, and later a group which starred Tim Holt. Exceptions were such films as John Ford's *Stagecoach* (1939), and some occasional offerings such as John Wayne's *Tall in the Saddle* (1944).

If westerns seldom appeared on the RKO schedule, so too did feature-length comedies of the pratfall-and-pranks variety (although by combining music and attractive girls with a comedy pair named Wheeler and Woolsey, the studio enjoyed more than small profits from this variety of comedy film).

One comedy with the Marx Brothers, *Room Service,* and a pair with Joe E. Brown, *Fit for a King* and *Riding on Air,* were typical of the occasional forays into feature-length slapstick which RKO occasionally made.

The firm gave stiff battle to the likes of MGM and Warners when it began turning out the very profitable Fred Astaire-Ginger Rogers musicals which were soon to set the tone for all RKO musicals, and indeed most of its own light comedies, such as those which starred Cary Grant, Katharine Hepburn and the like. Quickly, it seemed, a sort of

"RKO look" emerged: brightly lighted sets, done in glossy whites, the sets "posh examples of art deco dazzlement," as one critic said of them.

RKO also cornered the distributorship, for a number of years, of Sam Goldwyn's films, as well as the productions of Walt Disney. For further prestige, RKO occasionally managed to release a surprise blockbuster such as Orson Welles' *Citizen Kane* (1940).

The RKO logo also appeared on productions made independently by Sol Lesser, of which *Our Town* (1940) was perhaps the outstanding example. Lesser's minor musical dramas starring Bobby Breen also were for a time profitable, an excellent group of "B" budget attractions.

Down through the golden years of Hollywood, RKO developed a coterie of players who, if not exclusive "stars" of that studio, at least cropped up in many films made there, as witness Robert Mitchum, the Astaire-Rogers combination, Cary Grant, Rosalind Russell, Charles Boyer, Eddie Cantor, and many, many more.

The RKO release schedule called for a good many "B" films, many of which were of a "series" nature and often produced by independent producers who worked at the RKO lot. Such cheaply-made series as *Dr. Christian, Lum 'n' Abner,* and *Scattergood Baines* are examples. The pleasantly remembered *Saint* series, also issued from RKO, was a competently made group of films which were particularly good when they featured George Sanders and Wendy Barrie.

But the problems of maintaining a schedule of profitable releases were almost nothing as compared to maintaining some sort of stability in leadership of the studio. Pandro S. Berman was one of RKO's best studio chieftains.

RKO had always been possessed of a tumultuous history from the days when it had been born out of the remains of Joseph P. Kennedy's F.B.O. From about 1928 until nearly the end of 1950, Radio-Keith-Orpheum was the top holding company of RKO, yet even that upper echelon was splintered among individual stockholders!

To add to this confusion, RKO was in what is termed "equity receivership" from January 1933 through January 1940. Throughout much of this period, RKO's interests had been in the hands of a conglomerate called Atlas Corporation, which had acquired the outfit from RCA. A fellow named Howard R. Hughes had holdings in Atlas, so it is perhaps not surprising that Hughes eventually bought up control by acquisition of Atlas Corporation's stock in RKO.

As Hughes became more and more unorthodox in business and personal affairs, his attempts at running RKO were extremely unsteady. Hughes' heavy, unseen hand moved a succession of studio chieftains in and out of the firm; the operation began to languish, its output becoming more and more irregular in quality and quantity.

Lawsuits and other problems plagued Hughes, at which point he commenced selling off his stock in RKO Theatres Corporation, and later, in RKO Pictures Corporation, the latter sale announced in 1952 but proving abortive, causing Hughes again to take over the studio.

In December 1955, RKO was merged into General Teleradio, resulting in the name change, October 1959, to RKO General. As late as 1976 RKO Pictures continued to exist, although in name only and not as a viable studio, listed only as "a division of RKO General, Inc.," and by then having no Hollywood operations except for bookkeeping affairs and legal matters.

The final RKO film was released in the fall of 1959, though it was distributed on a primitive "states rights" basis, since RKO no longer had film exchanges of its own. RKO's final year of any real release program had been 1955, when a dozen features were offered by the firm.

It would have been far easier to recount this story if the end of RKO's history had come swiftly and cleanly. Instead, the vast chain of RKO theatres went into other hands; the studio itself fell to Desilu Productions; the vast library of old RKO releases (what ones had not disintegrated from age) were sold to television.

But the name, the barest skeleton of the firm, lingered on long after the spirit was gone, as it often is with Hollywood firms.

# Hal Roach

Around 1913, when Harold Lloyd first met Hal Roach, both young men were scratching out an existence as screen extras in movies, most often at the old Universal lot, then situated in downtown Hollywood. Roach, who was born in Elmira, New York, had earlier come to the West Coast area, first to the Pacific Northwest and Alaska. The ownership of a motion picture studio wasn't even a dream in Roach's mind when he came to Los Angeles and found work as a cowboy in J. Warren Kerrigan westerns. Roach and Lloyd paired up as friends, and the two found work wherever they could.

"Roach surprised me . . . one day by announcing that he got hold of several thousand dollars," Lloyd later wrote, "with which he intended making pictures on his own." What's more, Roach talked Lloyd into coming with him at $3 per day as the "top comic" in Roach's first film productions.

When Roach entered film production it was by way of rented

**Hal Roach Studios, neighbors to the MGM lot, Washington Boulevard, Culver City, California.**

quarters in an old mansion which was called simply the Bradbury house, at the time something of a landmark, at least among Los Angeles citizenry. Atop Court Street hill, the old structure glowered down upon downtown Los Angeles like an old maid upon a bevy of young debutantes. In the yard about the estate were a giant palm tree more than 100 feet tall and a huge rubber tree, which Lloyd described as having "roots that were pushing up the cement walks." Immense and drafty, the Bradbury house served as an early office complex for small-time film producers of that era. Here, Mary Pickford, Hobart Bosworth and other players had made pictures. The grand staircase of the structure was, reputedly, much photographed for early films, as were the grounds surrounding.

Setting up his operations in such tattered and faded surroundings, Roach decided first to turn out a profitable novelty film involving a bunch of kids, accompanied by a chauffeur (played by Lloyd), who cavort wildly at the beach, a one-reeler packed with boisterous shenanigans.

*Opposite:* The owner of Hal Roach Studios poses with the 1922 version of his popular screen players "Our Gang" (Reissued theatrically and for television as *The Little Rascals*). Shown besides Roach in the photo, from left to right: Jack Davis, "Farina" Hoskins, Jackie Condon, Mickey Daniels, Mary Kornman, Joe Cobb and "Sunshine Sammy" Morrison.

As the Roach-Lloyd relationship developed, Roach became enthusiastic about Lloyd's possibilities as a screen comic, urging Lloyd to "think up a character." Lloyd answered the request first with one which Roach and his comic christened "Willie Work." By Lloyd's own admission, many of Roach's first comedies were bad, so bad they were never released. Roach eventually began to turn out a surprisingly steady output of comedies acceptable to Pathe, which distributed them, and profitable to distributor and producer alike.

As Lloyd dropped the "Willie Work" character and moved on to one which he christened "Lonesome Luke," Roach moved his company to the Norbig studio, located but half a block from what was then the Keystone studio. While Mack Sennett was the reigning king of screen comedy, Roach was destined, a couple decades hence to usurp Sennett's throne.

While Roach was simply a tenant of the old Norbig studio, and not its owner, his company was by then big enough and sufficiently active enough to require the total area of Norbig.

Laurel and Hardy both came to work at Roach's studio and were fashioned into a comedy team destined to appear in about two-and-a-half-dozen short comedies made in the silent film format. Their initial two-reel Roach comedy, *Slipping Wives,* was released through Pathe on April 3, 1927.

Roach was one Hollywood production mogul who believed staunchly in living in the movie colony and remaining close to his fiefdom much of the time. However, whenever Roach directed one of his pictures, he often ran out of enthusiasm for the project before it was entirely shot and turned over the work of directing the final moments to one of his personnel.

From the Norbig studio, Roach moved his operation to a location on Santa Monica Boulevard soon afterward. He then moved again, back to his former quarters in the old Bradbury house on Court Street.

In 1920, Roach built his own studio, moving there while one of his films, a two-reeler titled *An Eastern Westerner* (which starred Harold Lloyd), was midway through production. Two of the subsequent Lloyd comedies, *Grandma's Boy* and *A Sailor-Made Man,* began as short subjects but were expanded during production to feature-picture length. This was to prove a wise move, indeed, marking, as it did the entry by Roach into production of full-length pictures — just about the only type of comedy picture which was to be sufficient to support a full-scale studio of the sound film era.

Lloyd ultimately left Roach's employ, and the age of silent pictures halted not long afterward. When the change to talkies occurred, several "comedy mills" were still hanging on, including those of Mack Sennett, Educational Film, Christie Brothers and Roach.

MGM happily and profitably assumed distribution of Roach's product during a period when Pathe was preparing to merge with RKO. While under the MGM aegis, Roach gradually phased out the Laurel and Hardy short comedies, making the successful transition to a group of L & H features. He attempted to do the same with films of comic Charley Chase, but did not succeed, and he let Chase go.

Of the short subject "teams" Roach employed, his kiddie comedies, "Our Gang," proved to have the longest-lived appeal. Not only did Roach carry on the series until late 1937, but he then sold the rights to Metro which continued it until 1944.

When talking pictures came into vogue, Roach revamped the stages at his studio, installing at the same time Western Electric recording equipment which was compatible with that being installed at the neighboring Metro. (Both Metro and Roach shortly afterward updated their recording gear to embody Western Electric "Noiseless Recording" attachments.)

The Roach lot at Culver City was one of which the owner had every right to be proud. His was a better looking "film factory" than even the MGM one, its facade an expanded copy of a Southern-style mansion in which respect it was similar to another Culver City lot, that of Thomas Ince.

Behind the neat, picturesque facade of Roach's lot were the various indoor stages—looking for all the world like aircraft hangars. Between these structures and the administrative building was an open area containing what came to be known as "Laurel and Hardy Lake," a combination swimming pool and replica of a natural lake (depending upon the direction the "lake" was photographed).

Farthest from Roach's administrative building was his "back lot," a sprawling outdoor area containing permanent, or semi-permanent, street sets and other exteriors which saw service in many productions made at the Roach studios.

Roach occasionally attempted to turn out films which were of other than a comic nature. He'd secured the use of Rex, the half-wild horse, and in 1924 released the feature *King of the Wild Horses*, for example.

Roach's foray into the field of melodrama was brief. From 1919 to the closing of his studio, most of his films, regardless of length, were of a comic nature. They rarely ventured into even subdued comedy such as that displayed in such feature pictures from the Roach studio as Joan Bennett and Adolph Menjou in *Housekeeper's Daughter* (1939); Fredric March and Virginia Bruce in *There Goes My Heart* (1938); or the modest *Zenobia* (1939), in which Oliver Hardy portrayed a small-town physician who together with his wife (Billie Burke), have their lives momentarily disrupted by an elephant whose keeper (Harry

Langdon) cannot separate his pet from the physician who saved the creature's life.

In 1937, Roach contracted with actor Cary Grant for a salary of $50,000 to appear in the cleverly mounted feature *Topper*, which co-starred Constance Bennett. (Sequels to the successful light comedy were later turned out at Roach, but none again featured Grant.)

By World War II, the Roach lot no longer made short comedies, instead relying upon productions of feature length in order to keep the operation profitable. The MGM distributorship of such Roach films had, by then, passed to United Artists under whose aegis Roach experimented with what he called "streamliner features," abbreviated, modestly budgeted light comedies designed for use as the lower half of double feature programs. The streamliner pictures were less than one hour in length and were cast with players who either were relatively unknown or were ones who otherwise proved inexpensive to hire. Bobby Watson turned up in a few (usually cast in the role of a comic Adolph Hitler, as in *The Nazty Nuisance*, 1944). Noah Beery, Jr., and Will Rogers' son, Jimmy, were paired in the feature brevities *Calaboose*, *Prairie Chickens* and others. William Tracy, Jimmy Gleason, Joseph Sawyer, William Bendix, Grace Bradley, Frances Langford, Johnny Downs, Marjorie Woodworth and scores of other second-string players were to be seen in these Roach films.

In 1942, Roach succeeded in getting himself commissioned as a colonel in the Signal Corps of the United States Army, at which point nearly all the Roach studios' facilities began to function as a training film headquarters. It proved an astute move for Roach, who thus managed to keep his studio financially solvent until the war ended.

Not long after the war the specter of television cast its ghostly flickering, but ever-brightening, visage across all Hollywood, promoting Roach to enter the field of television, for there was obviously no future for feature-film production.

Launching a few television series, Roach and his son set out to conquer the new electronic medium, only to find rather quickly that they were unable to compete successfully. By the beginning of the 1960s, the Roach studios were razed to make room for postwar building projects, the nature of which had rendered film studios dinosaurs within a world where properties in Culver City, California, were far too valuable for their continued use as mere fun factories.

# *The Joseph Schenck Studio*

The address was along New York City's East 48th Street, Manhattan, in what formerly had been an old warehouse. Even after Joseph Schenck had poured a great deal of money into refurbishing the structure and converting it into a movie studio it was still described by author Anita Loos as "ramshackle to a degree." Unimpressive the studio may have been, but it was the place where, on each working day, Norma and Constance Talmadge might be glimpsed leaving or arriving in their custom-built Cadillacs. One might have glimpsed Roscoe "Fatty" Arbuckle shooting scenes for the comedy *The Grocer Boy,* in which he introduced screen audiences to a veteran stage knockabout comedian named Buster Keaton.

Joseph Schenck had established his New York studio following an already rather successful career. He, his brother Nicholas, and their parents had come to America from Russia (where Joseph was born on December 25, 1892), being nine when he emigrated to the United States.

Just how quickly the Schenck brothers learned the path to commercial success in their adopted land may be judged by the fact that in 1908 the two had enough business acumen to operate an amusement enterprise, Paradise Park, at Fort George in northern New York state — an operation so successful that it permitted the two brothers to purchase, in 1912, Palisades Park, near Fort Lee, New Jersey.

As the two were so involved, they became associated with Marcus Loew, a theatre owner and operator in their region, the brothers soon coming into key positions with Loew's firm.

All those activities didn't prove to be enough for Joe Schenck: acquiring the screen rights to a magazine story, he engaged director Roland West and obtained the services of stage actress Josie Collins, producing a film which subsequently was released by Fox. Schenck followed that one with a pair of films in which he starred Elizabeth Nesbit Thaw.

These activities in film production served only to whet his filmic appetite. He signed ex–Keystone comic Roscoe "Fatty" Arbuckle for a series of comedies for release by Paramount.

In 1918, he became the producer for Norma Talmadge, a young actress whom Schenck had become aware of through an agent and promoter named Lewis J. Selznick. The first picture which Schenck was to produce with his new ingenue was *Panthea.*

His roster of contract players grew quickly. In 1919, he added Buster Keaton as a contractee and even before that, Constance Talmadge,

*Top:* At the Joseph Schenck Studio, New York City, Roscoe "Fatty" Arbuckle made numerous comedies. In this production *(His Wedding Night,* 1917) Arbuckle included in the cast a knockabout stage comic named Buster Keaton. *Opposite:* The Robert Brunton Studios, 5341 Melrose Avenue, Los Angeles, as it appeared a few years before its sale to Joseph Schenck and M.C. Levee (who renamed it United Studio). Today it is the site of Paramount. (Photo courtesy of Film Favorites)

sister of Norma. His studio became so busy that he soon found himself an important independent producer, eventually turning out Talmadge Films for First National and Keaton pictures for Metro.

Following his marriage to Norma Talmadge, Schenck had purchased the warehouse in New York for a studio, entering partnership with director Allen Dwan. Then, at the request of Schenck, John Emerson and his wife, Anita Loos, quit Douglas Fairbanks and traveled from Hollywood to New York City to devote their services to the Schenck operations. The initial picture that Loos and Emerson wrote for Schenck was the Constance Talmadge offering *The Bachelor*, followed by *A Temperamental Wife* and *A Virtuous Vamp*.

Until the 1920s Schenck's warehouse studio was the site where several film productions were made at the same time. Anita Loos recalls that in 1914 Norma Talmadge had her company of players, personnel and sets on the first floor of the warehouse when she was at work on *Poppy* with Eugene O'Brien, while her sister had her own company on the second floor. On the third floor, Fatty Arbuckle and Buster Keaton were at work. The top floor, you ask about? That one, according to Miss Loos, was occupied by sets, players and crew for the feature released as *Old France*, starring Erich von Stroheim.

In her 1978 volume *The Talmadge Girls*, Anita Loos wrote flippantly, "although we never knew it Art was beginning to stick his nose through the chinks of Joe's ratty old studio, summoned by the youthful genius of Buster Keaton, Erich von Stroheim and Greta Garbo."

*In Search of a Sinner*, one of the pictures made at Schenck's New York studio, brought together a cast which included, besides Constance Talmadge, such players as Gilda Gray and Ned Sparks.

*Love Expert* featured a third Talmadge sister, Natalie, a rather plain-looking girl who failed to achieve any audience-following as a result of this, her only film.

Operating a studio in the area in and around New York City had marked advantages: talent from the Broadway stage was available in an endless stream to film producers in the East; the financial hub for the motion picture had long been in New York City, as had the headquarters of nearly all the large studios.

Probably for one or all of those reasons (and possibly because of his connections with Marcus Loew, as well as his interests in New York amusement parks) Joseph Schneck continued to operate his Manhattan film studio until the end of the summer of 1921. In the late fall, he shuttered the studio on East 48th Street and moved his entire production operation to Los Angeles.

Anita Loos explains the move by Schenck: "The California sunlight was free, while Kleig lights in our Manhattan studio were expensive to operate." Her explanation seems an oversimplification, because even in the early years of the 1920s, while greenhouse-type stages were still in use in California, a great deal of artificial lighting already had come into use there. At any rate, the Schenck company moved into a studio on Hollywood's famed Sunset Boulevard, the players and personnel temporarily ensconced at the venerable, towered Hollywood Hotel.

Schenck's early Hollywood productions were turned out on an outdoor stage with the ubiquitous muslin travellers on wires over the stage to reduce the glare of the sunlight and to achieve a softer, more pleasant illumination, filled in by shiny reflectors to "bounce" sunlight off actors' faces and costumes.

When First National was organized, Schenck contracted with the new firm to release his feature films beginning with the 1922 picture *The Eternal Flame,* in which Norma Talmadge and Conway Tearle were starred, and which Frank Lloyd directed.

*The Eternal Flame* was filmed not on the outdoor stage on Hollywood Boulevard but at the former Brunton Studio, Hollywood, which Schneck had joined hands with M.C. Levee to jointly purchase in 1922. The two partners renamed this operation the United Studio, and began advertising it as a rental lot, claiming it to be the largest independent motion picture studio in the world. (It is now the Paramount Studio.)

In December 1924, Schenck was elected chairman of the board of directors of United Artists, which indirectly led him to co-found Twentieth Century Pictures, in which his partner was Darryl Zanuck. In May 1935, Twentieth Century, which had been releasing its product through United Artists, merged with Fox Film.

In 1941, while Schenck was yet head of 20th Century–Fox, he was convicted of tax evasion and perjury and served four months in prison. Upon his release he found himself demoted to a minor post as an advisor at Fox, his Hollywood career abruptly ended.

# Selig Polyscope

He marketed one of America's earliest weekly newsreels, and more than a dozen of its first "musicals," yet "Colonel" William N. Selig closed his film studios before World War I ended, his fortune made and his contributions to film history behind him.

The Selig name today is almost totally unknown except to serious students of motion picture history, though it was under the Selig banner that a Pennsylvania cowboy named Tom Mix made most of his pictures.

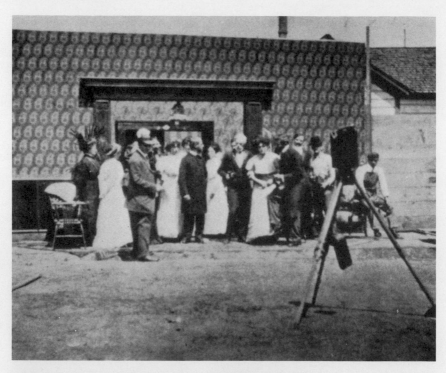

*Top:* **The first studio anywhere in California was established in Los Angeles in 1908 by Selig Polyscope.** *Bottom:* **1845 Allesandro St., Los Angeles. Originally the William Selig Studio, this Edendale, California, studio was briefly the William Fox Studio in 1916.**

**Selig Zoo-Studio entrance at 3800 Mission Road, Eastlake Park, Los Angeles, 1913. This facility was used for filming jungle pictures. Covering 32 acres of ground, it housed one of the largest animal collections in the United States.**

The Selig trademark also appeared on the first film version of Rex Beach's *The Spoilers*, as well.

When the motion picture firm of Selig Polyscope was at the peak of its earnings, Colonel Selig walked about grandly dressed, carrying a pearl-studded walking stick, the superb picture of a retired military man, though in truth he'd usurped the title of colonel in the days when he operated a fly-by-night medicine show, distinguished in later years only by the fact that it happened to employ for a time the great entertainer Bert Williams.

It was odd that when Selig entered the motion picture business, he chose Chicago as the site for his earliest studio, because, of all the early U.S. filmmakers, Selig probably knew California most thoroughly. After all, the Selig medicine show plied its trade primarily along the West Coast!

But Chicago wasn't so unlikely a place for a film studio when one considers that Selig cameras went "on location" for most of their westerns and outdoor films (and these productions were extremely numerous because Selig made one-, two- and three-reel pictures for the nation's nickelodeons). Besides, silent film studios were simple to establish, most comprised of nothing more complicated than "stages" which were raised platforms above which muslin sheets were arranged on wires so as to screen somewhat the harshness of the sun. By 1915 Selig had established branch studios in Jacksonville, Florida, near Prescott, Arizona (where Selig star and director Tom Mix made so many films), and at Edendale, California (a suburb of Los Angeles). Selig's crews had also been on location in Colorado, and to countless other parts of the United States.

There was this to be said for Selig's Chicago headquarters: The

*Wm. N. Selig* presents

# TOM MIX

in

## "GOING WEST to MAKE GOOD"

**Tom Mix, the quintessential screen cowboy, entered the movies by means of short films made by Selig Polyscope.**

Colonel found much star material in the Windy City or willing to journey there, players such as Bryant Washburn, Lester Cuneo, Kathlyn Williams, Victoria Forde, William Duncan, and Charles Clary.

In 1907 the colonel had dispatched a small film crew out to California, a group headed by a former stage director named J. Francis Boggs. Along with Boggs was a small cast of players and enough other personnel to establish a "rooftop studio" on a commercial building situated on 8th and Olive streets in Los Angeles. Once set up, the little company cranked out a one-reeler adapted from the storyline of the opera *Carmen,* while also accomplishing some location scenes for a picture which Selig studios in Chicago had already begun: *Count of Monte Cristo.* On stretches of beach from Laguna to Venice, and using a completely different cast of players than had appeared in the Chicago-made sequences, Boggs secured some surprisingly excellent footage which when sent back to Selig in Chicago, prompted the studio in 1909 to again rent studio space in Los Angeles, this time a back lot behind Sing Loo's Chinese laundry on Olive Street.

The following year, Selig proudly opened a full-scale studio in

California, in the Edendale area of Los Angeles, at 1845 Allesandro Avenue.

The somewhat quaint, quasi–Spanish studio was walled in by a fake adobe wall which was punctured at intervals by arched openings, within each of which hung a small replica of a mission bell.

The studio itself contained stages, dressing rooms, offices, and a modestly sized film laboratory. It was a layout which might have seemed more of an accomplishment to the colonel but for the fact that his most popular film cowboy, Tom Mix, was establishing still another studio for Selig, this one at Prescott, Arizona. In 1912 and 1913 Selig operated a branch studio in Canõn City, Colorado, producing weterns. It moved out of Colorado to Tucson, Arizona, in the fall of 1913. Then, too, Selig soon conceived the idea of constructing a larger California studio, at which a "Selig Zoo" could be operated year-round and thus provide the studio with a good part of its annual upkeep costs.

With that in mind Selig set crews to work in 1913 upon a piece of land totaling some 32 acres at 3800 Mission Road, Eastlake Park. Before 1917, Selig had left the studios on Allesandro to William Fox (who for a short time occupied that lot while Fox's studio on Western Avenue was being prepared).

While all these events were unfolding, Selig had made an arrangement with publisher William Randolph Hearst establishing a weekly Hearst-Selig Newsreel, which followed onto the market such pioneering newsreels as those of Pathe and Universal. Hearst and Selig were not newcomers to partnership; they had paired up before when Hearst had helped Selig to produce the serial *Adventures of Kathlyn,* which had starred sultry Kathlyn Williams. The storyline of the serial was worked with a "tie-in" of weekly installments of an *Adventures of Kathlyn* serialization in Hearst newspapers, whereby both Hearst and Selig profited.

A study of the colonel's other motion picture releases will reveal that on April 6, 1914, his firm was awarded copyrights for a "package" of 14 one-reel subjects, all featuring the Scottish folksinger Harry Lauder, and all of them "talkies" distributed with synchronized phonograph records on which Lauder lustily sang such Scottish favorites as "I Love a Lassie," "Roamin' in the Gloamin'" and a dozen more. (Moviemakers had realized the value of sound as accompaniment to film as early as 1894 when, in its Kinetoscope catalog, the Edison Company pointed out that it had in stock numerous cylinder recordings which were designed to accompany the short films it was releasing.)

Mention of the Edison Company calls to ths writer's mind the fact that Selig was sued by the Motion Picture Patents Company, of which Edison was a member in extremely good standing. On October 24, 1907, Judge Christian K. Kahlsaat of the federal court in Chicago ruled that Selig's motion picture cameras infringed upon Edison's patents. The ruling proved a definite contributory factor to Selig's tacitly agreeing to join the Motion Picture Patents Company!

Even today there is occasional mention of how Selig, a short-lived firm indeed, was a charter member of the Patents Company (a "pool" consisting also of Lubin, Essanay, Pathe, and Kleine).

Virtually all the original members of the Patents Company failed to make the sweeping changeover to full-length, multiple-reel feature pictures which occurred between 1912 and 1914. Only Vitagraph and Pathe were successful in doing so. Edison, Lubin, Essanay, and the other Patents members folded their camera tripods permanently at that time.

Selig Polygraph made a half-hearted attempt to introduce feature productions into its schedule. One ambitious feature was undertaken for Selig by Tom Mix, but never completed. (Mix left Selig's employ ultimately for a long-term contract with Fox.) Yet, when the gigantic Mark Strand Theatre opened along Times Square, New York, it was a full-length feature picture of Selig's which served triumphantly as the initial attraction, starring William Farnum, Bessie Eyton, Wheeler Oakman, and Thomas Santschi in the first filmization of Rex Beach's novel *The Spoilers*. Initially the novelist had demanded no less than $2500 for the screen rights to *The Spoilers*, but allowed Selig to talk him into accepting a royalty instead, something which turned a small fortune for Beach. It seemed, in fact, that several people connected with the Selig film fared exceedingly well on the picture; Farnum, a former stage star, went on to even greater stardom in films after he made *The Spoilers*, while Colonel Selig is said to have boasted often that he'd made a fortune on that single picture alone.

But Selig was not one to rest quietly on past achievements. He always had his "story scout," John Pribyl, contracting for new story materials, often with famous authors of at least Rex Beach's stature, including James Oliver Curwood, whose novels were then in great vogue.

As Selig's fame and properity reached their crest, surely the former medicine show operator must have looked smilingly over his shoulder, looking back on his beginnings in the film industry, and on days when his film studio was capable of turning out nothing longer, or more ambitious, than the early Selig one-reelers, such as *Trapped by Bloodhounds* or *Lynching at Cripple Creek*. Selig's first Chicago studio was then a mere hole-in-the-wall operation situated at 43 Peck Court, a place which in reality was little more than an alley. In those days, at a saloon nearby, Selig directors often recruited casts of untrained actors and extras for the one-reelers which Selig was making in great quantities. Such casts, for a Sunday's work, received no more remuneration than their lunch and a barrel of beer.

Ah, Selig probably thought as he recalled those first days of filmmaking, he'd come a long way since then!

In July 1910, it must have become clear to Selig that his fortunes in motion picture production were about to peak. A Selig film, made in Arizona and titled *Ranch Life in the Great Southwest,* showed a 10-second closeup of a cowboy who seemed possessed of such excitement potential that his mere appearance was able to lift the action contained in that prosaic film many times over. The cowboy's name? Tom Mix.

From that time on, the output of Mix's films from Selig was incredible. The maze of one- and two-reelers which Mix directed, often wrote, and very nearly always starred in, totaled very nearly a film per week through the pre–World War I period, including *Why the Sheriff Is a Bachelor* (1914), *Chip of the Flying U* (1914), *Bill Haywood, Producer* (1915), *Cowpuncher's Peril* (1916), *Tom's Sacrifice* (1916), *Tom's Strategy* (1916), and such three-reel pictures as *Pals in Blue* (1915).

The last-named picture, by the way, did not have a running time of 30 minutes as many, many film historians claim. Apparently those writers have forgotten (or else didn't know) that one reel of silent film, which was filmed at a speed of approximately 16 frames of film per second (not 24 frames as are all "talkie" pictures), ran 15 minutes. Thus, a three reeler in the silent mode ran very nearly as long as many "talkie" westerns, which ran about 60 minutes, whereas the three-reel silent subject ran 45. The overall output of Selig films, especially from 1913 to 1917, was immense, though most were but one- and two-reel subjects, it must be remembered.

Like most other members of the Motion Picture Trust, the Selig firm seemed unwilling or unable to gear facilities to turning out quantities of full-length feature pictures. But in 1915, Selig managed to produce a five-reel film version of an Agatha Christie novel, *The Circular Staircase,* the picturization having been directed by Edward Le Saint.

As the vogue for shorter films wound down, Selig continued in production. But, like the Edison Company, Lubin, and other film pioneers, the "Colonel" had banked a fortune on his effort and was unwilling to lose his money on expensive new feature pictures. By the time World War I was over, so too were the years of Selig activity.

He'd turned out a handful of full-length feature pictures, it's true, including not only *The Spoilers* and *The Circular Staircase,* but also *At Piney Ridge* (five reels, 1916), *The Barker* (five reels, 1917), *The Crisis* (a twelve-reeler made from a book by Winston Churchill, 1916), *The Cycle of Fate* (five reels, 1916), and *Danger Trail* (five reels, 1917). One of the last of the Selig feature pictures to be released was one titled, ironically, *Ghost of Yesterday* (1918).

For a ghost of yesterday was what Selig Polyscope had gradually, slowly become.

# Mack Sennett

Even dressed in meticulously tailored clothes, Mack Sennett looked to be nothing more than a simple country bumpkin, an appearance which was further accented by a shock of hair which usually hung in a sort of casual wisp on his forehead, highlighting his rural origins.

A confirmed chewer of strong "plug" tobacco, the Canadian, even after he'd begun his reign as the unquestioned "King of Custard Comedy," noisily chewed away on Bull Durham as he viewed his studio's latest films in his crowded screening room, where a rocking chair was Mack's throne, almost as well-known to film aficionados of today as the oversized, ornate bathtub in his office. There he often relaxed while holding court with his jesters, scribes and other figures from his wild kingdom.

For a filmmaker whose career has been well documented, there is much that even the most avid film buffs don't know or else choose to overlook.

One biography of Sennett, *Father Goose* by Gene Fowler, describes many of Sennett's idiosyncracies amusingly but never even approaches accuracy in recounting the basic facts of Sennett's career.

Born in Denville, Quebec, Canada, in about 1880 or 1884, Mickall Sennett (the original spelling of his surname was "Sinnott") migrated to the United States, eventually finding work at the American Mutoscope and Biograph studio in New York City—first as stagehand, scenery painter, and bit actor, but later as a disciple of and assistant to director D.W. Griffith.

By the time Griffith resigned from Biograph, Sennett had already departed, both men ultimately ending up on the West Coast, at first working for different film outfits. In Sennett's case, beginning in 1912, he was head of a comedy mill called "Keystone Comedies," one of a group of production units under control of a couple of one-time racetrack touts, Adam Kessel and Charles Bauman.

In those days, names for film companies were often purloined, usually from sources far afield from the motion picture. In the case of the comedy factory of Mack Sennett, an Eastern railroad was the source, specifically a timetable for the Pennsylvania Railroad, which utilized a well-known logo, consisting of an idealized outline of the Keystone employed atop an archway.

It is Keystone Comedies most film enthusiasts are speaking of whenever they point to what they often refer to as the "heyday" of Mack Sennett. The years when Sennett operated his "Studio City" did not begin until after his association with Kessel and Bauman and their New York Motion Picture Company.

By the time Sennett occupied his own studio, the one in North Hollywood, talking pictures were soon to cloud the horizon. Almost before Sennett could blink his bewildered eyes, he found himself obliged to equip his stages with equipment, acoustic material, and added personnel for sound recording.

The talking comedy quickly became part of Sennett's stock-in-trade, as did musical short subjects, many of the latter featuring a youthful baritone named Bing Crosby, and once Bing moved on, a replacement singer, Donald Novis.

In September 1932, Sennett stopped releasing his product through the Educational exchanges, leaving the remainder of his 1932 productions, and all his 1933 releases, for Paramount release, a move he was to shortly regret: Paramount entered bankruptcy in early spring 1933.

When he was titular head of Kessel and Bauman's Keystone Comedies, Sennett had shaped a frantic but successful schedule, a production machine with concomitant techniques which caused the operation to work profitably and unfailingly. When he established his own studio, he used the same methods.

Sennett's own studio was constructed on a "gift parcel" of land, 20 acres which had been deeded to the comedy producer by a group of enterprising real estate operators in the San Fernando Valley.

Sennett claimed he spent half a million dollars building the new studio, christened "Studio City," its main gate at 4024 Radford, the lot comprising a quasi-Spanish style two-story administration building, several stages, a few other structures, and a "back lot" for outdoor sequences, all spaced apart so generously that after the conglomeration passed into the hands of Republic Pictures, considerable other construction could be managed without giving the lot the crowded appearance.

At about the time his new studio was under construction, according to later claims by Sennett, his total financial worth was somewhere near $15,000,000. Sennett had come far from the time when every few dollars spent had to be justified to other men, including explanations to producer Thomas Ince, who at that time owned 100 percent of Keystone Comedies.

Contrasting with the former Keystone Comedies' lot in Edendale, the North Hollywood lot was strikingly different. The Edendale headquarters for Mack Sennett comedies, according to Chaplin, was "dilapidated, with a green fence around it. . . . The entrance . . . a garden path, through an old bungalow."

Chaplin theorized that the Edendale lot might once have been a farm, inasmuch as Mabel Normand's dressing room was part of an old bungalow near which stood an old barn which Sennett employed as the dressing room and costume storage area for use by minor players in the Keystone films. That was how Chaplin remembered the place, although others say it consisted in part of a former grocery store.

Whatever the exact appearance of the Edendale lot, Sennett could rightfully point with pride to the fact that his own studio, the one in North Hollywood, utilized no second-hand structures.

Unfortunately for Sennett, he was pouring a fortune into his studio just prior to this nation's great economic collapse, a debacle which followed in less than two years after Sennett opened his studio in 1927.

By the time the Great Depression had steamrollered its way across America (and, eventually, most of the rest of the world as well), Sennett had been forced to contend with the invasion of the talking picture, the "talkie" animated cartoon, and the double feature program which began to force its way into motion picture theatres everywhere, all of which seemed to militate against the continuation of the short slapstick comedy.

Sennett attempted to switch his production schedule so as to embrace a few light, breezy musical shorts, more than a few of which featured Bing Crosby.

W.C. Fields, a highly individualized comic who'd appeared on-screen as early as the era of voiceless films when he'd played in the D.W. Griffith features *Sally of the Sawdust* and *That Boyle Girl,* joined the Sennett ranks in the "talkie era."

Today the legion of lovers of Fields' misanthropic sort of comedy avidly collects such of his Sennett comedies as *The Pharmacist, The Dentist,* and others, ignoring the deplorable cheapness, the utter lack of production values of these films, and the fact that in the 1930s, when they were issued, numerous theatre managers, owners, and bookers complained loudly of adverse audience reactions whenever such films were on their programs.

But if his output of short films of that period was deplorable, it also embraced a few short subjects which were filmed in what the producer less than modestly named "Sennett Color." A bi-pack film akin to Cinecolor and Multicolor, and not at all a bad process, Sennett Color was the equal of the old two-strip Technicolor which was in use at that time. Sennett Color subjects such as *Movie Town* (1931) with George Olsen's Orchestra, and Sennett himself in a sort of guest role, reveal a color process which deserved wider use than Sennett was able to provide.

The output of the Sennett studio in 1932 had been entered for copyright before the end of September of that year, his productions after that time being copyrighted through Paramount or, in the case of the deplorable Moran and Mack feature *Hypnotized,* through a small firm which released through World Wide.

The final year in which Sennett's studio operated was 1933, a year in which the owner released but a handful of sadly cheap films.

Although his studio was not six years old, it shut down at the onset of the fourth year of the Great Depression, Sennett subsequently blaming Paramount for his bankruptcy.

Sennett himself got out with few assets other than personal belongings, most of his assets lost in the U.S. stock market crash and the collapse of his studio. "Studio City" remained empty while its fate was decided in bankruptcy court.

Nat Levine's Mascot Pictures took over the studio about a year after Sennett had entered bankruptcy, leasing with an option to buy the studio. Levine ultimately transferred the lease to Republic Pictures, which ultimately bought the studio outright. Today the facility is known as CBS Television City.

Sennett managed to find work within the industry, including that of director and author of the original story for the dreadful Moran and Mack feature film *Hypnotized* (1932). Later he directed a handful of short comedies for Educational including *Way Up Thar* with Joan Davis, *Timid Young Man* with Buster Keaton, *Just Another Murder* with Vince Barnett and Billy Gilbert, and others.

He also wrote and sold scripts to producer Jules White at Columbia and directed the 1944 Columbia comedy *To Heir Is Human,* which starred one-time Mack Sennett contractee Harry Langdon, and released *Down Memory Lane,* a compendium of some of his early pictures, which was distributed through PRC.

But probably the single factor which restored Sennett's financial equilibrium was that his late mother, using primarily funds she'd wheedled out of Mack back when his financial cup was running over, had enlarged the family farm in Canada, acquiring much additional acreage (on most of which, after her death, mineral deposits were discovered, including asbestos, oil, and gold).

With this new fortune, Sennett was again able to live comfortably, for the remainder of his life.

# Thanhouser

The March 25, 1956, editions of newspapers in New Rochelle, New York, devoted nearly half a column on an inside page to the death, a day earlier, of film pioneer Edwin Thanhouser. His passing was not so prominently noted elsewhere in the United States. Pioneers seldom are given much space in newspapers.

New Rochelle journalists paid their minor tribute to the man because he once had operated a full-scale motion picture studio in an abandoned skating rink in that city, and there had filmed the series of "Falstaff" comedies.

Thanhouser, ninety at the time of his death, had entered show business as a minor player in stage presentations. Born in Baltimore (or in Fort Wayne, Indiana, some sources say), he had pursued employment as an actor as early as the 1880s, gradually working his way into the managerial and production end of show business, all the while accumulating both experience and savings. By 1909 he was operating his own film studio, said to be the first to be operated by an experienced member of the theatrical profession.

Just what caused Thanhouser to establish his motion picture studio in the town of New Rochelle, New York, isn't entirely clear. It may have been that the place was far enough from New York City to have low taxes yet close enough to acquire Broadway acting talent whenever needed. At any rate the entrepreneur bought the physical facilities of a large skating rink situated on that city's Grove Avenue, directly across from Ruppert's Brewery.

Mr. Thanhouser was later to admit that he didn't know a lot about the film business, but neither did most of the stockholders in his new firm. "They knew nothing about actors, or the value of situations," Thanhouser said later. "They were from all walks of life and every business but the motion picture industry."

The new firm had rushed into motion picture production at a time when the powerful Motion Picture Patents Company formed to produce all the motion pictures needed by film exhibitors. To attain such a stranglehold on the industry, the Patents group (which included Pathe, Edison, Biograph, and a handful of others) claimed to have certain basic patents on motion picture cameras and projectors.

Yet, outside this elite circle, a growing group of independent film producers had come into being. Thanhouser joined the outsiders.

The Thanhouser studio's initial production was written by Lloyd Lonergan and Mrs. Thanhouser (a former stage actress). Their script was *The Mad Hermit*, a love story, murder, and a daring robbery all wrapped onto a 1000-foot reel. Filmed by a former Edison cameraman, the picture was shot in about two weeks.

There was some difficulty in marketing the film (all independent film production has always faced problems of distribution). Thanhouser followed the tried-and-true method of "states rights" distribution — dealing with film exchanges throughout the country and selling the rights to prints of their productions while hoping for rather prompt return of their initial investment.

Once these markets had been secured, the studio was able to undertake further production. *The Actor's Children* and a one-reel version of *Jane Eyre* followed, marketed much as the first Thanhouser film had been, with one exception: A film distributor from Australia came to New Rochelle and gave Thanhouser $10,000 cash for a set of negatives for all pictures which had been made thus far. "He cleaned me out," commented the film producer, "my first real return on my investment in the business."

From that extremely modest beginning, Thanhouser Film Corporation became a film producer of considerable repute. With reputation there followed an almost steady stream of profits, which in turn permitted the firm to set up a Florida studio in Jacksonville. Charles J. Hite had entered the firm as well as W.E. Snellenberger. Snellenberger brought with him a young graduate of an Iowa business school, W. Ray Johnston, who shortly after was placed in charge of finances (and went on to become founder and head of Monogram Pictures).

As with most film studios, the Thanhouser firm built a stock company of players. The firm's early stalwarts included a young leading man named James Cruze and a leading lady named Marguerite Snow who later married Cruze. Harry Benham, Florence LaBadie, Lila Chester and Sidney Bracy were among others of the regular players in pictures made in New Rochelle.

The former skating rink, which had been converted into a studio, provided not only an area for stages but also space for the film processing laboratory, screening and editing areas, and a small area in which the firm perforated its film, both negative and positive types (this was a time when the primitive orthochromatic negative stock and the printing stock, too, were supplied by manufacturers in unperforated, ribbon-like material).

On the afternoon of Monday, January 13, 1913, the Thanhouser Film Corporation's entire plant was completely destroyed by fire, the blaze apparently having started in the film perforating room, possibly from a faulty electric motor in one of the mechanisms. Although no lives were lost in the blaze, all cameras were lost as was most of the picture *Sherlock Holmes*, which was in production that day.

"All employees in the factory and studio had narrow escapes," reported the New Rochelle paper that day. "Miss Marguerite Snow, the leading woman, lost her entire new wardrobe which arrived this morning."

A Mrs. Hattie McCroskery was the heroine of the day, for she dared to dash into the film store room and hand out reels of film in tin containers to waiting helpers who tossed the film out windows to where they could be carried to safety. The newspaper reported that Mrs. McCroskery had remained in the blazing building as long as it was possible to do so.

Simultaneously, C.J. Hite, president of the studio, Bert Adler, the publicity agent, and an office boy named John Desmond removed other valuable contents, including office records.

The studio was totally consumed by flames within an hour after the outbreak of fire, the loss estimated at $60,000, on which there was no insurance.

Records aren't entirely clear as to Edwin Thanhouser's connection with the studio at the time of the fire. What is certain is that he sold his share in the firm some time before the fire, although he was destined to play a part as a manager of the firm during the period when the organization finally disbanded.

At any rate, Thanhouser himself appears to have had no monetary investment in the studio at the time of the fire nor in the new studio later established on Main Street at the corner of Evans. It was at the new studio that the Thanhouser firm reached what was to be its greatest degree of success, the production of a serial which was to prove one of the most successful of that era.

Some time prior to Thanhouser's entry into serial production, the *Chicago Tribune* had co-sponsored a serial titled *The Adventures of Kathlyn,* the film and simultaneous newspaper versions of which had tremendously boosted circulation of that paper. As a result, the *Tribune* was ready to undertake another such cooperative plan with whatever studio proved capable of turning out the serial, which was to be titled *Million Dollar Mystery,* the filmmaker to be selected through the advertising agency of Nichols-Finn of Chicago.

By an outlandish coincidence, one of the partners in that ad agency, Joseph Finn, happened to meet, in the smoking car of the train *Twentieth Century Limited,* the scenario chief of Thanhouser, Lloyd Lonergan who, in turn, introduced Finn to Charles Hite, president of Thanhouser. The three men proceeded to discuss the intentions of the *Chicago Tribune* and just how Thanhouser studio might be able to enter into the plans.

Terry Ramsaye in his book *A Million and One Nights* tells what happened then: "Now came the Syndicate Film Corporation, floated through John Burnham and Company of Chicago, to finance the *Million Dollar Mystery* to be made by Thanhouser and promoted as a newspaper feature by the *Tribune.*

"James M. Sheldon, famous football star in the days of his glory at the University of Chicago, became president of the Syndicate concern.

"At New Rochelle, Hite put the picture into production with a cast which included Florence LaBadie, Marguerite Snow, and James Cruze."

Lloyd Lonergan, head of Thanhouser's scenario department, wrote the script for the serial. The newspaper version of it was written for the *Chicago Tribune* by Harold McGrath.

*Million Dollar Mystery* was an amazing success. Its 23 chapters appeared eventually in 7,000 motion picture houses in America, a truly amazing record when one considers that there existed only about 18,000 U.S. theatres at that time.

Production costs of the serial were somewhere around $125,000. It is said to have grossed approximately a million and a half dollars.

But tragedy occurred close on the heels of the success of the Thanhouser serial: Charles Hite, president of the firm, was killed on the night of August 22, 1914, in an auto crash in which he plunged through the railing of a Harlem River viaduct. Stockholders of the serial concern thereby shared in a $100,000 insurance policy on Hite's life, netting the stockholders about a 700 percent profit on their stock.

Following Hite's death, Edwin Thanhouser returned to the firm he had founded (he and his wife had been residing in Switzerland) and proceeded to liquidate the affairs of the studio. It was a tangled web which required about two years for Thanhouser to accomplish. For this work he received a salary, for by that time he had no stock or other interests in the firm.

Years after his final association with the New Rochelle studio, Edwin Thanhouser and his wife revisited that city. A retired, wealthy man by then, Thanhouser had become well-known as a world traveller and a collector of art objects.

Prone to reminisce, he told a reporter for the New Rochelle *Standard Star,* "I have done with my life exactly what I wanted. I was in the theatre and made enough money, but most of all, I retired young enough to enjoy it."

What a pity more show business lives weren't the financial successes of Edwin Thanhouser's.


# Tiffany


Just why Tiffany is forgotten is something of a mystery. Few film fans recall it, and fewer still can remember any pictures which carried the Tiffany logo — a lack of recognition probably stemming from the fact that during its early formative years, the company chose to release its product through the larger, more prestigious Metro, and thus decided

**Tiffany Studios, Los Angeles. The firm collapsed in 1932. For a time it was known as Tiffany-Stahl when director John Stahl had a share in the firm.**

not to display its logo. When Metro Pictures merged with Goldwyn (and subsequently with Louis B. Mayer Productions) the resulting colossus no longer found it desirable to distribute Tiffany pictures.

On the eve of the talking picture vogue in 1927, Tiffany found itself both faced with setting up a new distribution channel and in converting its stages to sound film production.

Extensive research into Tiffany's output of films reveals about 200 features and westerns which either were made by Tiffany or were distributed through them.

A few of the Tiffany releases of more than passing interest include *The Last Mile,* a K.B.S. production, that provided audiences with a tense, low-key prison picture in which Preston Foster and George E. Stone portrayed doomed men within the shadowy confines of a prison set which seemed to have been inspired by similar films made by the brothers Warner.

There were several talkative comedy feature films issued by the Tiffany outfit, such as *The Medicine Man* (1930) in which Jack Benny appeared, *Lucky Boy* (1929) which presented filmgoers with a youthful George Jessel, and two features in which Joe E. Brown was top man, *Painted Faces* and *Molly and Me.*

When actor Conway Tearle decided to attempt a screen comeback in 1929, it was in a vehicle titled *The Lost Zeppelin,* on which Tiffany spent a huge budget only to have the picture panned unmercifully by film critics.

Technicolor had been around for years by the time Tiffany tried making a picture in that process, though the process had not been well received by the filmmakers themselves or by the audiences of that time. It was a primitive two-color process, its color rendition gaudy, when used in a short sequence of the silent version of *Ben Hur* as well as the entire feature film *The Gulf Between.* Despite this, Tiffany chose to film its 1930 offering *Mamba* in Technicolor.

Up to that time, Tiffany had ground out many features, one of which was the 1921 *Peacock Alley,* which proved so successful that the studio was to remake the picture in 1930. Tiffany's president during all of its busiest years was L.A. Young; William Saal was its vice president and general manager.

In 1930, also, there occurred a broadening of the kinds of films which Tiffany was to offer—though it must be admitted that most of the infusion of action pictures came from independent producers who simply released their output through Tiffany, as for example, K.B.S. Productions. The initials K.B.S. stand for the last names of Bert Kelly, Samuel Bischoff, and William Saal. Saal's earlier Quadruple Pictures became the K.B.S. production group in 1932, which changed its name to Admiral Productions in '33.

Bob Steele showed up on the Tiffany release list for 1930, appearing in such westerns as *Land of Missing Men, Near the Rainbow's End, Oklahoma Cyclone* and *Headin' North.*

At about the same time Ken Maynard was signed to several westerns for Tiffany release, though only one of them, *Fighting Through,* was completed in time for release in 1930.

Production of Tiffany westerns continued throughout the next year. Bob Steele rode triumphantly through *Ridin' Fool, Near the Trail's End, Nevada Buckaroo* and one called *Sunrise Trail.*

Ken Maynard, who had been in only one film released by Tiffany the year before, galloped through a half dozen such films in 1931: *The Two-Gun Man, Range Law, Pocatello Kid, Branded Men, Arizona Terror* and *Alias the Badman,* made by the K.B.S. production unit and released with Tiffany.

Other than westerns, Tiffany offered little among its '31 releases of any importance, although *X Marks the Spot* is mildly interesting. In August 1931, L.A. Young ceased to be with Tiffany; head of the firm then became Samuel Bischoff.

The Great Depression had most of the nation in its grasp in 1931, strangling countless American businesses into bankruptcy. In 1932

Tiffany production ground slowly to a halt, ending production with a few "chimp" comedies by independent producer Sigmund Neufeld, whose activities at Tiffany managed to keep a few persons employed, mostly sound engineers, post-production personnel and a few clerical workers.

There were also a few K.B.S. westerns entered for copyright by Tiffany in early '32: *Whistlin' Dan, Sunset Trail, Hell Fire Austin* and *Texas Gun Fighter*. The dying gasps of Tiffany were punctuated by withering gunfire of Ken Maynard, and the grins of a few chimpanzees.

# *Triangle*

Triangle seemed like an unbeatably superb idea when it was conceived. A simple enough plan, the firm was to consist of three top film producers, Thomas Ince, D.W. Griffith, and Mack Sennett. This triumvirate of producers would supervise production of films made for Triangle release.

Unfortunately, the company organizer, Harry Aitken, was obsessed with the idea that he could further insure Triangle success by signing up a wealth of overpriced Broadway "stars" and turning them over to his three producers.

Broadway stars may have impressed the show-going citizenry of New York City, but they meant almost nothing to most other Americans during the years of Triangle's existence. Aitken ignored that simple fact.

He and his representatives happily signed Sir Beerbohm Tree, Marie Doro, Weber and Fields, Joe Jackson, Elliott Dexter, and others whose names in front of film houses seemed more likely to drive audiences away rather than to attract them.

Among its stage-star acquisitions, however, a handful of performers did become successful on-screen, including William S. Hart and Douglas Fairbanks (although Griffith did not foresee a successful future in films for Fairbanks).

Harry Aitken had earlier been a founder of Mutual, a firm which had included Kessel and Bauman and D.W. Griffith. But when Griffith had undertaken the expensive Civil War melodrama which eventually was released as *The Birth of a Nation*, Mutual withdrew from backing production of the picture, allowing Griffith, with the help of Aitken and a few other backers, to buy out Mutual's share of that production. It was this move which probably started the wedge between Aitken and the Mutual firm and indirectly led to the founding of Triangle.

**Although the firm existed but a short time, Triangle once owned this sprawling studio at Culver City, California. Later it became the MGM lot.**

Aitken incurred no trouble whatever in obtaining all the Wall Street money needed to get Triangle into production. Smithers and Company, the same Wall Street banking house rumored to be connected with Standard Oil, was said to be the "angel" of Triangle.

Aitken was able to spend money freely in organizing Triangle. He acquired a lease on New York City's Knickerbocker Theatre to use as the glittering showcase for top Triangle productions. Usherettes decked out in uniforms topped by triangular-front blouses easily made customers feel they hadn't been overcharged at $2 a ticket to see the first Triangle film program on September 23, 1915. There was, suitably, a trio of pictures on the program: Ince's *The Iron Strain* with Dustin Farnum, Enid Markey, Louise Glaum, Fred Mace, and Mabel Normand; D.W. Griffith's *The Lamb,* which featured Douglas Fairbanks and Seena Owen and, finally, Mack Sennett's *My Valet* in which Raymond Hitchcock starred.

Even film exhibitors across this nation and elsewhere were impressed by the advance publicity of the Triangle corporation. Bookings for Triangle pictures flooded in to the exchanges, even though rental rates for the Triangle product were exorbitant.

Triangle film studio, located along Washington Boulevard in Culver City, California, had stages primarily of the "greenhouse" design, which was still prevalent during the years preceding World War I.

None of the three producers who made up the "corners" of the triangle really needed a studio. Ince was operating two separate studios, one just down the street from the Triangle operation, the other (known as "Inceville") in Santa Yñez Canyon near Santa Monica. Griffith was ensconced in what had once been the Majestic-Reliance lot in Hollywood. Sennett was operating his original California "Laugh Factory" at Edendale.

During its brief existence, Triangle employed many players including Eddie Foy, Polly Moran, Tully Marshall, Roscoe "Fatty"

**Mack Sennett shown as he directs a scene for a Triangle/Keystone 1915 picture.**

Arbuckle, Mae Busch, Henry B. Walthall, Eugene Pallette, William Desmond, Dorothy and Lillian Gish, and Robert Harrow.

The firm was "cashing in" on the names of Sennett, Griffith, and Ince, but did not call on the three to direct. Instead, a sizable team of directors was employed to work under the tutelage of one of the "name" producers. Christy Cabanne, Allan Dwan, John Emerson, W.S. Van Dyke, Jack Conway, Sidney Franklin, and Raoul Walsh were under Griffith's supervision.

Triangle operated for only about four years. The firm originally operated under a strict rule in which a theatre not holding a Triangle contract was not permitted to play Triangle product.

Like the United Artists Corporation, Triangle was merely a label under which it skimmed off 35 percent of the gross rental fees for Triangle pictures—plus certain other charges.

It required but a short time for Aitken to discover that his contracts with what turned out to be a warehouse full of overpaid, overage and frequently overweight Broadway players, could only bleed Triangle coffers sadly dry. By 1919, what remained of Triangle's unreleased forthcoming productions employed casts of players with less impressive names such as Wilbur Higby, J. Barney Sherry, and Jack Richardson.

Probably the best of all the Triangle offerings were those which starred William S. Hart. Although produced by Thomas Ince, these attractive westerns have largely been attributed to Hart himself; during the Triangle period Hart appeared in *Hell's Hinges,* one of the finest pictures he ever made. It was the films of Hart, together with those of Douglas Fairbanks, which were the top attractions offered by Triangle. (Unhappily, Hart left Triangle in 1917. The firm attempted, rather unsuccessfully, to replace him with Roy Stewart.)

While Hart and Fairbanks's releases through Triangle invariably proved profitable, its financial problems reached a climax when Aitken sold the chain of Triangle film exchanges in 1916 for $600,000 for 22 exchanges. The buyer: W.W. Hodkinson who, in making the purchase, agreed to continue to provide distribution for Triangle productions.

In 1917 Kessel and Bauman sold out their New York Motion Picture Co., which included Kay Bee, Broncho, Domino, and Keystone. Included in the half-million dollar sale were negatives of many releases. The buyer: Harry Aitken, in an action which permitted Kessel, Bauman & Co. to retire from motion pictures on January 31, 1917.

Less than two months afterward, Griffith quit Triangle, barely on the heels of Douglas Fairbanks.

Triangle boldly and optimistically had opened an East Coast studio along Riverside Avenue, the former estate of Clara Morris, in Yonkers, New York. Aitken, at the same time, moved executive offices from the overpriced Brokaw Building in New York City to the Yonkers address. Studio facilities were hastily constructed on the grounds and Allan Dwan moved east to command the remaining productions of the Triangle firm.

It was a vainglorious attempt to keep the firm in operation. Triangle inevitably closed down operation in 1919, as Adolph Zukor took over most of the remaining Triangle assets.

Harry Aitken ultimately retired. His three-sided battery of producers went their ways.

And Triangle? Its brief, unsuccessful story still haunts American motion picture history.

# Tulsa, Oklahoma, Studios

Just after World War I, Henry Starr, "the last of the outlaws" as journalists were calling him, was told by a friend, "There's more money in the motion picture business than in robbing banks." At least that's how author Glenn Shirley reported it in one of his books about western outlaws.

***The Cowboy and the Rajah,*** **one of a series of films which actor Franklyn Farnum appeared in while employed at a studio in Tulsa, Oklahoma, for producer
William Smith.**

Brother of the infamous Belle Starr, Henry thereupon temporarily
eschewed the ways of crime, turning his sights on a career in films. Fortunately there was no need for him to go to Hollywood; a fledgling film
industry had suddenly been spawned in Tulsa, Oklahoma, just after a
local theatre owner had bought, in 1912, a second-hand 35mm movie
camera. Most theatre patrons regarded motion pictures as a distinct
novelty, the theaterman knew, and so were likely to turn out in droves
to see a locally made newsreel. That $500 investment appears to have
been the motivating factor in spurring community interest in transform-
ing Tulsa into a movie capital of world renown, making pictures which
would create high excitement and thrills on motion picture screens the
world over.

In April 1915, the Tulsa Motion Picture Company was launched
under the guidance of H.A. Mackle, that production outfit followed
shortly by Longhorn Film Company.

Scout Younger, the infamous bandit, had already appeared in a
rough-and-ready three-reel featurette titled appropriately *The Younger
Brothers*, a film which supposedly detailed with accuracy the depreda-
tion of that outlaw clan. Younger, a friend of Emmett Dalton's, last

survivor of the Dalton gang, then teamed up with Dalton to appear in a two-reel production, *On the Texas Border.*

Those two pictures induced several Tulsa businessmen to invest in a western-movie street along Sand Springs Road, and to provide a few more or less permanent structures for use as offices and dressing rooms for movie companies.

About that time, temporarily reformed badman Henry Starr entered Tulsa's movie production scene, acquiring a one-fourth interest in Pan-American Motion Picture Company, it is said.

As his screen debut, Henry made a picture called *Debtor to the Law*, supposedly a filmic retelling of the daring double bank robbery in which Henry was leader of the bandits. To make his picture as accurate as he could, Starr hired many of the very employees and witnesses who had seen the actual robbery, even Paul Curry, the man who'd shot and wounded Starr during the affair.

Starr appeared in a couple more films for Pan-American, but appears to have been unable to collect his money for his efforts as an actor. Adding salt to his financial wounds, he'd been offered a job as a technical advisor at a California studio, only to quickly discover that were he to leave Oklahoma he well might be seized by officials who were seeking him to stand trial for at least one robbery in Arkansas!

At that juncture Starr is said to have been so bitter at being cheated out of money by the film industry that he assembled his gang once more and returned to bank robberies, more sure methods of collecting money. That decision led him to rob a bank in Harrison, Arkansas, where, in 1921, he was fatally wounded.

Before that time, the Tulsa Motion Picture Company was organized, and had acquired the use of the grounds of the International Dry Farming Congress, close to Lewis Avenue in Tulsa, and just south of the Frisco Railroad. The fairgrounds were quickly transformed into a motion picture lot, making it appear that the Tulsa area was heading for a large role in motion picture history.

Once the "western" street was completed, a one-reeler, *The Wrecker*, was filmed there, completed in August 1919, followed immediately by production of *The Cowboy Ace.*

A succession of films was soon to follow, all made in and around Tulsa, creating such local interest that one Tulsa businessman announced he was about to import some actors and actresses from New York City. He actually visited Manhattan, it is said, returning convinced that "city slickers" whom he'd encountered had tried to make a fool of him by attempting to talk him into signing a skinny-legged 16-year-old girl by the name of Norma Shearer. Who ever heard of such chicanery? the businessman asked.

Whether the story is true, Tulsa filmmakers appear again and again to have been just about that foolish, not even troubling to spend the few dollars necessary to copyright their films!

It is that sort of near-sightedness which probably caused the Tulsa studio to fail so quickly.

# The U.S. Moving Picture Co.

Before Hollywood began to emerge as the chief center of American film production, there were many other places around the country which attracted filmmakers.

Take the case of Wilkes-Barre, Pennsylvania.

Situated in a corner of lovely Wyoming Valley, the moderately sized city seems, even today, almost lost in what once was the colony of William Penn. Lakes and mountains abound in a year-round climate about as pleasant as one can find anywhere in northern United States. A mildly bustling city, Wilkes-Barre has yet to reach a population of 60,000. (Still, it's progressive enough to have possessed an electric streetcar line considerably earlier than many larger American cities.)

The officious title "U.S. Moving Picture Company" must have startled the Wilkes-Barre citizenry when first they encountered it. The company, with James O. Walsh as its president; Fred Herman, vice president; and Daniel L. Hart, secretary-treasurer; was organized little more than a decade or so after the turn of this century. Using the label "Black Diamond Comedies" the new firm began turning out a series of films, mostly one-reelers, many of them written and "worked out" (as the firm quaintly reported it to the U.S. Copyright Office) by company president Walsh.

One local tub-thumper wrote enthusiastically in the local chamber of commerce journal of April 1915 that Wilkes-Barre's new motion picture industry was going to enjoy a long, glowing future, considering how it would be aided by the area's "scenic beauty, atmospheric conditions and abundance of available good talent." In its October journal, the same organization continued its optimism, speaking of how Wilkes-Barre, "among . . . lofty mountains which surround the beautiful Wyoming Valley and near the broad expanse of the Susquehanna River, with lakes, forests and all the scenery needed in production of the moving picture" possessed genuine appeal and real potential for filmmakers.

But since U.S. Motion Picture Corporation had early set its sights upon making quantities of short slapstick comedies, vast scenic backgrounds weren't really necessary (and indeed would be somewhat of a detriment to material prepared strictly to obtain laughs). With that in mind, and also because of a need to possess indoor staging facilities for their productions, the embryonic picture makers began construction of a greenhouse-type studio.

Early in 1915, a Wilkes-Barre paper took a photograph inside the glassed-in stage of the United States Motion Picture Co., the photo showing a handful of the firm's officials in the foreground. "Film Factory Will Soon Be in Motion," ran the headline beneath the photograph. "Plays Will Be Staged in Our Valley and Surrounding Mountains" cried a subheading. The text of the article which followed virtually oozed unbridled enthusiasm: "Within a few days, probably at the end of the present week, the United States Motion Picture Company Corporation will begin the production of its first film play. The studios, which have been under construction for some time, have been completed and tests of lighting, apparatus and other equipment made with extremely satisfactory results. Motion picture experts who have visited the plant have pronounced it one of the most complete in the United States. The first play, *The Making of a Motion Picture Actor,* will be played with a local staging. The studio, which is situated in Forty Fort, is a large building of glass, measuring 40 by 83½ feet on the floor, and rising to a height of 32 feet. With the exception of a four-foot wall, the entire upper part of the building is of glass."

The article then took its readers on a sort of tour of the facility:

> In the basement are the dressing rooms, each one equipped with hot and cold water, and with shower bath nearby. The dark rooms for developing the films, the projecting rooms where they are tested, are also below stairs. Studio scenery is now being built and other arrangements made for beginning actual picture productions. Arrangements have been made by the local corporation with one of the largest distributing agencies in the country for a dispersal of the local plant's entire output.
>
> Expert motion picture people believe that there is a good field in Wyoming Valley for a motion picture manufacturing company. This is evidenced in the fact that two large corporations have only recently placed playing companies within a few miles of the city.
>
> High grade motion picture artists will be engaged to play in Wilkes-Barre within a short time. Work will not be confined to the studio, but plays will be staged all over the valley and on the mountains.

Throughout 1916 and 1917 Black Diamond comedies rolled from the cameras at Wilkes-Barre's "greenhouse studio." There may also have been a series of comedies which one or more local historians claim were made in imitation of Mack Sennett's "Keystone Kops" (these

supposedly utilized costumes which were imitations of the Pennsylvania State Police). Whether such bogus Keystone Comedies were
made cannot be supported by any evidence, however.

It should be noted that Wilkes-Barre amateur historians maintain
that United States Moving Picture existed for a longer time than would
be indicated by the U.S. Copyright Catalog, which indicates only that
the firm copyrighted about 14 short comedies, all in 1916 and 1917.

The titles of the Black Diamond subjects are not particularly
clever, although *His Ivory Dome* and *Their Counterfeit Vacation* (both
1917) seem intriguing.

Not surprisingly, the United States Moving Picture Co. collapsed
in late 1919. For one thing, the market for one- and two-reel films was
badly glutted. For another, the motion picture industry, right after
World War I, was undergoing both a depression and a change of needs.
Film audiences had switched allegiance to full-length feature films, the
type which were shown in plush, mansionlike surroundings of deluxe,
"downtown type" motion picture palaces. Fancy surroundings called for
fancy, high-budget films and "name" players. The nickelodeon showing
short films was dying.

Curiously, one type of short film survived this transition period; the
chapter play was still appealing to adult audiences everywhere. The
continuing craze for serial pictures prompted the formation of a production outfit which christened itself "Serico Productions" and which
moved into Wilkes-Barre in 1919. Not only that, the new firm took over
the old studio on Slocum Street and readied production of a 15-chapter
serial, *A Woman in Grey,* for which the firm brought to Wilkes-Barre
mildly famous Arline Pretty and Henry G. Sell to play the leads in the
serial.

The finished production revealed a surprisingly well photographed
chapter play which had taken adequate advantage of such exteriors as
street scenes in Wilkes-Barre, the Jessie Ford Smith mansion situated
in nearby West Pittston, a conservatory garden and bridle paths which
at that time existed on the River Commons of Wilkes-Barre. Serico also
managed to turn out its serial with but two "stars" in the cast, the supporting players in the picture being recruited locally.

Once the serial was ready for release, Serico officials let it be
known that the picture had cost some $90,000 to produce, though that
figure is highly questionable, especially considering salaries and the
costs of materials at the time. (If such a budget figure were even re-
motely evidenced by bookkeeping records, some truly "creative" jug-
gling of costs had been applied!)

There is no denying that Serico was a shoestring operation. It was
a relatively open secret that the company was relying upon a quick,
sizable profit from *A Woman in Grey* in order to finance any future

productions. Alas, like so many filmmakers, Serico was eventually to find that it was more difficult to find honest distributing outfits than it was to produce a picture. By the time the serial was sold to distributors on "states rights" deals, and by the time those firms had returned profits to Serico, it was much too late. The "greenhouse studio" in Wilkes-Barre again was empty, save for a few years of later use as a "clothes drying room" for a local laundry. The building was demolished in 1934.

Lyman H. Howe, another Wilkes-Barre film producer, didn't fare as badly. A pioneer motion picture exhibitor, Howe managed to make the transition from exhibitor to film producer, turning out a series of short subjects called *Lyman H. Howe's Hodge Podge* series—from 1922 to 1933, a popular monthly release in the United States and various foreign markets.

Carol Nelson, an educational television producer employed at Public Broadcasting's WVIA in Pittston, Pennsylvania, researched the history of the film industry in and around Wilkes-Barre, with considerable emphasis upon the work of Lyman H. Howe. The results of her task were woven into documentary production for television, detailing accounts of the exciting years when the films of that section of Pennsylvania were on movie screens of the world.

# *Universal*

By midsummer 1909, a diminutive German-Jew named Carl Laemmle had already parlayed a nickelodeon theatre called the "White Front" into one of Chicago's busiest places of film entertainment. What's more, he pyramided that one theatre into several others, and served all of them from his own system of film exchanges—the latter securing their material from independent, small-time filmmakers.

It was at that moment that "Pop" Laemmle determined to become a film producer, supplying assured quantity and quality of product to his own exchanges.

Actophone Studio, in New York City, was chosen by Laemmle as the place to start. Renting production space, he employed ex-Vitagraph director William Ramous, actress Gladys Hulette and others. The 1909 result was a one-reel drama titled *Hiawatha*. It was not only Laemmle's first production, it was also the first film to bear the "IMP" trademark (the initials "IMP" stood for Independent Motion Picture Co.).

In practically no time, Laemmle's new film production outfit was in a battle against the huge, overpowering Motion Picture Patents Company.

*Top:* Diminutive Carl "Pop" Laemmle, one of the several founders of Universal, who ended up owning most of the firm. He sold out in 1936. *Bottom:* An early view of the Universal City lot, today one of the most active of all studios.

**Soon after Universal entered film production this was its earliest outdoor studio, along Dyckman Street, New York City. This picture was taken in 1909.**

As the strengths of such independent filmmakers as IMP and William Fox's Box-Office Attractions Co. grew, Laemmle lured to his outfit the actress whom Biograph had made famous to the public as simply "the Biograph girl," her real name never revealed by Biograph. When Laemmle hired her however, he publicized her real name, and the fact that she now was "the Imp girl." In doing so, he started what became known as the "star system."

King Baggott signed on with Laemmle, adding to the growing fame of "IMP," by then a thorn in the side of the Motion Picture Patents Company. "IMP" decided to try to escape the Patents Company by undertaking film production in Cuba.

Soon after it had succeeded in signing both Mary Pickford and her husband, Owen Moore (Mary at $175 a week, incidentally), the Pickford-Moore troupe departed for Cuba with their director, Thomas H. Ince.

Ince had been around films since the fall of 1910, when as an out-of-work stage actor he'd found employment in films, as a villain in pictures made in New York by IMP.

Ince deserted IMP for work at Biograph, but was taken back into the IMP operation as a director, *Little Nell's Tobacco* being his first directorial assignment.

**Filming an early Harry Carey western at Universal, 1917. *Love's Lariat* was directed by Fred Kelsey. Note the onlookers on the observation balcony, a forerunner of today's public tours of Universal City.**

When "Little Mary" and her husband joined IMP they brought along others of the Pickford clan: Jack, Lottie, and Mary's mother.

Mary Pickford, however, was slave to no employer; she departed Laemmle's IMP studio for Majestic, at a salary reputed to be $275 weekly.

When Laemmle returned to New York from a visit to his birthplace at Laupheim, Germany, Mary Pickford was an ex–IMP, as were David Miles, Anita Hendrie, Herbert Prior and a lot of others.

About this time Kessel and Bauman of New York Motion Picture Co. acquired the services of another departee from IMP: Thomas H. Ince, who left IMP while earning a mere $60 weekly, and climbed into a director's chair with Kessel and Bauman at a salary of $150.

IMP, founded in 1909, was incorporated into Laemmle's so-called "Sales Company" in 1910. The consolidation was short-lived, however; in 1912 Laemmle incorporated his production interests into a new corporation, Universal Pictures, other major partners besides Laemmle being Robert H. Cochrane, Pat Powers and Mark Dintenfass.

In 1914 Laemmle conceived the idea of constructing one huge, sprawling studio, Universal City. Since there wasn't a large enough plot of land in Hollywood available for a reasonable price, Laemmle in March 1914 bought 230 acres in San Fernando Valley, 10 miles out of Los Angeles, along the old El Camino Real, the thread with which Spanish

An early "series" picture made in 1928. Universal always has had a reputation with owners of less than "deluxe" theatres for its production of a good many "bread and butter" offerings which, while available at modest rentals, nonetheless frequently proved to be "mortgage lifters" for certain theatres.

settlers had connected together a group of missions all the way from San Diego in the south to San Francisco in the north.

Laemmle paid $165,000 for the 230 acres, breaking ground for Universal City in October 1914, and completing the vast complex by March 1915. When it opened, Universal City had a main stage measuring 400 feet by 50 feet, 80 dressing rooms, many offices, three pumping stations, a water reservoir, a hospital, two restaurants capable of serving 1200 persons simultaneously, shops, forges, garages, mills, and even a school. By 1930, the immense layout was to include six stages, all equipped for sound recording, and a back lot with "streets of the world."

The first picture made at Universal City was *Damon and Pythias*, followed by such films as *Richelieu, Washington at Valley Forge*, and internationally famous swimmer Annette Kellerman's picture *Neptune's Daughter*.

Lon Chaney found work at Universal as a "character actor" at $35 weekly, Harold Lloyd as an "extra" at $5 per day.

Other early stars on the roster of Universal included Pearl White,

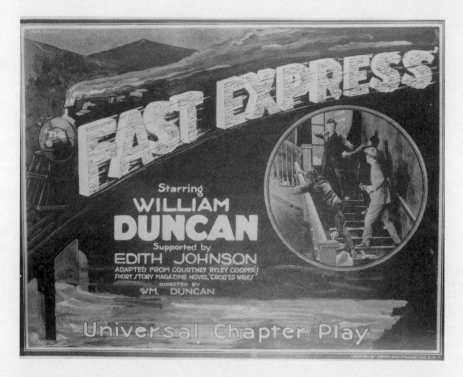

Universal had already been in existence for more than a decade when, in 1924, the firm released this serial. Railroads were still exciting to film audiences, and trains invariably offered scriptwriters countless opportunities for "cliffhanger" endings on chapters. Universal, Republic, and Columbia continued to offer chapter plays into the 1950s.

Mae Murray, Marie Prevost, Sarah Bernhart, Lew Cody, Harry Carey, Art Acord, Betty Compson, Erich von Stroheim and Rudolph Valentino.

Von Stroheim had come to Laemmle with a scenario for a picture titled *Blind Husbands,* which Laemmle not only bought but also signed Von Stroheim as director and leading actor of the film.

*Blind Husbands* succeeded financially for Universal, although Von Stroheim's extravagances resulted eventually in the parting of the ways for Laemmle and the director. Von Stroheim made four features for Universal.

But Laemmle had bigger things on his mind than problems with Von Stroheim: "Uncle Carl" found that his partners were even more of a problem, and accordingly, Laemmle and one of his partners, R.H. Cochrane, in 1920 bought out P.A. Powers.

In 1914, when Universal City began operation, Hollywood was completely different from what it was to be a decade later; in his book

*Charmed Lives,* author Michael Korda commented, "Nor did Los Angeles in the late '20s resemble in any way the city we know now. It was before the age of air conditioning." Korda continues, "The houses of the rich were built with thick walls and small windows . . . to keep the heat and sunshine out. When the dry Santa Ana wind began to blow, igniting brush fires in the hills and sending the local suicide rate soaring, half the city retired to nurse a migraine, while the rest huddled in bars seeking relief in heavy drinking and an occasional murder."

It was in such a Los Angeles region that talking pictures took over the film industry. Universal, like all other studios in Hollywood, installed sound recording equipment, sound-speed cameras, and dialog coaches. Stars who had reasonably good voices (as far as the microphone was concerned) stayed around and found adequate work. Those who didn't faded quickly into oblivion.

Optimistic about sound, Laemmle spearheaded such early Universal talkies as *All Quiet on the Western Front* which starred Lew Ayres, and *King of Jazz* which featured Paul Whiteman, his orchestra, and some early two-strip Technicolor. Laemmle was bold and imaginative, except when it came to avoiding nepotism!

In simple terms, "Pop" Laemmle had early shown considerable tendency to employ as many of his family as possible. It was so pronounced a tendency that it became a joke around Hollywood. "Did you hear the latest?" in those days was often followed by "Laemmle's about to open three gigantic branch studios, just so he can employ more of his relatives!"

Accordingly, in 1929, Carl Laemmle, Jr., was appointed director-in-chief at Universal City, and while many of the senior Laemmle's critics scoffed, "Junior" turned out the now-classic 1930 feature *Frankenstein* and the later offering *Dracula.*

Still, the Hollywood wags swapped jokes about "Pop" Laemmle, such as the time Laemmle supposedly had been told that the great Albert Einstein, the father of the theory of relativity, was about to visit Universal. The studio chieftain is supposed to have groaned wearily and then said, "With all my family working here, this bum's gonna come along and tell me anything about *relativity*?"

Not just Laemmle's relatives were creating jokes about Universal. Bosley Crowther claims, in his book *Hollywood Rajah,* that in 1912 during a vicious fight for control of the newly formed company, Lewis J. Selznick (father of David O.) discovered that a personal battle was being waged between Laemmle and Pat Powers. Into this crazy world wherein those two partners weren't even speaking to one another, Selznick took over an important position within the studio—totally an outsider, Selznick was hired by neither Powers nor Laemmle.

As Selznick placed himself on the Universal payroll, brazenly ordering stationery with Universal's name and *his* on it, he was allowed to continue, simply because Laemmle and Powers each thought the other had hired Selznick.

Eventually, Laemmle discovered the truth, but by that time General Manager Selznick, the ex-jewelry seller, had learned enough about the movie business to strike out on his own.

As 1912 moved speedily onward, Laemmle bought stock formerly held by Mark Dintenfass, Laemmle acquiring the stock for $75,000. Laemmle had either learned from Selznick of the Dintenfass stock being for sale, or else had purchased the stock through him. In either event, that did not prevent Laemmle from firing Selznick once he learned how the latter had bluffed his way into that job.

The purchase of the Dintenfass stock gave the little promoter control of Universal, though when Powers learned that, he forced Universal into receivership, a move which didn't succeed because, at the 1913 meeting of the board, Laemmle thwarted all moves to wrest control of Universal from his hands.

During the more than 20 years that Laemmle remained at the helm, Universal was a profit-making studio, weathering internecine battles and such violent industry changes as talking pictures.

In his book *The Life of Bette Davis,* author Charles Higham avers that at the coming of talkies Universal had financed its way through the transition largely by re-releasing many of the studio's silent movie hits, adding music and sound effects to those films. The studio's initial sound film was *Lonesome,* a part-talkie which was not popular at the box office.

Universal soon after made a stab at adapting to the screen a talkie version of the stage play *Showboat,* based on the Edna Ferber story. Involving sequences in sound and silent footage, it was still a step away from the "full sound" feature *All Quiet on the Western Front* (1930).

Higham describes the Universal lot, circa 1930, as a "scattering of wooden, verandaed buildings and rambling palm-lined streets."

Because Higham is mostly concerned with downgrading that studio where actress Davis found less than fame and fortune, he tends to be exceedingly harsh on the Laemmles. "Although 'Uncle' Carl Laemmle was the ostensible head of the studio . . . he handed over the reins of power to his singularly uninspired son, known as 'Junior.' At the age of 21, Junior was a depressing example," writes Higham, "of the results of nepotism. His sausage-machinelike approach to making pictures, based on second-rate novels or plays, resulted in works of surpassing mediocrity."

What a British writer such as Higham may think matters little; the facts remain that Universal, long known as producers of "bread-and-butter" pictures, was turning out films which drew crowds, delighted patrons, and brought them out again and again to revel in such minor fare as *The Cohens and the Kellys,* and almost endless Frankenstein films, westerns, serials, and others.

Either Carl Laemmle just happened by pure luck to turn out consistent money-making pictures, or else those he hired did so.

In the book *Hollywood* (1967) Garson Kanin provides a much kinder picture of Laemmle and his productions: "Laemmle [at] 75, seemed as venerable as the Grand Lama. He was to die the following year, but when I met him, he was bright and cheerful and funny and loved to talk about the movie business."

Kanin continues, "I had been anxious to meet him because he seemed to me . . . one of the most fascinating and imaginative of the motion picture producers."

Laemmle retired in 1936 from his position as head of Universal, just 30 years after he'd opened his first movie theatre in Chicago. He died September 24, 1939, about 25 years after he'd helped found Universal.

The studio operation he founded is today one of the only consistently profitable major studios which survive. In the years since Carl Laemmle died, Universal has passed through the hands of many groups, including those of J. Arthur Rank and the present one, M.C.A.

# *Vitagraph*

There had not been such things as motion pictures for very long when, in 1897, a newspaper cartoonist named James Stuart Blackton joined hands with a bookbinder named Albert Edward Smith and a Harlem coin-machine operator named William "Pop" Rock and came up with the word vitagraph ("vita" meaning life and "graph" implying pictures). They applied their new word to a film studio which the three entrepreneurs organized that year.

Less than a year earlier, working as a newspaper reporter, Blackton had been dispatched to interview the famous Thomas A. Edison. In order to amuse Edison during the interview, Blackton did some cartoonlike sketches while the inventor looked on. Not only was the "Wizard of Menlo Park" pleased with Blackton's artistry, he retained the youth to do some of his cartoon sketches for the Edison camera. What's more, the inventor ended up selling Blackton an Edison 35mm projector with which to set himself up as a motion picture exhibitor!

Blackton not only showed films, but studied the projector mechanism carefully until he transferred the basics of projector to a motion picture camera!

**The Vitagraph Studio at the corner of Prospect and Talmadge, Los Angeles. Founded in New York City in the late 1800s, the firm's first "studio" was a rooftop operation on the Morse Building, Manhattan.**

Edison unwittingly had created a Frankenstein!

The Vitagraph threesome set up a studio, a rooftop affair on the Morse Building along Nassau Street in New York City. There the three filmmakers began turning out numerous one-reel subjects, the making of which frequently was interrupted while clouds of unwanted steam, smoke from nearby chimneys, or other rooftop-type interferences crossed the lens of the Vitagraph camera. Obviously, a rooftop studio, while providing sporadic but free sunlight, was no substitute for a protected motion picture studio.

In the Flatbush section of Brooklyn, the three partners poured the profits from their early films into the construction of a totally glass-enclosed studio, where soon the firm was undertaking the production of one-reel, then two- and three-reel subjects to help meet the growing needs of thousands of store-front nickelodeons which were popping up, mushroom-like, across the nation.

The seemingly insatiable appetite of film audiences for longer and more complex pictures filtered upward to the Vitagraph triumvirate. By 1914 the firm not only was turning out a large program of the new "feature films," but had acquired the Criterion Theatre on Broadway as a showcase for all the new Vitagraph features.

The initial capitalization of Vitagraph is set by some at a paltry $1,000 or less. Film historian Terry Ramsaye, in his book *A Thousand and One Nights,* claims Vitagraph start-up funds at approximately six times that amount.

About the time when the Edison Company was producing *Life of an American Fireman* (1902), Vitagraph busied itself turning out its own little milestones such as *A Gentleman of France,* a one-reeler featuring Kyrle Bellew. This film preceded, by almost three years, the production of Vitagraph's *Raffles, the Gentleman Cracksman,* a one-reeler made atop the Morse Building and which starred J. Barney Sherry and was produced for Vitagraph by Gilbert M. (Broncho Billy) Anderson.

Florence Turner was recruited by Vitagraph just as the firm was preparing to move from its rooftop studio to its new operation in Flatbush. Miss Turner became the first of a Vitagraph stock company of players, a group joined shortly afterward by Maurice Costello who was fresh from a stint at Edison Studios.

Not long after Vitagraph began operations at its new Flatbush studios, an extremely rotund comic showed up looking for work in pictures. One of John Bunny's earliest screen successes at that studio was the short comedy *The New Stenographer,* in which he was co-starred with Flora Finch who also became a regular member of the stock company at Vitagraph.

Bunny soon had a tremendous following among movie theatre habitues. But, for a time, he nearly lost his following when he undertook a severe diet, which resulted both in his losing 40 pounds and much of his appeal. "Fat is funny" was an edict of the 1912 era.

As the Vitagraph roster of players grew, the three Talmadge sisters, Norma, Constance, and Natalie, eventually made screen appearances there; two of the sisters going on to long screen careers.

Of the three founders of the firm, J. Stuart Blackton was the most prominent since he functioned often as one of the directors of productions at the studio, directing such films as an early version of *A Tale of Two Cities.* This was placed into production at a time when the studio was enjoying a period of great profitability and was employing 29 directors and literally hundreds of players, carpenters, and other employees.

It should have been a period in the company's history when Blackton would be extremely contented. Unfortunately, such was not the case, for at Vitagraph's studio in Flatbush, Blackton had become relegated to a role as sort of a "paper pusher," a nonentity. It was at that point he withdrew entirely from Vitagraph, selling out his share of the firm and starting an independent production unit allied with Adolph Zukor's Famous Players.

Blackton did not remain long with Zukor; he left America to go to England where he had been born. There he employed a color film process called Prizma Color in which he produced *The Glorious Adventure.* After that he remained in Britain producing a handful of other features before returning to America and to a position as producer-director at Vitagraph, where he remained until the company was sold to Warner Bros. in 1925.

As early as 1912, Vitagraph had become so profitable that it was grossing between five and six million dollars annually, out of which the partners drew generous salaries for themselves, and paid all costs of operation, including stars' wages, while still clearing more than a million dollars per year!

By 1910, the Vitagraph studios in the East consisted of many glass-topped "greenhouse style" indoor stages, behind which was a studio "back lot" comprising ersatz streets and other outdoor locations. It was, in its time, a very complete and well-equipped operation.

By the close of World War I, Vitagraph had also built a new studio situated in Los Angeles, at the corner of Prospect and Talmadge avenues.

At its East and West Coast studios, Vitagraph always maintained a sizable output of motion picture serials, the genre having been launched by the Edison studios in 1912. Output of Vitagraph serials continued until the firm sold out to Warner Bros. in 1925, the sale including all 34 Canadian and U.S. film exchanges of Vitagraph.

Oddly, Warners carried the name Vitagraph on its film exchange system through the years until the end of World War II and had also christened its "talking picture" sound-on-disc system "Vitaphone" as a variation of the Vitagraph name. (Warners also carried on the name "First National" for years after it had acquired that firm, which the company purchased the same year as Vitagraph.)

The pennant-on-flagstaff trademark of Vitagraph is very old, but like so much of the history of the American film, refuses to disappear behind the veil of the lost or forgotten yesterdays.

# Warner Bros.

It required the acting services of a dog to keep Warner Bros. solvent during the closing years of silent pictures. Old Rin-Tin-Tin, who ended his days romping endlessly through cheap Mascot serials and the

WARNER BROTHERS presents

RIN·TIN·TIN

in

"FROZEN RIVER"

Directed by F. Harmon Weight

**Rin-Tin-Tin seemed so amazingly talented that his films packed theatres everywhere and in doing so, kept Warner Bros. financially viable through some of that firm's most trying times. Actually the original "Rinty" was represented onscreen by several different dogs.**

like, once was Warners' most consistent moneymaker and at times about the only star to pull in profits for that studio.

Those were days when a fellow named Darryl F. Zanuck was scripting Rinty's soundless exploits, inventing thrills for theatre audiences who watched intently as the German shepherd courageously guarded hydroelectric plants, captured entire gangs of miscreants, and helped lighthouse keepers to keep ships from piling their bones on rocky shores.

Like many another too-eager storyteller, the present one has plunged into his tale not at the beginning, but at somewhere near its midpoint. In reality Sam, Jack, Harry and Albert Warner entered the film industry years before Rin-Tin-Tin did. Like many others involved in film production, the Warners had bowed into the industry by way of exhibition of motion pictures, with a hand-cranked projector and well-worn copy of the Edison Company's 1903 one-reeler *The Great Train Robbery*, a film which was still drawing crowds in 1905 when the brothers Warner set out.

Although there were four brothers to split the profits, the Warners managed to accumulate enough funds with which to set up a small nickelodeon-type movie house, The Cascade, in New Castle, Pennsylvania. From there the brothers went on to establish a film exchange, then on to states' rights distribution of independent production and finally, in 1913, into film production.

Initial productions proved successful, so much so that by the end of the First World War their firm purchased about the final 40 acres along Sunset Boulevard in Hollywood of what once had been the sprawling Beesmyer Ranch, there constructing a studio.

Dreadfully underfinanced, the studio was somewhat successful for a time, though soon unable to cope with competing firms which began producing quantities of expensively made films.

Harry Warner, financial chieftain of the brothers, then borrowed from the Los Angeles Trust and Saving about a million dollars with which the brothers not only upgraded the quality of their productions, but also signed such players as John Barrymore and Irene Rich, who were to prove, for a time, money-making stars at the studio.

In spite of the infusions of capital, Warners continued to be short of cash. In his book *History of the Movies* Benjamin B. Hampton states that Warners went on "slipping downhill because of insufficient theatre connections," apparently dooming them "to go the way of the great majority . . . of the industry."

That downhill slide had about reached bottom when brother Harry decided that what the firm ought to do was simply to take the chance of re-equipping one of the studio stages for the recording of "talkies" and attempt to create a new market. Bell Telephone, through its subsidiary Western Electric, had developed a clumsy and imperfect system for sound-on-disc "talkies" and, having received the cold shoulder from all the rest of the film industry, was prepared to license the system to Warners at a reasonable price.

The silent films of Warner Bros. were, in the meantime, being refused by more and more first-run theatres, so WB quarterly reports had long since fallen into the loss column and seemed likely to remain there. The deeply troubled Harry Warner, it is alleged, aged three years in twelve months; even as his brother Sam passed away.

*Opposite, top:* The Warner Bros. studio on Sunset Boulevard, Los Angeles, as it appeared in the 1930s. Note the radio transmission towers; Warners operated its own AM radio broadcasting station. *Bottom:* This famous studio facade faces on Sunset Boulevard, Los Angeles. The Warner brothers entered the industry as film exhibitors, struggling financially and on the verge of bankruptcy until the firm's promotion of a Western Electric sound-on-disc process which changed the fortunes of the brothers.

In 1925 the remaining three brothers bought out Vitagraph, Inc., along with that firm's 34 U.S. and Canadian film exchanges and soon after that First National Pictures, as well.

In the late spring 1926, Warners introduced their new Vitaphone "talkies" even as William Fox entered the market with a sound-on-film system called "Movietone."

By the fall of that year, neither Fox nor Warners "talkies" had really excited a large segment of moviegoers. Such apparent apathy should hardly have been unexpected; after all, attempts had been undertaken to wed silent films to audible devices almost as long as there'd been such a thing as movies. Some even worked fairly satisfactorily. Yet, when the devices were displayed the public just didn't seem to care sufficiently for films that talked.

Still, by fall 1927, there seemed a positive, unmistakable shift in the degree of acceptance by the public in the talking picture, as the three Warner brothers were quick to point out. Even the increasing popularity of the Vitaphone talking short subjects seemed proof. Warners decided to completely immerse their company in the making of talking feature films, beginning with a synchronized film version of a Broadway show, *The Jazz Singer.*

Having purchased screen rights to the play, the Warners next approached George E. Jessel who'd played the key role in the Broadway version of the play. Jessel wasn't interested, so another Broadway star, Al Jolson, was signed for the movie, which was to contain songs but no talking sequences.

While the film was being shot, however, the exuberant Jolson suddenly uttered a few words which, fortunately, were allowed to remain in the final version of the picture. It proved conclusively that audiences wanted to hear players speak as well as to just sing.

By the time Warners had readied its first "all-talking" feature, *Lights of New York*, all of the film industry seemed agreed that the talking picture was destined to be around for a while.

Just why the talkies succeeded by the time of the late 1920s when they'd failed repeatedly during the years earlier may be explained by the fact that radio had come onto the scene, accustoming the public to "canned" speech and other sounds.

Warner Bros. studio found itself suddenly a profitable entity and at least two large steps ahead of all other Hollywood studios save William Fox's, with its competing "Movietone" sound system, an invention which was to prove far superior to Warners' sound-on-disc system.

By 1930, Warners found itself in the position of phasing out its sound-on-disc Vitaphone and going to that of sound-on-film, a variable-density sound track, impinged along its releases a photographic image of sound, traced there by light beams.

Just how profitable the talking picture enabled Warner Bros. to become may be gleaned from the fact that while the firm had shown nothing but financial losses during 1925, 1926, and 1927, there was a complete reversal in 1928, accompanied by profits of between two and three million dollars.

On Sunset Boulevard near Bronson Avenue, Warners built a huge, colonnaded administration building behind which several of the largest indoor stages in the film industry were constructed. This lot was augmented by the Vitagraph and First National lots in Los Angeles and production facilities on the East Coast.

As the firm grew in size, it also constructed the Warner Bros. Theatre in Hollywood, which on April 26, 1928, opened its doors with the Delores Costello, Conrad Nagel film *Glorious Betsy.*

Numerous stars have reigned at the Warners, the studio continually maintaining a stock company of contract players, major and minor in stature, a memorable list which has at one time or another included Bette Davis, George Raft, Olivia de Havilland, Errol Flynn, Humphrey Bogart, Joan Blondell, Ann Sheridan, Dick Powell, Alan Hale, Ruby Keeler, James Cagney and others.

For good or otherwise, Jack Warner was a staunch Democrat, a political leaning which during the years of World War II not only influenced the Warners' choices of film subjects but brought aid from U.S. government sources whenever help was needed in filming pictures at military facilities! It also helps explain the World War II penchant which Warners had for patriotism, which was mired deeply in the sort of things near and dear to the heart of President Franklin D. Roosevelt.

Warners seemed always to be aware of the public's tastes in pictures, more so perhaps than nearly any other studio. When gangster films sold quantities of theatre tickets, Warners flooded the market with pictures of that genre, pictures remembered today for their heavy, low-key lighting, strong silhouettes and shadowy staircases spidering upward along sets depicting a sleazy world.

Musicals came and went in vogue beginning in the late 1920s; Warners geared up for such whenever the audience tastes warranted.

A 1946 list of U.S. motion pictures which had grossed $2 million or more, not surprisingly, proved to have several Warners' pictures on it: *This Is the Army* (1943), *The Singing Fool* (1928), *Yankee Doodle Dandy* (1943), *Sergeant York* (1941), *The Jazz Singer* (1927), *42nd Street* (1933), *Gold Diggers of Broadway* (1929), and *The Doughgirls* (1944). Only MGM and United Artists, with 12 winners each, had better track records.

On July 15, 1967, a subsidiary of Seven Arts Productions, Ltd., acquired the assets and the trade of Warner Bros. Pictures, Inc., the resulting merger being known for a short time as Warner Bros.–Seven Arts, which in turn was swallowed up by Kinney National Service, July 1969.

The studio facilities of Warners are yet situated in Burbank, California, but the lot is shared with what remains of the Columbia Pictures firm, the latter now a property of Coca-Cola. As with every other studio in the country, Warners is deeply involved in production of TV shows.

The main studios currently comprise 102 attractively landscaped acres on which are all structures necessary for production of motion pictures. This celluloid city has its own police and fire departments, school, hospital, library and so on, beneath which buildings and grounds are miles of water, gas, and power lines, the latter feeding enough electricity to illuminate a city of 40,000. The complex has restaurants spacious enough to comfortably serve 1000 persons simultaneously.

The transportation department possesses some 300 pieces of motorized equipment ranging from limousines and convertibles to buses, trucks and bulldozers. On the lot there are also shops, mills, a foundry, and laboratories where nearly anything from a watch to an airplane can be produced quickly.

Ten principal thoroughfares and dozens of paved streets cross-hatch the lot, a total of more than 12 miles of roads, some leading along the back lot where one can wander through picturesque copies of "foreign" towns, bits of New York, and typical American towns and villages.

There is at the heart of this sprawling immensity a cluster of 21 sound stages, in 17 of which most interior filming is done, the remaining ones providing recording facilities or are used for storage.

The tallest of the stages, the highest one in the world, is Stage 7, which has a 72-foot clearance from the floor to ceiling joists. The largest sound stage, Number 22, has nearly 37,000 square feet of floor space, an area of 120 x 308 feet.

The most enormous building on the back lot is the Crafts building, where 400 workers and a wealth of machinery serve the mechanical and construction needs from a space totalling 131,000 feet.

Twenty miles from the studio is the 2800-acre Warner Ranch, used for much of the company's exterior shooting, and providing several western sets.

In the California of today where space is at a premium and taxes overwhelming, the Burbank Studios and nearby ranch seem an almost unbelievable luxury, a costly example of why film production voraciously chews up an endless amount of the gross profits at theatre box offices of the world.

# The Washington Motion Picture Corporation

The first hint that Spokane, Washington, residents had that their community was about to become a second Hollywood probably was a news item published in their *Spokesman-Review,* Thursday, January 10, 1918: "Dietz to Enter Spokane Movies," shouted a headline above a column in which the plans of W.H. "Lone Star" Dietz were detailed, including the information that Mr. Dietz, a one-time football coach who later had turned vaudevillian, recently had bought a share of the new motion picture studio at Minnehaha Park.

The former Washington State football coach, being partly Sioux Indian, announced that he intended to film motion pictures of a variety he felt were needed: "The moving picture has never given the Indian a square deal," he told reporters, hinting at the pictures he intended.

Whether or not Dietz actually put any money into Washington Motion Picture Corporation is not known at this time; what is known is that a few days after his initial news report, the same paper on January 27 reported that Dietz had "put his name to a contract the other afternoon," one guaranteeing his services for a year as an actor and director.

By February 17, 1918, the studio at Minnehaha Park was said to be nearing completion, mostly occupying buildings which had existed before motion picture filmers had found their way to Spokane. The structures, leased from the Spokane Park Board, were remodelled, while at the same time new structures such as the open-air stage was built, alongside which was a 60 x 100 foot building with a 22-foot ceiling, in which scenery painting could be accomplished. The outdoor stage, 60 x 80 feet in size, was to be topped with muslin "travellers" which could be shifted about to provide for controlled use of sunlight.

The administration building, a former beer garden, provided office space for auditors, the president of the firm, and general offices for other officials. On the second floor of the same building were the dressing rooms for stars and principal characters in the productions, and a covered walkway from this upper floor was to be connected to the indoor and outdoor stages.

The enclosed stage, which a reporter referred to as "the indoor theatre," was scheduled for later construction, although the motion laboratory was completed by late February 1918. "Our mechanical building will contain on the first floor the laboratory, consisting of special rooms for developing, drying, printing, cutting and assembling films," explained General Manager C.J. Ward, who added, "In this department there is a reinforced concrete fireproof film vault. Space is also provided on this floor for restaurant and cafeteria for employees and visitors." The second floor had provided space for camera repair and storage, the property room, and other facilities.

The construction sounds from the Spokane Park were, in effect, heard all the way to California, for in its February 20, 1918, issue a Spokane newspaper headlined a story "Movie Men Eye Spokane," and sub-headed the story, "Vitgraph People to Send Agent Here in Spring." The text of the article indicated that if California producers were to become convinced that the state of Washington was the filmmaker's paradise, the Minnehaha Park studio would be a rousing success.

Adding fuel to the local fires of enthusiasm, actor Tyrone Power, Sr., who had already made a name for himself in such pictures as Selig's *The Texas Steer* and *Thou Shalt Not Covet*, as well as the Bluebird production *The Eye of God* and Universal's *Where Are My Children*, announced that he would star in several forthcoming films made by the Washington Motion Picture Corporation.

Before long, it appeared Spokane would possess its own actors' colony. "Tyrone Power, our star, will arrive from Los Angeles on Monday night," C.J. Ward told reporters on May 11, 1918. When asked about other motion picture stars who had been added to the roster, Ward answered by naming Florence Turner, who was to be Power's co-star in his initial Spokane production, *Marshall Strong*. He supplied newspapermen with still other names of film players, such as Wellington Playter, Evelyn Brent and Kempton Greene who was to essay the juvenile role in Tyrone Power's film.

Laurence Tribble was prepared to begin production on *Marshall Strong* by mid–May 1918; unfortunately, rain and cold prevented his doing so. The studios of the Washington Motion Picture Corporation were off to an extremely bad start.

But to mask the ill beginning and at the same time to hold public attention on the place which sought to become "Hollywood North," a score of Spokane school children were invited to the studio to witness a rehearsal on May 26, following which various officials of the city including its mayor, C.M. Fassett, presented studio dignitaries with a profuse and verbose welcome to the city.

By mid-summer local newspapers had become infected with "movie fever": "Thrills Abound in Work of Movie Picture Actors at Minnehaha," a headline stated excitedly in the *Spokesman-Review*, July 7, 1918. The author could never have visualized that Washington Motion Picture Corporation would soon be placed into receivership.

"Receiver for Washington Motion Picture Corporation Is Appointed," stated a headline in the August 29, 1918, issue of the

*Spokesman-Review.* In the accompanying story were accounts of how stockholders charged that the firm had been riddled with dissension, and filled with acts of deception and extravagance.

At the time of the bankruptcy it was disclosed that actor Tyrone Power had been dropped from the payroll fully two months earlier in an effort to reduce operating costs. Only one picture, *Fools' Gold* with Tyrone Power and Victor McLaglen, had been produced by the company; its cost was $32,000, only a pittance of the total that the firm initially raised in its sale of stock.

Several months afterward, on August 21, 1919, newspapers disclosed that the studio and equipment had been purchased by Wellington Playter, who already was taking steps to begin operations under his Playter Photo Players. In doing so, Playter pointed out that he had retained the services of Irving Cummings and Anna Q. Nilsson as his leading actors. Other personnel were also retained, including film directors J. Winthrop Kelly and Elizabeth Mahoney.

In spite of the debacle involving the original operators of the studio, local stockholders reportedly were again interested in financing Playter — a truly surprising development when one considers that early in 1918 citizens of the Spokane area had purchased a great deal of worthless stock in "Titan Feature Photoplay Company," which had leased property on the city's Caste Hill (later renamed Rimrock Drive) but the firm simply had expended stockholders' money and quickly disappeared!

The bid, $20,000 for the lease and equipment of the studio, was the sole offer received by the receiver for the Washington Motion Picture assets. In putting up a $2,000 certified check with his offer, Playter told newsmen, "Workmen will be employed at once to put the plant in shape with a view to starting work on the first picture in two weeks. We expect to finish that film in one month."

The first and only production of the ill-fated Washington Motion Picture firm had fallen to the receiver of the assets of that company. It was not until July 11, 1920, that the negative was sold to Arrow Film of New York City. The agreement brought the creditors a total of $20,000, it was reported by F.K. McBroom, the receiver for Washington Motion Picture Company, an amount reportedly $8,000 more than was anticipated.

By the time Playter took over the studio, he came up with an idea for getting some cash into the firm's coffers without the need for too much delay: He opened an acting school at the studio where for $10 per lesson amateurs reputedly could be adequately trained so as to find work in motion pictures. Some 150 students signed up.

Soon after, actress Nell Shipman (Her son, Barry, attending military school at this time, grew up to be a scriptwriter, working for Republic Pictures, and thus carrying on the Shipman name in films.)

entered the picture, raising sufficient funds for local business people so she could move her production unit, which included a "wild animal compound," from Los Angeles, and establish herself as a rental account for part of the Playter studio. *The Grub Stake,* directed by Bert Van Tuyle, was Miss Shpman's initial production at Spokane.

*The Grub Stake* utilized 11 sets, all built specially by the three-man carpenter crew. One of the sets, "Dawson Variety Theatre," occupied all of the outdoor shooting stage. The set comprised two bars and the replica of the stage at the original Dawson Theatre, including rows of private boxes along a wall of the theatre, as well as a section of orchestra seats of the miniaturized "auditorium." All of it was made in the carpenter shop which occupied what formerly had been the pavilion when the premises were occupied by a summer park.

But after working at the five-acre Playter complex for a few months, the Shipman company found itself in deep financial trouble, necessitating its withdrawal to a site near Priest Lake, Idaho, and a good deal of refinancing of Nell Shipman Productions.

Occasionally other independent producers made limited, sporadic use of the studio which by 1924 was managed by Lionel Campbell and was by that time known as the Minnehaha Photoplay Studio. A film about Indian life was announced, and even the "stars" chosen for the picture: Lucy and Nellie Garry, aged daughters of the Indian Chief Spokane Garry. Whether the film was ever made is not known.

Although the city of Spokane had grown greatly, especially since World War II, parts of the old studio in its park remained intact even until the 1970s (one building, a stone structure, with its windows and doors boarded up).

The wild dream of turning the area into "Hollywood North" had long since died.

# The Whartons

When producer Theodore Wharton went to Ithaca, New York, to film a football game in 1912 (Cornell vs. Penn State), he was no stranger to the area. In fact, he had relatives living in nearby Ludlowville. Still, that visit served to remind Wharton how scenically attractive the Finger Lakes region of New York state was. What a spot in which to make impressively scenic entertainment movies—a regular flow of interesting pictures, he doubtless thought.

Wharton was employed as a producer-director by Essanay Film of Chicago, one of the co-owners of which was George K. Spoor. It was

*Mysteries of Myra* teamed Jean Sothern with Howard Estabrook. The 1916 serial of 15 episodes was made by the Whartons for release through Hearst's International Film Service.

Spoor who authorized Wharton to return to Ithaca in the late spring 1913, this time in company with Wharton's brother Leopold, a small but complete production crew, and with a stock company of Essanay players including Francis X. Bushman and Beverly Bayne.

While motion pictures weren't the fashionable thing they would be once they'd outgrown the dingy, dusty nickelodeon movie houses to which they were restricted in their early reign, movies and movie players early fascinated a great many persons, Ithacans among them.

"Francis X. Bushman of New York City, leading man of the Essanay Moving Picture Company, arrived here in Ithaca Hotel," reported the *Ithaca Journal* on May 14, 1913. "Theodore Wharton, general director of the Essanay Co. is expected in town tonight," continued the story. "As

soon as scenarios are written these will be submitted to George K. Spoor, head of Essanay picture department. . . ."

Apparently Wharton got somewhat behind schedule, for it wasn't until Monday, June 2, that the newspaper noted: "Theodore Wharton, general manager and director of the Essanay Co. who arrived here yesterday, announced plans for making scenic films here in the next three months. The company," added the newspaper, "has leased a residence on Thurston Avenue to be used as living quarters . . . the studio will adjoin."

Besides Bushman and Wharton, the paper disclosed, the company would include William Bailey, Frank Dayton, John Breslin, Beverly Bayne, Helen Dunbar, and Juanita Delmorez, as well as Mr. Wharton's assistant Archer McMakin. Essanay's carpenter was to be J.E. Grooms of one of the local theatres, while the cameraman would be David Hargen.

It was all very impressive, and must have seemed more so to the citizenry of Ithaca, then a very small town indeed.

It was to prove a busy summer as far as filmmaking around Ithaca was concerned. In mid–August 1913, the "Pathe Players" came into the area to film some sequences for their Pearl White serial *The Perils of Pauline;* on-location company Pathe had sent Louis J. Gasnier to be in charge.

Pearl White quickly gained a reputation in the community as "one of them fool movie people who do just as they durned well please," roaring along the streets of Ithaca and nearby towns in her canary-yellow Stutz Bearcat sports car. In Ithaca, many oldtimers still talk of Pearl, as colorful a person onstage as off. Pearl smoked cigarettes and wore slacks on the streets! Arrested for speeding through the town of Trumansburg, New York, she was fined $5 by an elderly justice of the peace. Miss White promptly rendered $10, contemptuously announcing to the judge, "Keep the change. I'm going out of this town a damn sight faster than I came in."

During that time, Miss White was ensconced at one of Ithaca's several hotels, at another of which lived Lionel Barrymore who, unimpressed by the community, spent his spare time resting and reading.

The first production scheduled by Wharton was a two-reeler, *The Hermit of Lonely Gulch,* with Bushman in the leading role.

On an island in Fall Creek, Wharton's carpentry crew built what the *Ithaca Journal* described as "a picturesque cabin . . . below the falls, which will be used in the film starting tomorrow, June 6."

**Opposite:** This disparate collection of structures was the studio of Wharton, Inc. When the Whartons abandoned the studio, it for a short time housed Grossman Pictures.

But filming had to be delayed until Monday, June 12, when several actors for the film proved to be detained at Essanay's Chicago studio. Production of the picture started on Wednesday, June 11, and was completed late in the afternoon four days later.

In the meantime, work had been underway on a "studio" on Thurston Avenue, an outdoor stage with muslin sheets draped above it to filter the sunlight so that what were known as "exterior-interiors" could be shot without need for artificial lighting.

This crude method of lighting sets seems ironically appropriate: Ted Wharton's very next film was titled *Sunlight,* much of which was photographed in the vicinity of State and Tioga streets, Ithaca.

On the 26th of June, local papers reported that the Essanay group was at work in the gorges of Fall Creek making an unnamed production from a story by Archer McMakin, a film which was completed at the studio on Thurston St. soon afterward.

Before June came to an end, Wharton's cameras were again busy, this time filming in a fraternity house on the campus of Cornell University a scene for the picture *For Old Times' Sake,* which had been scripted by Ted Wharton. The producer told newsmen that, on the Saturday previous, his company had turned out *The Way Perilous,* an Essanay short drama which Wharton described as being a "character Southern play, which could not have been better if it had been rehearsed for two weeks." Eugene Gladsby played the "old darky servant" in the picture, Gladsby almost proving himself to be the "image of Uncle Tom," as Wharton so quaintly put it.

In spite of Essanay's Ithaca facilities being so crude, Wharton continued grinding out short dramas at a bewildering pace. By July 5, the Ithaca group was already at work on the Archer McMakin story *The Whip-Hand.* At the same time, Essanay's main office in Chicago was announcing that *The Hermit of Lonely Gulch,* the "first photoplay enacted in Ithaca," would be released sometime in the middle of August. Wharton was so far ahead in his filmmaking schedule that by the time *Hermit* was ready to go into release, Wharton was already at work on *Little Ned,* a drama featuring the young son of Professor L.A. Fuertes of Cornell University.

On Saturday, July 19, the *Ithaca Journal* gave a page-two position to a small article noting that "C.J. Evans, an Ithaca young man who has been working with the Essanay Motion Picture Company here, had a narrow escape from death on the rocks of Taughannock Gorge yesterday afternoon following [the taking of] the scene of an automobile dropped down a cliff." As the news story explained it, "A long rope had been tied to a tree and extended down to the foot of the gorge. Evans was wanted down in the ravine. Rather than take the time of climbing down the embankment . . . he got the idea that he could get down much quicker and easier by going hand over hand down the rope.

"When about half-way down the rope," continued the newspaper account, "he missed his grip [and] managed to hang to the rope . . . but his hands were terribly burned by the speed with which the hemp travelled through them."

Amid such minor mishaps, filming by Wharton's unit continued unabated all during that summer, interrupted occasionally by visitors from nationwide publications, such as Hugh Hoffman, an editor of *Motion Picture World* who came to Ithaca in mid–July, ostensibly to spend a two-week vacation in Ithaca. Upon his return to New York, Hoffman said he intended to write a piece "descriptive . . . of his impressions of the Essanay Company's work at Ithaca."

On July 21, Wharton told local newsmen that he had already started work on a one-reel drama, *Antoine, the Fiddler,* a short picture in which Francis X. Bushman was cast as the Italian violinist, and which would include, almost incongruously it seemed, the holdup of a stagecoach.

While Wharton was arranging his *Antoine* cast before one camera, his assistant, Archer McMakin, was directing a film called *The Right of Way,* while also preparing to make a two-reeler, *Love Lute of Romany,* a film for which McMakin bought (and would send up in flames) an old sanitarium near Dryden, New York. In addition to the exciting fire scenes, *Love Lute* included scenes of a band of gypsies. Tobert H. Townley, an Ithaca youth, appeared in the role of a vagabond gypsy in love with the gypsy chief's daughter.

While Essanay's production group at Ithaca was scheduled to close down its operation just past mid–August, the group hurried into production *Dear Old Girl,* a one-reeler which involved a realistic-appearing train wreck. That picture was completed just four days after its filming began.

On Saturday, August 23, the Ithaca group of Essanay returned to their Chicago headquarters, assuring newsmen that they'd return to Ithaca the next year.

As reinforcement of that promise, George K. Spoor had come to Ithaca earlier the same month; he too gave reporters the impression that when Essanay returned to Ithaca, it well might build a permanent studio there.

Unfortunately, Spoor's interest in his company—and the partnership which involved G.M. ("Broncho Billy") Anderson—was fast waning, the firm near dissolution. Only Theodore Wharton's interest in Ithaca as a film production center remained alive.

The citizenry of the town weren't aware, of course, of Essanay's internal affairs. On August 20, Ithaca's Star Theatre was filled to capacity;

the large audience had come to see Archer McMakin's production of *The Whip-Hand,* one of the pictures made early in the summer season by the Essanay crew when it had visited the community.

"All the actors . . . did very capable work," reported the *Ithaca Journal* the next day, but criticized the fact that "the scenario fails to arouse any enthusiasm." The plot, further carped the newspaper, "did not seem very strong, despite the excellent work of the principals."

Scenes for that film had been photographed in areas between the towns of Ludlowville and Portland, the paper reported, which added that the picture had a cast that included Francis X. Bushman, Juanita Delmorez, Frank Dayton, William Bailey, Harry Carr, Otto Breslin, Helen Dunbar, Edna "Babe" McClellan, and Beverly Bayne—all of whom performed their roles capably, the paper added.

The summer of 1914 saw the absence from Ithaca of further film production by Essanay. Theodore Wharton was back, though, but this time as an independent producer. Moreover, Wharton had brought his brother Leopold; obviously they were distilling ambitious plans.

A band of Onandaga Reservation Indians was brought to Ithaca early in July, and taken by trolley car to the Wharton studio, (the former Essanay layout along upper East State Street). Forty Indian men and ten women went to work as "Aztecs," their scenes being filmed at Fall Creek Gorge, outside Ithaca. In order to enlarge the number of extras, numerous Cornell College students, garbed as Indians, also were utilized, the studio reported.

That same month, the Whartons secured the use of J.E. McIntosh's palatial yacht *Calypso* for use in the film *The Shanghai Man,* a four-reel feature which starred Thurlow Bergen.

Activities at the Wharton lot seemed to involve an unbroken production schedule; apparently the brothers had been able to find ready, profitable distribution for a great many films. On July 20, the firm announced that its crews were at work on a third feature, *The Kiss of Blood,* being filmed from a scenario by Ted Wharton. Described by a local scribe as "a fascinating story," the picture involved location shooting in the foyer of the Ithaca Hotel, and along the tracks of the Ithaca Street Railway (the latter involving a sequence in which an overage trolley car is shown plunging off a bridge just outside the town of Ithaca).

Early in August, Wharton Studios announced still another "photoplay," *The Warning,* a picture which would include in its cast Katy Mayhew, Frances White, and the "new juvenile member of the company," Creighton Hale.

Pathe Freres, the name under which Pathe was then operating, was at that time distributing most, if not all, of the Whartons' output of pictures.

"When Wharton Inc. began making motion pictures in Ithaca,"

groused the *Ithaca Journal* on August 13, "it was announced that there would be a statement on every film that the pictures were made by Wharton Inc. at Ithaca, N.Y. The first of these was shown in the Star [an Ithaca theatre] . . . without the promised announcement."

The Whartons hurried a telegram to Pathe which replied to the effect that the trademark of Whartons had reached their "factory" rather late and so was omitted.

The Whartons continued their lighting production pace. "Ted Wharton had his moving picture actors on North Tioga Street this morning," local papers disclosed on August 19, "starting work on his new photoplay, which deals with a mountain feud." While Ted Wharton was so engaged, his brother Leo had completed the picture *The Warning*, after which its "juvenile lead," Creighton Hale, was permitted to return to New York City, though subject to recall for further roles at the Wharton Studio. While the summer season was fast drawing to a close, the Whartons still had pictures to make that year, as witness a company announcement of September 18, 1914: "scenes were taken for the new three-reel photoplay *The Fireman and the Girl* . . . . Thurlow Bergen and Elsie Esmond have the leading roles."

In mid–October, the studio started production of another three-reeler, *Slats*, and readied production of a four-reel picture, *The Prince of India*, even though the Wharton brothers indicated that brother Theodore had been obliged to go to New York City to secure a State Censor's seal for their new film *The Two Sisters*.

By early November, the picture *Slats* was completed, Ted Wharton directing three-and-one-half reels of film in just three days, which the Whartons declared was something of a new record. Completion of *Slats* marked the close of the Whartons' production schedule for 1914.

On January 1, Leo Wharton and his wife were scheduled to depart for Florida for the winter, while Ted remained in Ithaca to take some exterior scenes before he departed for New York City to do some unspecified work at the Pathe Studio.

Ithaca once again was dependent upon the college activities at Cornell for what excitement might be generated in and about the town. The Whartons' movie cameras were still, the studio empty until spring.

In the spring of 1915, the Ithaca, New York, newspaper announced enthusiastically that the community's venerable Renwick Park was on the verge of becoming a fulltime, full-scale movie studio! Wharton, Inc., was about to move to Renwick from their previous downtown "studio."

When the Whartons turned out episodes for Pearl White's 1915 serial *New Exploits of Elaine*, among which was Chapter 19 *(The Saving Circle)*, the Ithaca newspaper commented, "If the Whartons expect to produce similar work in Ithaca this summer there will be some unique 'movie' scenes enacted in the vicinity." (Ithaca citizenry began having a look at the opening chapters of that serial during weekly showings at the Star Theatre.)

May 17, 1919, the paper at Ithaca announced that "Within a week, Ithaca will be the temporary residence of a galaxy of brilliant moving picture stars who will enact a series of novel screenplays for the Wharton Moving Picture Co." The newspaper added how J.W. Buck, business manager for Whartons, while staying at the city's Ithaca Hotel, had announced that the ensuing nine chapters of *New Exploits of Elaine* would be produced locally. The announcement meant, of course, that the streets and business places of the community would continue to teem with such motion picture players as Lionel Barrymore, Paul Everton, Creighton Hale, Bessie Wharton, and others who were appearing in the serial.

With Pearl White in town, there was a plethora of grist for the publicity mill. Pearl seemed to generate sparks wherever she went, shocking even her co-workers at Whartons', who, incidentally, loved her dearly in spite of her slight eccentricities — such as wearing slacks, smoking cigarettes, and driving her canary-yellow Stutz Bearcat through Ithaca traffic at such unbelievable speeds as 40 miles an hour. (What a pity Miss White didn't elect before her death to write the true story of her life.)

Pearl was, without question, the serial queen of pre–World War I era, although she never successfully made the transition to feature films (one of her features, *Hazel Kirke,* was turned out by the Whartons in 1916).

Even her dissertation on some of the exciting moments which occurred during the production of her serials would be intriguing. Take, for example, one sequence for the *Elaine* serials. An abandoned bridge near Ithaca, slated for destruction by the county, was blown to pieces before the cameras of Wharton, Inc. The feat was accomplished with the use of 20 pounds of dynamite placed, not only along the bridge supports, but in the stream flowing beneath. As an explosives man stood by the triggering mechanism, Pearl, accompanied by co-star Creighton Hale, sped across the span, supposedly racing away with plans for a new, secret torpedo sought by foreign spies. The bridge, of course, was triggered so as to blow up just after Pearl, her co-star, and their automobile cleared the span.

By July 3, *The Romance of Elaine,* one of the continuation titles of the *Elaine* serials, had reached episode 27, far enough into that serial so that the Whartons were also able to devote some time to a *Get-Rich-Quick-Wallingford* series, which, in the opening episodes, featured Frederick de Belville as Wallingford, and for the remainder of the dozen two-reelers, Burr McIntosh in that role. (Max Figman appeared as "Blackie Dew" and Lolita Robertson in the feminine lead.)

As the *Wallingford* series was getting started, about three weeks more of shooting remained on *Romance of Elaine,* after which 150 prints of that serial were made ready for distribution, even as Pearl White, Lionel Barrymore, and Creighton Hale were preparing to leave Ithaca.

*Romance of Elaine* had reputedly grossed something around a million dollars, even before the Whartons had turned out the final episode.

For that reason, there was high excitement when, on May 9, 1916, Wharton studio officials told reporters that when the Whartons' newest serial, *The Mysteries of Myra,* appeared it would be as popular with the public as were the Pearl White offerings.

First announced as *Mystery of Mona,* the new serial would include in its cast Howard Estabrook, Jean Sothern, Allan Murname, M.W. Rale, and Bessie Emerick (Mrs. Leopold Wharton).

On April 5, 1916, it was announced that the famous dancer Irene Castle would arrive in Ithaca April 5, 1916, to appear in *Mysteries of Myra.*

The completed serial ended production in July, and was immediately readied for release through William Randolph Hearst's International Film Service. The Hearst releases called also for two other serials to be made by the Whartons: *Beatrice Fairfax* (originally titled *Letters to Beatrice)* which cast Grace Darling as the famed lovelorn columnist, with Harry Fox as her love interest. The screenplay for the serial was said to have been prepared by Beatrice Fairfax of the *New York Journal* and Basil Dickey; Ted and Leopold Wharton jointly were directors of the episode play.

Irene Castle didn't appear in *Mysteries of Myra,* instead she arrived in Ithaca on July 11, 1916, to appear in the third of the serials for International Film: *Patria.* The serial included in its cast Milton Sills, Warner Oland, Dick Stewart, M.W. Rale, Allan Murname, and George Majeroni. The directors were James Gordon and George Lessey.

On August 22, Miss Castle made headlines when she unwittingly fell into Lake Ontario near Rochester, New York, where she was appearing in scenes for *Patria.* Needless to say, Miss Castle was fished out of the lake relatively unscathed, though she remained under a physician's care for several days after the incident—or so the papers reported.

Throughout the three-year period of 1916–18, the Wharton outfit turned out not only serials, but such full-length feature pictures as *The Lottery Man* (1915) which comprised an unnoteworthy cast of players including Thurlow Bergen, Lolita Robertson, Ethel Winthrop, Harry Carey, and Howard Teachout, and *The City* (also 1915), which featured Mr. and Mrs. Thurlow Bergen, but with William Berry Hatch and Allan Murname.

In 1916, it was rumored that the Whartons and William Randolph Hearst were about to join hands in the construction of a huge motion picture studio in Ithaca, one far larger than the existing studio at Renwick Park. The new studio, it was publicized, would be called, as the reader may already have suspected, "Hearst-Whartons."

Then something occurred which caused the cancellation of that plan. In early 1917, even the feature picture *The Black Stork* (made by Whartons ostensibly for release through the Hearst film distribution network) was abruptly thrown into "states rights" distribution by a combination which announced itself as "Wharton-Sherriott."

Possibly the failure of the serial *Patria* had been blamed by Hearst on the Whartons. The serial possessed a good cast of players including, besides Irene Castle (in those years rather pompously being hailed as "the best dressed woman in the world"), such players as Warner Oland, Milton Sills, George Majeroni, and Dorothy Green.

*Patria* smacked of many of the hates and suspicions of William Randolph Hearst. The script almost seemed at times to have flowed directly from Hearst's own pen. The Japanese and Mexican governments and people were held up for scorn throughout the serial.

Just how costly the production of that chapter play was may be inferred from such pieces of location shooting as that of mid–December 1916, when the entire cast and crew of *Patria* journeyed west to the Universal Ranch near Hollywood. There the work crews built a "typical Mexican town" and nearby a sprawling outdoor stage on which "outdoor-interiors" were filmed as needed. Thousands of extras were claimed to have been used in roles there, including those of cowboys, aviators, troops, Indians, artillerymen, and even as Japanese soldiers.

Such lavish examples of location shooting came on the heels of an October 2, 1916, *Ithaca Journal* news story which told its readers "Flames that illuminated the sky for miles around destroyed a village of almost 20 buildings last night to furnish Wharton Inc. a sensational scene for the new serial *Patria*," adding that about 250 extras had appeared in this scene, which was filmed near Ithaca.

On January 4, 1917, the Whartons announced completion of *Patria*, a production on which they claimed to have exposed 150,000 feet of negative.

*Patria* became a source of trouble almost as soon as it began to be shown. Formal protests were made about the picture by the Japanese and Mexican governments, cries that reached United States president

Woodrow Wilson who almost immediately wrote Hearst asking that the serial not be exhibited.

By mid–January 1916, there appeared other darkening storm clouds over the Whartons' film enterprises, which doubtless had something to do with the fact that J. Whitworth Buck, business manager of the studio, and incidentally, a brother-in-law of the Whartons, announced that he'd sold his interest in Wharton, Inc., in order to enter business in New York City.

If this weren't adequate evidence that something was seriously wrong, on February 3, 1917, the Whartons announced they would henceforth be both independent producers and distributors, indicating that things had gone awry between the Ithaca firm and both its distributors, the Pathe Exchange and Hearst's International Film Service.

As the storm clouds thickened, Leopold Wharton went ahead putting finishing touches on his script for a feature *The Great White Trail,* a picture which was to star Doris Kenyon and Paul Gordon.

On November 12, 1917, Whartons announced a new 20-chapter serial, *The Eagle's Eye,* made from a story by Chief William J. Flynn, United States Secret Service, and which purported to show the "inside workings of German intrigue in America." Filming began in New York City, then moved to Washington, D.C., and eventually to Ithaca. King Baggott and Marguerite Snow were the featured players.

The public doubtless was unaware by then that anything at all was wrong with the financial affairs of the Whartons, especially when the 300,000 reputed readers of *Photoplay* magazine were told that the complete story of *The Eagle's Eye* was to be published serially in the pages of that magazine, a serialization, incidentally, which would be written by Courtney Ryley Cooper, who already had prepared the screenplay for the serial.

Production of *The Eagle's Eye* necessitated a new, gigantic storage building with a floor space of more than 2500 square feet. These and other rather large expenses involved in enlarging the studio facilities at Ithaca were aggravated by the costs to the Whartons of establishing a suite of offices on the third floor of the famous Longacre Building, New York City (of which office the Whartons named Charles Hankel the manager).

Somewhere around this point, the clouds which had gathered over the Whartons opened up! The cost of film production had risen dizzyingly since the outset of World War I, accompanied by falling receipts at motion picture theatre box offices.

So perhaps it was not altogether surprising that on May 9, 1919, the *Ithaca Journal* reported, "In 1917, financial difficulties beset Wharton, Inc. . . . debts had accumulated against the concern culminating in the necessity of appealing to interests outside the firm. . . . Wharton, Inc. struggled along bravely . . . but odds were too formidable." The article concluded by saying that the studio equipment was to be sold to satisfy creditors of the firm. "Only motion picture production paraphernalia will be sold," added the paper.

When the sale was concluded, a mere $12,000 was all that had been raised. It was pitifully little to represent the value of Wharton, Inc.

But only days after that, "Whartons Form New Company in San Antonio" called out a minor headline inside the Ithaca newspaper, the text stating that various Texans had already subscribed to $150,000 in preferred stock of a firm to be known as Antonio Pictures Corporation, of which organization Maclyn Arbuckle was to be head, and which would produce at least three motion picture serials under a contract held by Theodore Wharton of Wharton, Inc., with Pathe Company, New York City. "The Pathe Company will select the . . . casts," added the paper, noting also that "Mr. Wharton says he will remain in Ithaca, going occasionally to San Antonio to supervise picture production there."

For some reason, apparently nothing further came of the Antonio Pictures venture, for less than a month later the *Journal* carried a story that the Wharton Company was indeed going down to Texas, but this time asserting that the firm's new headquarters would be in Galveston, not San Antonio!

As if the blizzard of confusing newspaper accounts weren't already sufficient, a July 12, 1919, story in the Ithaca paper happily announced that Theodore Wharton, having just signed a contract with Pathe for a new serial, *The Crooked Dagger*, was hoping he could produce that picture in Ithaca.

Less than a week after, Ted Wharton released still another tidbit of news to reporters: Jack Norworth, who had gained fame as the stage partner of singer Nora Bayes, had just signed a contract to star in Wharton's new 10-chapter Pathe serial.

While plastering newspapers with such news as this, Theodore Wharton apparently had parted company with brother Leopold; now whenever he returned to Ithaca he was alone.

Other questions arose at this time. Fr example, Where in Ithaca was Ted Wharton to establish his new studio? The Renwick Park location was unavailable, a motion picture company named Grossman Pictures having taken over that facility.

Undaunted, Ted Wharton returned to Ithaca, announcing cavalierly that a new Wharton studio was to be established in Ithaca, and that there would be a "full season of motion picture production," each film budgeted at $50,000 to $75,000, and all of them released through a new "Wharton Releasing Company."

Jim Gordon, one of the Whartons' directors, standing under the propeller of a plane used in stunts for movies made at Ithaca, N.Y. Standing at left in the foreground (light suit and hat) is Leo Wharton, one of the two brothers who owned the firm. Others are officials of the Ithaca airplane factory at Ithaca.

On July 23, the Ithaca newspaper disclosed that Wharton had leased the large, abandoned skating rink on West State Street and was already converting the building into a film studio, Wharton quite literally "raising the roof" so as to provide about 20 feet of additional height to the structure. A new "rotary converter" was also being installed in the studio, which would convert conventional AC power to DC in order to produce flick-free images on all scenes shot in the studio. The new place was to be called the Theodore Wharton Studio.

By this time, Pathe itself had undergone many changes. For example, it was no longer Pathe-Freres, as the firm had been when it was first established in the United States. The name on this side of the Atlantic would now be Pathe Exchanges. The firm was more determined than ever it would not accept for release independently made productions which did not measure up to minimal quality standards set by the Pathe firm's review board.

It would not be long before autumn would begin splashing its gaudy colors all about the Finger Lakes area, yet Ted Wharton still was not ready to roll the cameras on his new serial. Frederic Chapin, scenario editor from Pathe's main offices, spent a week in Ithaca in August, conferring with Wharton about the forthcoming serial *The Crooked Dagger* which, it was said, would involve a spectacular sequence in which an actual dirigible was to be burned while flying high above Lake Cayuga; moreover, Wharton told members of the press that he'd already made arrangements with a firm called Thomas-Morse Corp. to have planes bomb and destroy the dirigible, all to add a touch of realism and some further thrills to *The Crooked Dagger*.

On September 4, 1919, filming got underway on the serial, even though workers still were putting fininshing touches on the new Theodore Wharton Studio. Wharton, his cast and crew headed for Sayre, Pennsylvania, to do location shooting for the serial, a junket which, by the way, supposedly required a five-car train to transport cast and crew.

Even as Theodore Wharton and most of his personnel were shooting their new serial, some work was being done in Ithaca, financed by a few local business people, to completely re-edit and re-title the earlier Wharton/Hearst serial *Patria,* turning it into a feature picture which was to be called *The Red Peril.* (Such a metamorphosis was a comparatively easy thing to accomplish with a silent picture.) A New York Senator Lusk, having seen the newly revivified Wharton production, told the press that the film as re-edited would do much to fight Bolshevism. (Shades of Senator Joseph McCarthy!)

An article on page 3 of the *Ithaca Journal,* November 20, 1919, carried bad news regarding both Grossman Pictures and Theodore Wharton's new studio: Pathe, according to the news story, had rejected both Grossman's *A Million Dollars' Reward* and Wharton's serial *The Crooked Dagger.*

Theodore Wharton next appeared in Los Angeles looking about, he declared, for "studio accommodations" in which to produce a "spectacular film feature from the story 'Tangled Flags' which was based upon the Boxer Rebellion in China."

Entrepreneurs of film production enterprises, it seems, just don't know the meaning of defeat!

# Afterword

Although far more than half a hundred U.S. film studios are treated in some detail in this volume, a good many other less-than-significant ones were omitted, as was the case with such Florida studios as Ivan Tors, Capitol, Davis Island, Shamrock, and Rainbow.

As this book discloses, the number of American film studios which have come and gone is immense: competition, mismanagement, internal squabbles, poor choices of stories, stars, and a myriad of other problems have driven studios out of business.

Yet in spite of the demise of many, new ones are occasionally created. The Zale Magder Entertainment Corporation, a Canadian firm, only recently announced its acquisition of 250 acres in the eastern area of North Carolina, where the firm intends to build a complete "film city" comprising three sound stages, carpenter shop and support facilities, aiming at continuous production.

Elsewhere in the Tar Heel state, the E-O Corporation operates a modest-sized film studio at Shelby, where it specializes in action feature films highly favored by audiences at drive-in theatres.

Along the coast line of that state in the city of Wilmington where Dino DeLaurentiis has a 32-acre layout originally called "North Carolina Film Corporation," now known as D-E-G. Films made here included Natalie Wood's final one, *Brainstorm*, and the comedy *Private Eyes* with Tim Conway and Don Knotts.

The D.E.G. studio grew out of a rental by DeLaurentiis of an empty warehouse which a production crew utilized during the making of the George C. Scott feature *Firestarter*.

Presently the D.E.G. studio comprises five huge sound stages and a sprawling back lot which includes an impressive New York Chinatown set and others. Estimated value of the new studio: $17,000,000.

Near Orlando, Florida, the Walt Disney firm is working with MGM in construction of a joint studio which, when complete, will enter into feature film production, at the same time offering visitors guided studio tours quite like those in California afforded by Universal studios.

Studio construction throughout the South appears to be something

**The Filmworks Studios, Atlanta, Georgia.**

of a bellwether for return of a great deal of theatrical film production to areas east of the Mississippi.

Not to be outdone by other Southern states, Georgia is continually alert for opportunities which may assist in boosting the production of motion pictures within that state. The former Lakewood Fairgrounds has already begun to undergo transformation into a production complex, its four one-time exhibit halls, any of which is sizable enough to serve well as a full-scale motion picture stage, being more than two stories high. Operating as "Filmworks USA" the Atlanta complex boasts 4,000 parking spaces, 250,000 square feet of indoor space, 24-hour guard service and a tall security fence enclosing the entire facility, within which there is a 20-acre lake surrounded by a one-mile dirt racetrack with grandstands. All four buildings are heated. Streets within the complex are all-weather types, making running shots easily possible without the need for leaving the studio grounds. Filmworks Studios is situated midway between downtown Atlanta and the Atlanta international airport.

Georgia also recently opened an operation called the Atlanta Production Center at which there are two sound stages. Both commercials and theatrical features can be filmed at the two Georgia facilities.

One of the "rental accounts" at Filmworks Studios, Special Effects International, Inc., specializes in what the firm describes as "anything from rainstorms to blizzards, fog to windstorms" and adds that its licensed explosive experts can handle pyrotechnics as minute as autobody bullet hits to creating effects for multiple explosions in entire groups of buildings. The firm's credits include such productions as

*Opposite:* As a tenant of Filmworks Studios, Atlanta, a firm known as PS—A rents camera cranes and dollies.

*Sharky's Machine, Stroker Ace, Last Days of Frank and Jesse James* and *Purple Rain.*

The migration of the film industry away from the West Coast is unquestionably due to the outrageously high costs of land and labor there. Organized labor with its incessant demands for higher pay has contributed heavily to increased costs of every foot of film exposed, processed, and run through post-production phases on the West Coast. "Long ago, things in California had reached such an impasse," explained one producer, "that we were forced to deal with about 20 employees for every two-man job—union requirements, you see."

By contrast most southern states have "right to work" laws forbidding the union's "closed shop" with its accompanying demands for specified numbers of workers, the restriction of work to only union members, and restrictions as to the type of duties each may perform. (Although this author is an experienced cameraman, he was forbidden by his union to operate a camera once he became a scriptwriter-director, though he was a member of the union which represents cameramen and laboratory workers.)

Certainly factors other than these also are strangling West Coast film production. Even the San Andreas fault which knifes through California, north to south, seems to have diminished interest in building studios along the West Coast, although as early as 1935 filmmakers were all too aware of earthquake problems. Paramount officials were reminded of that when production of the feature *International House* was halted by immense earth tremors which rocked the sound stage on which comic W.C. Fields happened to be performing at the time. Even more deadly quakes have now been forecast by modern seismologists. The mysterious magic of the name "Hollywood" is being shaken severely, possibly triggering the return of the motion picture industry to almost the same region where it had its origins!

Tomorrow's Hollywood studio may therefore be in Wilmington, North Carolina, or somewhere in that region.

# Bibliography

Alicoate, Jack, ed. *Yearbook of Motion Pictures, 1938–1942.* New York: Film Daily, 1942.

Aaronson, Charles S., ed. *International Motion Picture Almanac 1970.* New York: Quigley, 1970.

Balshofer, Fred J., and Arthur C. Miller. *One Reel a Week.* Berkeley: University of California Press, 1967.

Bell, Geoffrey. *The Golden Gate and the Silver Screen.* New York: Cornwall Books, 1984.

Brownlow, Kevin. *The Parade's Gone By.* New York: Alfred A. Knopf, 1968.

Capra, Frank. *The Name Above the Title: An Autiobiography.* New York: Macmillan, 1971.

Clarke, Charles C. *Early Filmmaking in Los Angeles.* Los Angeles: Dawton's Book Shop, 1976.

Crowther, Bosley. *Hollywood Rajah: The Life and Times of Louis B. Mayer.* New York: Holt, Rinehart & Winston, 1960.

Fowler, Gene. *Father Goose: The Story of Mack Sennett.* New York: Friede Covici, 1934.

Gish, Lillian, with Ann Pinchot. *The Movies, Mr. Griffith, and Me.* Englewood Cliffs, N.J.: Prentice-Hall, 1969.

Hampton, Benjamin Bowles. *History of the Movies.* New York: Friede Covici, 1931.

Higham, Charles. *Bette: The Life of Bette Davis.* New York: Macmillan, 1981.

Jacobs, Lewis. *Rise of the American Film: A Critical History.* New York: Harcourt, Brace, 1939.

Kanin, Garson. *Hollywood: Stars and Starlets, Tycoons and Flesh-peddlers, Moviemakers and Moneymakers, Frauds and Geniuses, Hopefuls and Hasbeens, Great Lovers and Sex Symbols.* New York: Viking Press, 1974.

Korda, Michael. *Charmed Lives: A Family Romance.* New York: Random House, 1979.

Peters, Lloyd. *Lionhead Lodge.* Fairfield, Wash.: Fairfield Press, 1967.

Ramsaye, Terry. *A Million and One Nights: A History of the Motion Picture.* New York: Simon and Schuster, 1926.

Ramsaye, Terry, et al., eds. *International Motion Picture Almanac, 1939–40 to 1942–43.* New York: Quigley, 1943.

Ramsaye, Terry, ed. *International Motion Picture Almanac 1934–35 to 1937–38.* New York, N.Y.: Quigley, 1938.

Robinson, David. *Chaplin: His Life and His Art.* New York: McGraw-Hill, 1985.
Sennett, Mack. *King of Comedy.* New York: Doubleday, 1954.
Smith, Albert E., and P.A. Koury. *Two Reels and a Crank.* New York: Double-
day, 1952.

# Index

Entry numbers in **boldface** indicate photographs.